THE GIRO

Herbie Sykes

100 tales from the corsa rosa

Rapha.
EDITIONS

For Gavin, Michelle and Thea

THE GIRO 100

100 tales from the corsa rosa

Herbie Sykes

The Giro 100
© Herbie Sykes, 2017

All images © the 100, 2017

First published in 2017
by Rapha Racing Ltd
Imperial Works,
18 Tileyard,
London, N7 9AH

Published for Rapha Editions,
in arrangement with
Bluetrain Publishing Ltd
bluetrainpublishing.com

Rapha founder and CEO: Simon Mottram
Publishing director: Daniel Blumire
Design directors: Jack Saunders and Eve Isaak

rapha.cc

Editor: Taz Darling
Publishing editor: Guy Andrews
Art direction: Bluetrain
Copy-editor: Mark Ralph
Image retouching: Linda Duong

Book design: Melanie Mues,
Mues Design London

Printed in Italy by EBS

ISBN 978-1-912164-00-4

Cover Photograph: Attilio Benfatto of Filcas
Front endpaper winners: Young Virginio Levati
winning, proud Dad with flowers
Tail endpaper Charlies: L-R Roger DeVlaeminck,
Patrick Sercu and Giancarlo Bellini

CONTENTS

9   INTRODUCTION
    UN UOMO SOLO
    É AL COMANDO
    (Herbie Sykes)

10 PROLOGO
    CESARE SANGALLI,
    CARTOGRAPHER OF THE
    GIRO D'ITALIA

12 GIROTAPPA 1
    I SOGNATORI
    (The Dreamers)

18 GIROTAPPA 2
    LE MAGLIE ROSA
    (Race Leaders)

30 GIROTAPPA 3
    ALCUNI VINCITORI
    (A Few Winners)

38 GIROTAPPA 4
    I SECONDI
    (Some Runners-up)

47 GIROTAPPA 5
    LE ALTRE MAGLIE
    (The Other Jerseys)

59 GIROTAPPA 6
    GREGARI D.O.C.
    (The Gregari)

73 GIROTAPPA 7
    QUELLI CHE NON CE
    L'HANNO FATTA
    (Those Who Didn't
    Quite Make It)

84 GIROTAPPA 8
    LA FAVOLA DEL GRUPPO
    SPORTIVO FILCAS
    (The Fairytale of
    G.S. Filcas)

99 GIROTAPPA 9
    È UN PO' …
    COMPLICATA
    (It's a Bit …
    Complicated)

109 GIROTAPPA 10
    L'ORGANIZZAZIONE
    (The Organization)

123 GIROTAPPA 11
    QUELLI CHE
    RACCONTANO
    (The Storytellers)

133 GIROTAPPA 12
    I NOSTRI AMICI
    STRANIERI
    (Our Foreign
    Friends)

142 GIROTAPPA 13
    GRAZIE A DIO …
    (There but for the
    Grace of God …)

149 GIROTAPPA 14
    IL CLIMA
    (The Weather)

156 GIROTAPPA 15
    I VINCITORI DEL 85°
    GIRO D'ITALIA
    (The Winners of the
    85th Giro d'Italia)

173 GIROTAPPA 16
    UN GIORNO DA LEONE
    (One Day as a Lion)

184 GIROTAPPA 17
    ALTRE STORIE DEI
    GREGARI
    (More Stories
    from the Gregari)

201 GIROTAPPA 18
    DIETRO LE QUINTE
    (Behind the Scenes)

211 GIROTAPPA 19
    I DIRETTORI SPORTIVI
    (The Sports Directors)

220 GIROTAPPA 20
    I GIGANTI DEL
    GIRO D'ITALIA
    (The Giants of
    the Giro d'Italia)

224 ACKNOWLEDGEMENTS

13 MARIO GARAVOGLIA *ST VINCENT, 1960*	**66** MARCELLO BERGAMO *IN THE SOUTH, 1969*	**124** GIAN PAOLO ORMEZZANO *ITALY, 1967*	**180** ALESSANDRO PAGANESSI *ARABBA, 1983*
15 FRANCO BOCCA *PIOSSASCO, 1969*	**70** AURELIO CESTARI *OSPEDALETTO, 1957*	**126** GIOVANNI TARELLO *BORGO D'ALE, 1973*	**182** PAOLO LANFRANCHI *BRIANÇON, 2000*
19 UGO COLOMBO *SAN LORENZO, 1971*	**71** RENATO LAGHI *IL CIOCCO, 1975*	**128** PAOLO VIBERTI *GIRO D'ITALIA, 1994*	**185** MATTEO CRAVERO *SAVONA, 1969*
22 GIORGIO ZANCANARO *ALESSANDRIA, 1967*	**74** LORADANA BARATELLI AND ADRIANO PASSUELLO *CATANIA, 1965*	**129** ABRIZIO DELMATI *PASSO DELLO STELVIO, 1975*	**186** REMO ROCCHIA *SAN GIACOMO DI ROBURENT, 1977*
26 SIMONA CAMERONI *SCHIO, 1998*	**75** PIETRO ZOPPAS *TERMINILLO, 1960*	**131** CLAUDIO GREGORI *FRANCE, 1923*	**188** VIRGINIO LEVATI *SCANNO, 1969*
27 PIETRO GUERRA *BRINDISI, 1971*	**78** FIORENZO TOMASIN *VESUVIAS, 1959*	**134** GLENN MAGNUSSON *NAFPAKTOS, GREECE, 1996*	**190** FLORIDO BARALE *THE ABRUZZO, 1990*
31 FRANCO BALMAMION *PASSO VALLES, 1963*	**80** CLAUDIO COMINO *CUNEO, 1977*	**135** GEORGE MOUNT *IN THE APENNINES OR CENTRAL ITALY, 1982*	**192** ENNIO SALVADOR *RHO, 1982*
32 GIANNI MOTTA *TRIESTE, 1966*	**82** PIERGIORGIO CAMUSSA *AREZZO, 2008*	**137** MICHAEL RASMUSSEN *BOLZANO, 1990*	**194** BRUNO VICINO *VILLORBA, 1967*
36 FAUSTO BERTOGLIO *PASSO STELVIO, 1975*	**85** GRUPPO SPORTIVO FILCAS *ITALY, 1970–1974*	**139** HARRY LODGE *AVERSA, 1992*	**198** ORLANDO MAINI *BOLOGNA, 1979*
39 ENRICO ZAINA *PASSO PORDOI, 1996*	**100** GIANNI ZOLA *PESARO, 1986*	**140** PHIL EDWARDS *RIONERO SANNITICO, 1980*	**199** ANGELO OTTAVIANI *PASSO DEL SEMPIONE, 1965*
41 GIANBATTISTA BARONCHELLI *LEFFE, 1974*	**102** DOMENICO CAVALLO *VATICAN CITY, 2000*	**143** CLAUDIO RAVASIO *SCIACCA, 1986*	**202** RICCARDO BATTILOSSI *TURIN, 1962*

43 ITALO ZILIOLI
ITALY, 60s

45 TOMMY PRIM
TRE CIME DI LAVAREDO, 1981

48 LUCILLE LIEVORE
GHISALLO, 1967

50 MARC ANTONIO DI RENZO
PLAN DI MONTECAMPIONE, 1998

52 MASSIMILIANO STRAZZER
MILAN, 2001

53 THE BORTOLOTTOS
ORSAGO, 1977

55 MARCO GROPPO
PARMA, 1983

57 MARIO BECCIA
SPOLETO, 1977

60 OSCAR PELICCIOLI
CAPITELLO MATESE, 1994

62 GIANCARLO BELLINI
JAFFERAU, 1972

65 DORINO VANZO
MANERBIO, 1976

104 CARMINE CASTELLANO
CUNEO, 2002

105 DENIS LUNGHI
VALKENBURG, 1998
CHIETI 2002

107 MARCO PINOTTI
OSIO SOTTO, 1995

110 MAURO VEGNI
SICILY, 1994

111 ANNA PORTINORO
CASALE MONFERRATO, 1962

113 CESARE SANGALLI
PASSO DELLO STELVIO,
1953

115 SERGIO MEDA
APELDOORN, HOLLAND, 2016

117 STEFANO DICIATTEO
CUNEO, 2009

118 ANTONIO PENATI
NIBBIONO, 1988

120 THE TORRIANI BROTHERS
SAN GIOVANNI ROTONDO,
1947

145 OLIVIERO MOROTTI AND
MINO DENTI
PASSO CROCEDOMINI, 1970

147 ELKE WEYLANDT
GHENT, BELGIUM, 1984

150 ALBERTO DELLA TORRE
BORMIO, 1988

151 ALDO BERALDO
PASSO ROLLE, 1962

153 DARIO ANDRIOTTO
CORVARA, 2007

154 SIMONE FRACCARO
PASSO VALLES, 1978

157 I VINCITORI DEL 85°
GIRO D'ITALIA EUROPE AND
NORTH AMERICA, 1920–2002

174 GIOVANNI MANTOVANI
SORRENTO, 1980

175 BENEDETTO PATELLARO
BORNO, 1981

178 MARCO SALIGARI
SONDRIO, 1992,
VALLE VARAITA, 1993,
CASERTA, 1994

204 ALDO GIOS
MILAN FAIR, 1971

205 BRUNO RAGONA
TRENTO, 1979

207 SERGIO LEONE
BIELLA, 2016

209 ENNIO DORIS
TOMBOLO, 1909

212 FRANCO CRIBIORI
BRIBANO, 1976

213 MARINO VIGNA
MONTE GRAPPA, 1968

216 DAVIDE BOIFAVA
NUVOLENTO, 1961

217 GIGI STANGA
MILAN 1990, 1999

221 ANGELO MARELLO
TURIN, 1960

223 FILIPPO GHIRON
PECETTO, 2016

The cycling industry has always portrayed itself (or, more accurately, hawked itself) as in some way "heroic". The mountains, the terrible physicality, the camaraderie, the exposure to weather. Oh woe is us, and the unremitting cruelty of all that is best in life.

Notwithstanding the current vogue for gratuitous stages and for cheap thrills (everything, in point of fact, that is the opposite of long-distance bike racing), sufferance still just about sells. Journalists and photographers pursue its leaden narrative, the endless auto-celebration an end in itself. Denuded almost entirely of creative impulse, a small army of us repeat the tired old Dolomite mantra. Blithely and guilelessly, we continue our pitiable appropriation of geological and temporal decree.

Of late, it's all become a bit too clichéd, a bit too self-reverential. Cycling *is* about the mountains and about suffering, but it's also about so much more besides. I've interviewed hundreds of professional bike riders, and not one has ever blathered about the majesty of the mountains or the innate nobility of the *gregario*. Mercifully, cyclists – at least the real ones – aren't like that. They don't think like that, because, if they did, they wouldn't be cyclists.

As such, this book, celebrating the constituents of a hundred *giri* through a hundred disparate voices, is an unashamed reaction against traditional cycling methodology. The good, the bad and the downright ugly of the photography is derived not from some faceless digital archive, but from the cupboards, scrapbooks and photo albums of the participants. They chose the images just as they chose the stories, so I make no apology for the fact that there are no sweeping Stelvio panoramas, no "dramatic" snow-capped Gavias. Been there and done that, and arrogantly I assumed that you might, just for once, like something a little bit other.

A Giro winner once told me that 90 per cent of the race was both instantly forgettable and invisible to the viewing public. Likewise, only a tiny minority of its protagonists perforate the wider consciousness, and these facts have significantly informed what I'm optimistically calling the narrative.

For every winner there's a loser, for every loser a few dozen *gregari*. For every *gregario* there's a family, a multitude of facilitators and well-wishers, a thousand wannabe *gregari* by the roadside. The Giro is its winners and losers, but also their nearest and dearest, their *tifosi*, sponsors and suppliers. It's the managers, journalists and poker-faced officialdom, the unpaid volunteers, fundraisers and myriad public servants.

My own *gregario di lusso* was a ninety-three-year-old cartographer. Cesare Sangalli began mapping the Giro in 1953 – the first time it went over the Stelvio – and would see off Coppi and Bartali, Anquetil and Merckx, Hinault, Moser and Pantani. The great unwashed never saw him and never heard from him, but without him there would have been no superhuman Alpine exploits, no tales from the *gregariato*, no spellbinding denouements. There would have been, quite simply, no Giro d'Italia.

In his humility, wisdom and unstinting dedication, Cesare was one of the true bulwarks of the race. I therefore prevailed upon him to begin a second working life, to reconfigure the stage profiles he'd created for the 1962 Giro. We wanted to pay homage to those, like him, who helped build the legend, and so he set about rewriting their names into the profiles just as meticulously and painstakingly as ever. Thus, to my immense pride, he has been instrumental in the creation of this, our literary Giro d'Italia.

Enjoy.

PROLOGO
CESARE SANGALLI, CARTOGRAPHER OF THE GIRO D'ITALIA

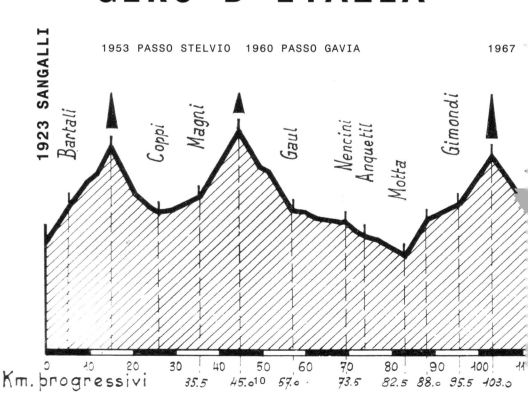

"*The cyclists needed to know the length of the climbs, the gradient and the state of the roads, and the fans needed to know where to go to watch the race. So I played my part, because everything was decided according to the drawings I did, the timetables I drew up and the architecture of the stages we put together.*

"*Someone worked out that I did more than 200,000 kilometres, five times round the equator. I was the cartographer of the Giro d'Italia for over fifty years …*"
— *Cesare Sangalli*

E DI LAVAREDO   1990 PASSO MORTIROLO

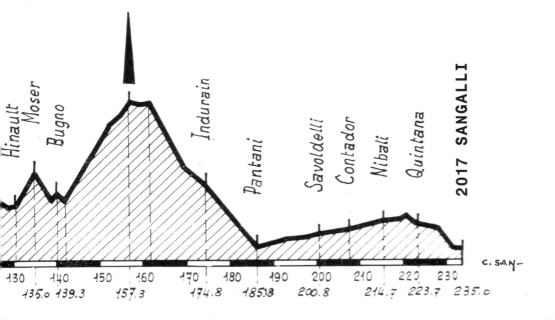

2017 SANGALLI

Hinault · Moser · Bugno · Indurain · Pantani · Savoldelli · Contador · Nibali · Quintana

C. SAN-

130   140   150   160   170   180   190   200   210   220   230
135.0 139.3   157.3   174.8 185.8 200.8   214.7 223.7 235.0

GIROTAPPA 1

I SOGNATORI

(THE DREAMERS)

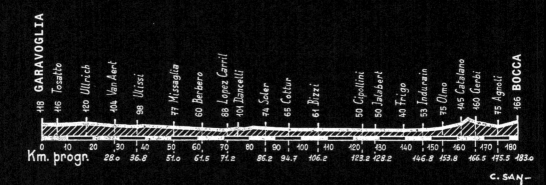

GARAVOGLIA | 118 Garavoglia | 116 Tosatto | 120 Ullrich | 104 Van Aert | 98 Ulissi | 77 Missaglia | 60 Berbero | 88 Lopez Carril | 101 Dancelli | 74 Soler | 65 Cottur | 61 Bizzi | 50 Cipollini | 50 Jalabert | 40 Frigo | 53 Indurain | 75 Olmo | 145 Catalano | 160 Gerbi | 75 Agnoli | 166 BOCCA

Km. progr.   0   10   20   30   40   50   60   70   80   90   100   110   120   130   140   150   160   170   180
28.0   36.8   51.0   61.5   71.2   86.2   94.7   106.2   123.2 128.2   146.8 153.8   166.5 175.5 183.0

C. SAN-

**MARIO GARAVOGLIA
SPRINTER (AGED 8)
ST VINCENT, 1960**

I was eight, but I remember it like it was yesterday …

One of our neighbours was a guy named Tino Rolle. He was a commissar and jury president on a lot of big races, including the Giro. He worked with my dad, so he was a family friend. He often had cyclists at his house, and sometimes he'd invite me round to meet them. I met Gino Bartali and Fausto Coppi there, and once I even got to present Coppi with a prize. In fact, Coppi's death was a terrible tragedy for me. I was crestfallen.

When Coppi died, I started supporting Miguel Poblet, the Spanish sprinter. He was small like me, and he was always smiling. He was simpatico, unlike Rik Van Looy, and I used to cry when Van Looy beat him. I used to say to Tino, "When are you going to bring Poblet home?"

Tino had always bought me my bikes, and just before the Giro he bought me my first drop-handlebars racing bike. It was a Frejus Junior, an exact replica of the one that Poblet rode for Ignis.

Anyway, the stage was on a Tuesday morning, and when I woke they told me there was a surprise for me. I was being given a day off school, and we were off to watch the Giro. They told me my bike was already in the boot of the car, and then Tino gave me a parcel. I opened it up, and there inside was an Ignis jersey, just like Poblet's.

We got to the start and waited for the Ignis riders to show. Then, when they arrived, Tino said, "Quick, come with me. I'll introduce you to Poblet." So there I was, and he said to Poblet, "This little guy is your biggest fan, but he reckons he can outsprint you."

Poblet got on his bike, but then he said, "Hang on a minute. This is an uphill sprint! You know I'm not a climber, and you're bound to beat me if we do it that way." So we had to turn round and do the sprint in the opposite direction. It was about fifty metres, and I think it was a dead heat.

Next I heard the announcer calling my name over the PA system. I had to go on stage and sign on with the rest of the *gruppo*, and then I went to get my musette. After that I went to the start line for the *partenza*. Jos Hoevenaers had the pink jersey, and I lined up on the front row with him and all the other stars.

Then they lowered the flag, and I took off at full tilt. Everyone else just stayed where they were for a moment or two, and so for about fifty metres I, Mario Garavoglia, was *in fuga*. I was on my own, leading a stage of the Giro d'Italia.

RAI [Italy's national public broadcasting company] were there with their cameras, and they filmed the whole thing. I watched it on TV later that night on the highlights show …

Miguel Poblet's Ignis team was the brainchild of Giovanni Borghi.
A manufacturer of home electronics during the economic boom of the
1950s, Borghi was a sporting visionary. In addition to road and track
cycling, he sponsored basketball (Ignis Varese), the world champion
boxers Sandro Mazzinghi and Duilio Loi, and other high-class athletes.
    Spain's cycling was light years behind that of Italy and France,
and so too was its economy. Thus, Spain's cyclists earned a
comparative fortune in Italy, and nobody more so than the great Miguel
Poblet. He won twenty Giro stages all told, including three in 1960.
    The race, a genuine epic, was narrowly won by Jacques Anquetil.
On stage 14, a 68-kilometre time trial at Lake Lecco, he produced
arguably the greatest crono in Giro history. Half the peloton — fifty-
three riders — were over the time limit, forcing the race organizers
to rewrite their own rule book. The original 12 per cent time limit was
increased to 20 per cent, and all but three lived to ride another day.
    Mario Garavoglia still has the bike — and is still nuts about
bike racing.

FRANCO BOCCA
HOTSHOT
PIOSSASCO, 1969

I was a big cycling fan, and had started writing about it when I was sixteen. I wrote articles for a weekly sports paper, but then, when I was twenty, I was sent to Rome for fifteen months' military service. I carried on going to bike races, but I stopped riding my bike.

Then, at the end of the season, I decided to take my leave, and went home. My cousin was organizing a "gentleman's race", and he asked me if I wanted to take part. They were two-up time trials of about twenty kilometres, and each team was composed of a professional rider and a local amateur or cyclo-tourist. They did them at the end of every season after the Tour of Lombardy. I hadn't touched the bike for a year, but my cousin said, "It doesn't matter. It's not really a *race* as such, and we're all friends anyway."

Three or four days before the event I started a strict training regime. By the end of it, I reckon I'd have done at least 100 kilometres …

The way it worked was that there were about fifteen teams, and they drew lots to decide who you rode with. I got Ugo Colombo, which was great for me because I was a fan of his. He was one of the best *gregari* in the business; he'd won a stage at the Giro that year and finished fifth on GC. He rode for Filotex, so he gave me a jersey exactly like his. He said, "Just go steady, eh? It's not a real race." I said, "Don't worry. I'm just on leave from military service and I haven't ridden," and off we went. My dad, who followed us in our car, was immensely proud.

The first part of the circuit was pan-flat, and I figured it would be best if I put myself on the front. That way, Colombo wouldn't drop me straight away, and I wouldn't make a fool of myself. It seemed to me to make sense, but then I went and got carried away with it all and went full gas. I did a massive turn, and I could hear Colombo shouting at me to take it steady. I wasn't having that, though. I could see the couple in front coming back to us now. They'd started two minutes earlier, but they were getting nearer and nearer. I got us to within maybe two hundred metres, but then we hit the climb and my legs just … *exploded.*

I'd gone too deep on the flat, and I'd nothing left. My legs were like lead, but Colombo said, "Just grab my thigh and I'll take you up the climb." He'd have been used to doing that for Franco Bitossi, and now it was my turn. I grabbed his thigh and he started towing me up the climb. It was incredible that he could go that fast with me hanging on to his leg, but there we are. When we got to the village at the top of the climb, I let go of his leg and started the descent. But I haven't got the faintest idea what happened next.

All I know is that I ended up on my back in a field. Obviously, I was physically destroyed after such a major effort, and it could be that the extreme fatigue had a hand in it. Anyway, it seems that my bike-handling skills let me down, and the consensus seems to be that my front wheel may have got caught up in Colombo's chain.

As I understand it, Colombo carried on, and didn't notice that his captain was lying in a field with a suspected fractured vertebrae. When I came round, I was in the back of a minibus. I'd lost my glasses, and I was quite confused. I looked around and saw that Colombo and Carlo Chiappano, another of the professionals, were sitting with me, and that there was a bike on the floor. Then I noticed I had an Italian team tracksuit on, but I couldn't quite work out why. I knew I liked cycling, but I hadn't realized I'd been selected to ride for the national team …

Franco Bocca has been writing about amateur and junior cycling for more than fifty years. He does so principally for La Stampa, *although as the junior scene contracts there's progressively less to write about. There are all sorts of reasons for the decline, among them*

The intrepid Franco Bocca (centre), with Ugo Colombo (left) and Carlo Chiappano.

Italy's obsession with football and the proliferation of such "new" sports as basketball.

Moreover, the advent of the World Tour has had catastrophic consequences for the sport lower down the food chain. The Italian under-twenty-three circuit, for decades the most fertile breeding ground in world cycling, has been decimated.

Franco Bocca capsizes; he's gone and got carried away.

GIROTAPPA 2
LE MAGLIE ROSA

(RACE LEADERS)

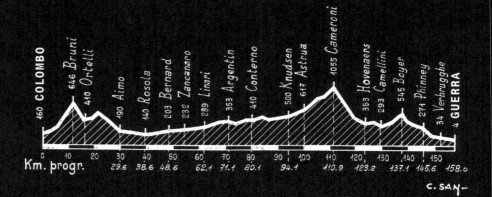

C. SAN-

I was probably the first road captain, yes. I enjoyed helping others …

In 1969 I'd been a *gregario* for Italo Zilioli and Franco Bitossi, but I'd won a stage and finished fifth without trying for the GC. Afterwards, there were offers from Salvarani and others, but I chose to stay with Bitossi at Filotex.

I finished third in 1971, but that Giro is my biggest regret, and I've never really come to terms with it. It still pains me even to think about it because I could have won that Giro if I'd had some help, but I got nothing whatsoever. I got nothing from my DS, nothing from my team and nothing from anyone else.

Let's just say that certain agreements were made, and certain things happened that were quite … *strange.* They're things you don't see on TV, and things that don't get reported in the media. In cycling, you have to look beyond the pictures and the newspapers, and try to understand where the power lies.

It was a Giro with no Eddy Merckx, so it began with four joint favourites. You had Gianni Motta and Felice Gimondi from Salvarani, then Gösta Pettersson and Zilioli from Ferretti. I was riding for Bitossi, but he wasn't really a GC rider. He was more about stages and the points jersey, and he wasn't in great shape anyway.

Gimondi missed a break and lost eight minutes, then Motta was positive at anti-doping. So that left Zilioli and Pettersson, the two from Ferretti, as favourites. Then you had Herman Van Springel from Molteni, because in Merckx's absence he became their GC rider.

Stage 5 went to Gran Sasso, in the Abruzzo. I remember Motta and Gimondi having a massive row, and Bitossi telling me to try to get in the break. That's what I did, and it earned me the *maglia rosa.* However, that was when it started to get complicated.

Gimondi had lost the Giro, but that didn't mean he didn't have a lot riding on it. Like everyone else, he was used to being beaten by Merckx, but he thought being the best Italian set him apart from the rest of us. So the last thing he wanted was for Zilioli to win the Giro, and still less for someone like me to win it. That would have been a disaster for him psychologically, but also economically. The pie is only so big, isn't it?

I started the seventh stage with seven minutes on Pettersson, and a good chance of winning the Giro. However, you can't win the Giro on your own, and certainly not when you're riding against five teams. I say five because I was riding against Salvarani, SCIC, Ferretti and Molteni, and I'm pretty sure I was riding against my own team as well.

Everything was well organized, and the trap was set for the feed at Paganico, 90 kilometres from the finish. I'd have been about fifteenth approaching it, but as they started distributing the feed, the riders surrounding me began causing mayhem. Prior to that, things had been relatively calm, but there had been a strange feeling about the whole day. My teammates should have been protecting me, but for some reason they were all at the back of the group. Anyway, amid the confusion Gimondi pulled a dirty trick and attacked. Ten of them got away, and the point is that everyone except for us and Eliolona, the poorest team in the race, was represented. That was proof that the whole thing had been organized in advance.

I wasn't one for doing deals. It wasn't in my character, and I wouldn't have had the resources to honour them. It was up to the team to do those things anyway, but Waldemaro Bartolozzi, the DS, did nothing. It's likely that both he and Bitossi were in on the deal, and I'm convinced that Vincenzo Torriani's fingerprints were all over it too. Maybe he thought that for a thirty-one-year-old *gregario* to win the Giro would have represented a loss of prestige for the race.

I needed help but I got nothing. Even Zilioli, who was my friend, couldn't pull because his teammate Pettersson was in the lead group. When the gap was still 150 metres, I called the

Ugo Colombo and Franco Bitossi are all smiles. For now.

car but nobody came and none of my teammates gave me a hand. I was on my own, trying to bring back a group including guys like Gimondi, Pettersson and Van Springel. I gave it everything, and the gap was hovering at 100 metres for a long time. In the end, though, we hit a long stretch of flat road, they all pulled and that was it. Gimondi had his moment of glory and his stage win, and I lost more than six minutes.

What Gimondi did was wrong, and most people watching couldn't understand what he hoped to achieve by it. I was *maglia rosa*, so from an Italian perspective there was nothing to be gained from it. All he'd done was drag Pettersson and Van Springel, two foreigners, into GC contention, and eliminated Zilioli. However, those who knew Gimondi understood that that was precisely the point.

The thing I never could stomach was that there was no one around to give me a hand, not even the guys from my own team. I'm sure they were in on it as well. Bitossi had seemed pleased when I'd taken the jersey. He'd told the journalists that he was convinced I could win the Giro, but after that his behaviour became ambiguous. Instead of helping me, he seemed to be riding for Claudio Michelotto. Michelotto was riding for SCIC, and was one of my rivals.

On stage 17 we rode up the Grossglockner. Michelotto was *maglia rosa*, Aldo Moser was second, then Pettersson, then me in fourth. We still had the Dolomites to come, though, and I was really strong. So despite everything, I still had a good chance of winning the Giro.

My brother was waiting on the mountain with some friends. He had two flasks of hot tea with honey and sugar ready, one for me and the other for Bitossi. I went up with Pettersson, Van Springel and Gimondi, and got my tea. Then my brother looked down the mountain with his binoculars. He saw Bitossi, and he was helping Michelotto, the *maglia rosa*, up the climb!

That evening, Bitossi was at the hotel with his family. But when my brother turned up, all hell broke loose. He had a temper on him, my brother, and he totally lost it with Bitossi. He said, "All that my brother's done for you for all these years, and instead of helping him you're helping Michelotto?"

Why would Bitossi be helping a rider from another team? Think about it for a minute …

Ultimately, Sweden's Gösta Pettersson won the incredible Giro of 1971. Van Springel was second, while Ugo, by common consent one of the nicest guys in the peloton, finished third at +2'35". As with almost every edition back then, there were — and remain — infinite conspiracy theories and all manner of accusations of skulduggery and subterfuge.

While many Giro riders complained about the roads, the heat and the chaos of the south, Ugo was in his element down there. In point of fact, all his Giro stages and each of his maglie rosa *were won in the dry heat of Abruzzo.*

Ugo's last hurrah came on the seventh stage of the 1974 Giro. By then thirty-four, he was the oldest in the race, and the night before he'd decided to pack it in. As he rolled out of Foggia (at 7.40 in the morning), he resolved to call his wife that evening to tell her he'd had enough. They had two children — Stefano and Cristina — and she'd been agitating for him to come home for a while. He decided it was time and, demob happy, told maglia rosa *José Manuel Fuente he was off for a ride on his own. Some seventy kilometres and two hours later, Ugo arrived in Chieti, still on his own.*

There are thousands of *maglia rosa* stories, but I'm pretty sure there isn't another one like mine …

I was a good climber. I rode the amateur World Championships in Switzerland, and I won a stage and the mountains jersey at the Tour de l'Avenir. My first pro season was 1962. I abandoned in the Giro in a blizzard on Passo Rolle, but they sent me to the Tour and I rode well. However, the team folded at the end of the season, so I signed for two years with San Pellegrino, Gino Bartali's team.

At the 1963 Giro there was a scandal over the *maglia tricolore*, the Italian champion's jersey. Two riders claimed to be the rightful owner, and they each started the Giro in the jersey. One of them, Marino Fontana, was riding for us, but in the end the Italian cycling federation decided to award the jersey to the other guy. They announced the ruling mid-Giro, but the riders' union refused to accept it, and so did San Pellegrino, our sponsor. They pulled out of cycling there and then, halfway through the Giro d'Italia.

So there I was, third on GC, and our sponsor had pulled the plug. The organizers told us we could carry on, and that the *Gazzetta* would pay our expenses. We stayed in the race, albeit with a plain jersey and no sponsorship on the team car. The following day was really hot and really hilly, perfect for me. I rode away and won the stage to La Spezia, so now I was second on GC. I was going really well, but suddenly my teammates were riding for a contract, ergo for themselves. I finished third behind Franco Balmamion and Vittorio Adorni, but I rode thirteen stages on my own. I literally had no team whatsoever, and I still maintain that if I'd had a few *gregari* I'd have won the Giro.

A new sponsor came on board for the rest of the season, but we never got paid. So in 1964 I signed for Carpano. I won the Tour of Tuscany easily, so they gave me a free hand at the Giro. Italo Zilioli was the leader, but I didn't have to work for him, and I won a stage down in Caserta. The trouble was that I developed a gastric problem and couldn't keep my food down. I felt terrible, and my teammates had to push me round. Carpano wanted to finish the Giro with all ten riders, and somehow I made it back. I weighed 56 kilograms when I got home, and at the end of the season Carpano folded as well.

I signed with Maino for 1965, but the stomach problems didn't go away. I wasn't able to digest my food, so I had no energy and just felt permanently tired. I didn't get a contract for the next season because I hadn't been competitive, but eventually I met a herbalist guy and, with his help, began to feel a bit better. I signed up with my old club and started training, and I still had my professional licence. I'd put some money aside, and I trained in the hope that people would remember that I'd almost won the Giro just a few years earlier. I was hoping something would turn up, and eventually I took a call from Gastone Nencini.

Nencini said he was putting a new team together for Max Meyer, and he needed fifteen riders in a hurry. I was in decent shape, so I agreed to give it another go. At the end of March they announced the route of the Giro, and lo and behold the first stage finished in Alessandria, my home town. It was a sprinters' stage, but it motivated me all the same. People round here knew me, and I wanted to get into the break and prove that I was still a rider.

I didn't much like talking to the press, and I knew there would be a lot of fuss afterwards. I didn't want to get caught up in it all, so I told Rita, my wife, to park the car just beyond the finishing line. That way, I'd be able to make straight for the hotel in Novi Ligure.

The sprinters' teams were all watching one another as we approached Alessandria, so I thought I may as well give it a shove. I did so, and as luck would have it five others jumped across. You had Balmamion, Giuseppe Milioli and Pietro Guerra, and then Roberto Poggiali and Adriano Durante from Salvarani. That was good because Durante was fast and Poggiali was strong. I didn't think for one minute we'd stay away, but then I realized they weren't coming back to us.

I was no match for Durante in a sprint, but I knew the road like the back of my hand. I knew there was a roundabout about five hundred metres from the line, and I managed to get myself last wheel headed into it. I was hoping against hope they'd go round it on the right side, and that's precisely what they did.

I couldn't believe my luck. I attacked on the left – the shorter side …

Rita: This is a big cycling town, and Giorgio was a hero. He won't admit that because he's shy, but everyone in Alessandria knew who my husband was, so people couldn't wait for that stage. I've never seen the town so packed in all my life.

So there I was waiting by the car, and suddenly I heard the announcer shout, "He's done it! He's won in his home town!"

Festivities marking the 50th Giro were to have started the previous midnight, with a series of sprints around Treviglio. However, US troops had invaded the demilitarized zone in Vietnam, and protesters had blocked the percorso.

Giorgio Zancanaro's day of grace began at 1.30 and, for the Belgian Roger Kindt, finished at 1.35. Kindt, a twenty-one-year-old neo-pro, had driven all the way from Brussels. However, he ploughed straight into a guard stone before he'd reached the city limits. He abandoned again the following year, and failed even to reach the start in 1969.

Three weeks previously, he'd won the Milano—Vignola semi-classic in record-breaking time. Two days before the partenza, however, the results came back from the anti-doping lab … Arrivederci Roger Kindt.

And Giorgio? He lost the maglia rosa the next day. He walked away from the sport the following year, appalled by much of what he was seeing and what it was becoming. He took everything he had (jerseys, shoes, caps, shorts, etc.), put it all in a box and dropped it off at the local bike shop.

Actually, not quite everything he had. He does retain one of his cycling jerseys …

Giorgio Zancanaro was a brilliant climber.

The magic of the Giro. Giorgio Zancanaro receives the *maglia rosa*.

SIMONA CAMERONI
WIFE, MOTHER, EVERYTHING
SCHIO, 1998

I married Andrea Noè in 1997, and the following year he won the *maglia rosa* …

My uncle was Giovanni Mantovani, and he'd been a professional bike rider. When I was a kid he and I were really close, and he always said, "Do what you want and marry whomever you like. Marry for love and only for love, but please don't marry a cyclist." Andrea became my boyfriend in 1992, and he turned pro the following year. My uncle came round in the end …

When Andrea was at a stage race we'd usually speak two or three times a day. He'd ring before and after the stage, and then in the evening before he went to bed. If he was going badly, he would barely say anything; but if he was feeling really good, he'd complain endlessly. I guess that's why they call him "Grumpy", but the night before this particular stage, he said it was hopeless, that he didn't have the legs, that he ought to just pack it in … I figured he must have been going really, *really* well.

The stage was tailor-made for Marco Pantani, but Andrea got in the break and was the only one who stayed away. He'd waited five years for a win, and now he'd beaten Pantani to get it.

I didn't really like the chaos around the races, and I'm quite a reserved person anyway. I preferred to watch on TV, but it was my birthday two days later so I made an exception and decided to go. Maybe it was divine intervention, but Andrea finished fourth and won the *maglia rosa*. A teammate of his won the stage, and they ended the day with all three jerseys. It was quite a birthday party, as you can imagine.

I was always Andrea's main adviser and his greatest supporter. Every time he joined a new team, or had to make a big decision, we did it together. You're right to say that he was a model professional, but being a model professional cyclist and a model husband aren't necessarily compatible. He was *extremely* meticulous about his career, and I mean every single detail. That was fine, because you can't be a top professional cyclist if you're less than 100 per cent committed. I come from a cycling family, so I was always around it and I understood it, but even for me it was difficult at times. So he *was* great, but also extremely lucky. He had someone – *me* – who took care of all the mundane, day-to-day things. And I mean *all* of them.

Camilla was born in 2000, and even that was a bit of an adventure. She was due mid-April, and we had it all worked out. Andrea would be home for the birth, then train at home for a month or so before heading off to the Giro mid-May. On 16 March he was away in Portugal doing a stage race. We spoke before the stage as usual, and then I went out in the car to do some bits and pieces. On the way home a young girl went straight through a red light and hit me head-on.

It took them two hours to cut me out of the car, and then they helicoptered me to the hospital. I'd broken my pelvis and some ribs, and had head injuries, internal bleeding … The baby was all right but the placenta was displaced so they had to

A near miss, but Simona Cameroni and daughter Camilla are getting started.

perform an emergency caesarean. I was awake through the whole thing, and thankfully she was OK.

When Andrea finished the stage, his DS told him he was a father. The problem was that, with my injuries, I was completely immobile for two weeks, then a month in a wheelchair, then crutches ... I don't suppose it was the best preparation for the Giro, but he finished fourth that year. I think maybe he was in a rush to get home!

I don't know if Andrea could have been an outright leader. There were a lot more champions back then, but he finished fourth at the Giro twice while riding as a *gregario*. He never really had enough belief in his talent, and that's one of the reasons he sometimes came across as a bit of a pessimist.

Andrea rode the Giro sixteen times, so if you think about it he spent eleven months of his life – or eleven months of *our* life – at the Giro d'Italia.

Andrea "Brontolo" Noè finished all but two of his tours of Italy. He began his final edition, that of 2011, aged forty-two. It was to be his cycling swansong, and he was to sign off in his home town, Milan. However, Noè — an exemplar of professional cycling — fell ill during the race and was forced to abandon. Simona told me she believes he will "never fully get over it".

Four years earlier Andrea had become the "least young" maglia rosa in the history of the race. He held the jersey for two days before his captain, Danilo Di Luca, relieved him of it in the Alps. The symbolism was lost on no one, and Noè's altruism was rewarded, with Di Luca holding on to claim overall victory.

PIETRO GUERRA
MAGLIA ROSA – OF SORTS
BRINDISI, 1971

The *maglia rosa*? It's a long story ...

In the early 1970s the Giro was a one-man show, and it was clear that Eddy Merckx couldn't be beaten. So a lot of Italian teams were closing down, and foreign teams didn't generally come to the Giro back then. So you had nine Italian teams and one from Spain, KAS. It was the famous "Giro 100", the Giro of a hundred riders.

Vincenzo Torriani was always looking for ways to stimulate public interest. He decided to start the race in the south because they were starved of cycling down there and he knew the crowds would be huge. Big crowds add to the occasion, right?

I was riding for Salvarani, with Felice Gimondi as the leader. The problem was that Merckx had won everything the previous season, and Gimondi hadn't been able to compete. So Salvarani approached Gianni Motta, and he agreed to join us. The idea was that the two of them would work together, and that collectively they might be able to overpower Merckx. It seemed like a good idea, and it was *certainly* a good publicity stunt, but Gimondi and Motta couldn't actually stand the sight of each other.

Gimondi had been the best when we were juniors, but then Motta had come along. He'd started late, but he was just this perfect cycling machine. I remember because I was one of the better amateurs in Italy, one of the "Gimondi group" that was destined to turn professional. I won two World Championships in the team pursuit, but Motta was ten times the rider either I or anybody else was. Gimondi was a sensational bike rider, but as regards natural ability there

PIETRO GUERRA

PIETRO GUERRA *
G. S. SALVARANI *

G.S. **Bianchi** *Campagnolo* prodotti speciali
biciclette

SALVARANI   cucine e arredamenti componibili

was no comparison. Motta rode like he didn't have a chain, and it really needled Gimondi.

In the event, Merckx got sick in the spring, so he didn't come to the Giro. So that was the situation at the beginning, and Torriani's big idea was to replace the prologue with a 62-kilometre relay race. It ran from Lecce to Brindisi, and each rider rode 6 kilometres with a baton. Then he passed the baton to the next guy, and so on and so forth. It was just like an athletics relay, but on bikes, and as a time trial.

The teams set off at two-minute intervals like in a standard time trial. We won the thing, which meant we began the opening road stage with all ten Salvaranis wearing the pink jersey. I guess it was a nice idea, and the public seemed to enjoy it.

Stage 2 was the longest of the Giro. It was 260 kilometres to Potenza with barely a metre of flat. A group that included Michele Dancelli attacked with about eighty kilometres to go, and Dancelli was a dangerous rider. Motta and Gösta Pettersson jumped out of the group to chase, and took Franco Bitossi and Enrico Paolini with them. Italo Zilioli lost three minutes, but Gimondi caved in completely. He lost nine minutes, so in effect Motta's counter had eliminated his "teammate" from the Giro. Motta had put himself in a great position to win the Giro, but you can imagine the atmosphere around the dinner table that evening. Gimondi was a grumpy so-and-so at the best of times, but that night he had a face like thunder.

The Giro rolled on, and a few days later we were in Umbria; Orvieto, I think it was. There were rumours going round that somebody had tested positive, and after the stage they announced it: Gianni Motta, on the stage to Potenza …

Gianni Motta's positive test for ephedrine, two years on from Merckx's expulsion at Savona, plunged Italian cycling into a new crisis.

Motta had already failed a doping test at the Giro, in 1968. So too had a number of others, among them Gimondi. The Italian Ministry of

Health had intervened on Gimondi's behalf, but Motta had been stripped of his stage win.

On this occasion, a tearful Motta predictably proclaimed his innocence, but elements of the "Potenza affair" do bear closer inspection. He came in with four others, and finished second in the sprint. Anti-doping regulations back then stipulated that only the first two would be tested, along with two riders selected at random. Motta couldn't have failed to know this, which begs the question of why he contested the sprint. In so doing, he guaranteed he'd be called to anti-doping, so he was either incredibly stupid or incredibly stitched up. Regardless, in one afternoon he'd contrived to sabotage not only Gimondi's Giro but also his own. Astonishing.

GIROTAPPA 3
ALCUNI VINCITORI

(A FEW WINNERS)

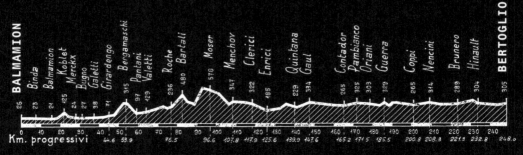

BALMAMION · Binda · Balmamion · Koblet · Merckx · Bugno · Galetti · Girardengo · Bergamaschi · Pantani · Valetti · Roche · Bartali · Moser · Menchov · Clerici · Enrici · Quintana · Gaul · Contador · Pambianco · Oriani · Guerra · Coppi · Nencini · Brunero · Hinault · BERTOGLIO

26 23 21 25 24 27 38 71 315 97 429 236 480 570 347 322 185 229 334 265 325 303 329 265 314 289 304 305

Km. progressivi   0 10 20 30 40 50 60 70 80 90 100 110 120 130 140 150 160 170 180 190 200 210 220 230 240 248.0
4.6 53.9 76.5 96.6 107.8 117.9 125.6 139.9 147.9 165.2 171.5 185.5 200.8 208.3 221.3 232.8

C. SAN-

In 1960 I was working in the spares division at Fiat and riding for the factory team. I'd won the biggest amateur stage race, the San Pellegrino, and had offers to be a professional. I was always quite conservative by nature, though, and Fiat meant security and peace of mind. There was very little of that in professional bike racing, and most careers were quite short. Obviously, the champions did well from it, but the majority didn't even last five years.

So I didn't want to burn my bridges at Fiat, just in case I crashed, didn't like professional racing, or didn't make it. I asked them to give me a year's unpaid leave – just in case – and it suited them because I was a good rider and I was good at my job. I kept popping in to work, though, to make sure they didn't forget about me …

I signed with Bianchi for 1961 and rode my first Giro. On the opening stage I nearly won the *maglia rosa*, just along the way from where I worked. I attacked, but then a group of three came across to me. One of them was Miguel Poblet, and there was no way I could beat him in a sprint. I got second, though, and was fourth after the first week. Then I missed the break on a stage down in Campania and lost twenty minutes. I finished the Giro twentieth, but the most important thing was the final week. I went well, and I recovered well.

The best result I got that season was third at the Tour of Emilia, so in some respects I wasn't that much further on. With that in mind I decided to go back to Fiat and ask for another year's leave. They said that was fine, so I signed on again. The problem was that Bianchi wound up its cycling team, and that left me in a bit of a spot. In the end, Carpano offered me a contract, and I finished up winning the Giro. At that point Fiat decided that I might just make it as a cyclist, and that it might be as well for me to resign. So that's what I did. I resigned and, I suppose, became a true professional cyclist.

I won the Giro the following year, 1963, as well. Vittorio Adorni had the jersey leading into the last-but-two stage, and I needed to find 22 seconds. So I forced a selection on the Passo Rolle, which meant that he and I were alone on the Valles. I dropped him there, rode a good descent, and put more time into him on the San Pellegrino.

Bravo Franco Balmamion.

They said I'd been lucky the previous year, and some journalists wrote that I'd only dropped Adorni because he'd lost his balance momentarily and lost my wheel. He may well have slipped, but that doesn't explain the fact that I put nearly three minutes into him. It's important to remember that what you read doesn't always correspond with what actually happened. And besides, I'm not sure you can win successive *giri* by being lucky.

I'm known as the guy who won the Giro twice without winning any stages. There are lots of reasons for that, but you don't win the Giro by winning stages. You win the Giro by not losing it, by conserving as much energy as possible, getting the jersey as late as possible, and beating the people who matter. So I *could* have won some stages, but it wouldn't necessarily have been very smart …

The 1963 Giro was a great race, and the battle between Balmamion and Adorni was a gripping denouement. The Piedmontese won the Giro with his head, while Adorni — tall, classy, aggressive in his racing style — failed to manage adequately his own resources.

As a metaphor for sport in the new television age, Balmamion and Adorni's head-to-head in the Dolomites was perfect. Balmamion was highly intelligent, but also quiet and reflective. He wasn't particularly expansive on the bike (and even less so in front of the cameras), but his modesty and decency ensured that he had no enemies in the gruppo. Adorni, on the other hand, was televisual gold. He was young, handsome and charming, and had Italian housewives tuning in to watch his post-stage interviews. The media portrayed him as the Giro's moral victor, not because he deserved to win the thing — he didn't — but because his on-screen performances were so sugary.

Adorni also had an innate understanding of how to play to the gallery. He knew that the more time he spent on TV, the greater his value to actual and putative sponsors, and he studiously cultivated the idea of himself as a "personality". He won the Giro brilliantly in 1965, and later hosted a TV game show, Ciao Mamma, with the actress Liana Orfei. It wasn't up to much, but his 200-kilometre solo win at the 1968 World Championships made up for it. Sort of.

GIANNI MOTTA
FLAWED GENIUS
TRIESTE, 1966

The first thing to say is that winning the Giro makes you wealthy. It makes you a celebrity, and celebrities earn a lot because people pay to be associated with them. So I earned a lot of money, and of course the way I won the Giro left a lasting impression. I was never that good again, but people don't forget, do they?

The celebrity thing is interesting in retrospect, but it wasn't something I gave much thought to back then. I was twenty-three years old, I was used to people telling me I was a star, and, if I'm honest, I found cycling easy. The other riders were always grumbling about how much they suffered, but for me it wasn't like that. It had been simple for me as an amateur, and as a professional I just carried on in the same vein. I expected to win every time I raced, and, if I didn't, I knew there was another win just around the corner.

I finished fifth at the 1964 Giro, having just turned twenty-one. Then I won Lombardy in the autumn, and my form was good the following spring. I was convinced I could win the Giro, but I got hit by a press car at the Tour of Romandy. I finished up with my leg in plaster for ten days, and I was a month off the bike. They sent me to the Tour de France instead, and that's probably where I became a bike rider. A Spanish guy, Julio Jiménez, kept attacking on Mont Ventoux, and so of course I kept chasing him down. I did it because I was young and conceited, and because I thought it was fun. It was my first Tour and I wanted to show off, so I was behaving like a clown. And eventually I blew. It cost me the Tour de France, and I ended up finishing third behind Felice Gimondi and Raymond Poulidor. Had I been fit, they wouldn't have got near me, but it was partly my own fault for being arrogant. Anyway, such is life, and, if nothing else, Ventoux taught me a valuable lesson.

I can't say I was suffering when I won the Giro. I was more watchful because of what had happened on Ventoux, but I won it easily. I was in a moment of grace, and I remember whistling as we rode along. On the stage to Moena it snowed on the Costalunga and it was cold. So we did more than half of the stage under a deluge, at 2,000 metres in the Dolomites. And that was one of the times I told you about, when I was eating while we climbed the Costalunga. Why eat? Firstly because I could – I had much more breath than the others – and secondly because it made sense. Being able to eat on the climbs meant that I was able to attack on the descents, and as a consequence the others couldn't eat on them …

People say I was a champion, but I never felt like one; in fact, I maintain that I wasn't one. There are two reasons for this. The first is that I only won for three years, although that's largely because one of my arteries calcified as a consequence of the crash in Switzerland. The main thing, though, is that winning came too easily for me.

A real champion is someone like Eddy Merckx, and not just because he was so much better physically. He was exceptionally talented, but what set him aside was the ability to push himself beyond the pain barrier; the harder it was physically, the stronger he was psychologically, and the better he got. He willed his body into doing unbelievable things. There were a lot of good Italian riders back then – Gimondi, Italo Zilioli, Vittorio Adorni, Michelle Dancelli – but sometimes Eddy just left you speechless.

Gianni's 1966 Giro, won with crushing authority from Zilioli and Jacques Anquetil, ought to have presaged a brilliant career. Gianni was more gifted than his great rival Gimondi (and, some argue, even than Merckx), but for all sorts of reasons his best years were behind him by his twenty-fifth birthday.

The incident with the press car at Romandy caused a hardening of one of his arteries, and he freely admits that he was riding "with one leg" for much of his career. In addition to excruciating pain, he also suffered from fragile self-esteem. Then he entrusted his physical well-being to Aldo De Donato, one of cycling's more nefarious "physicians". Gianni won sporadically until his retirement in 1976, but never again made the podium of the Giro d'Italia.

The bike factory he built sponsored an American team at the 1984 Giro. That was mind-boggling for the man in the Italian street, but even more so given that it had a woman, Robin Morton, as its DS …

The 1975 Giro was designed for Tista Baronchelli. He'd almost beaten Eddy Merckx the previous year, and that's why they decided to finish the 1975 race at the top of the Stelvio. It was a legendary climb and it was Fausto Coppi's climb, so they thought it was worth taking a risk with the weather. Baronchelli started as favourite, with Felice Gimondi and Giovanni Battaglin. I was working for Battaglin, but he collapsed so I took the jersey on the time trial. That was very tough for Battaglin psychologically, but it wasn't my fault he had a *défaillance*.

I lived the *maglia rosa* day to day. I didn't read the papers, and I didn't feel under any particular pressure. People were saying I'd crack sooner or later, but it didn't bother me. I figured that, if I collapsed, I collapsed. But I was sleeping well and recovering well.

I began the final stage 43 seconds in front of Paco Galdós, the Spanish guy. We did the San Pellegrino and the Costalunga, and I remember Roberto Poggiali, one of the sports directors, coming up to me and saying, "It's a hell of a long way up there, Fausto", as if I didn't know. The whole point of finishing on the Stelvio was to create a show, to try to replicate the Tre Cime di Lavaredo stage of the previous year. Vincenzo Torriani wanted more of the same, but of course Merckx and José Manuel Fuente weren't there. Then Gimondi was out of it and Baronchelli didn't have the legs, which just left me and Galdós fighting for the Giro.

Galdós attacked about four kilometres from the top, but I was able to go with him. After that he tried six or seven times, but he didn't have Fuente's change of pace. He was strong, but after the first two or three surges I knew he couldn't hurt me. People assume it was hard, but in reality the only thing I was really concerned about was a puncture. He kept asking me for the stage win, and in the end I gave it to him. That actually cost my teammates quite a lot. If I'd come round him, I'd have won the Cima Coppi and the green jersey as well, but there you go.

The real touch-and-go moment occurred the previous day, when Galdós and Roger De Vlaeminck attacked at the bottom of the Pordoi. I had two minutes on Galdós at the time, but I wasn't too worried about him. He couldn't descend, and from the top of the Pordoi to the finish it was 30 kilometres. The problem was De Vlaeminck, because he was going like a train and he was a good descender. I spoke to Fontana in the team car, and he said, "Don't worry about them. Baronchelli's more dangerous, so stay with him instead."

Everyone had been saying that Baronchelli was going to attack and break the race apart, but it was obvious to me that he didn't have it in him. De Vlaeminck and Galdós were up the road, and at a certain point I thought, "This is stupid!" and started going across. Gimondi came up and told me that if I didn't drop him on the climb, he'd help me out on the descent.

I'm not so famous. I'm Fausto Bertoglio and not Fausto Coppi, and I'm quite shy by nature. Also, that was the first post-Merckx Giro, and he'd been so dominant that the rest of us looked small by comparison. So maybe that's a reason why people forget, that and the fact that it wasn't live on TV that year. Whatever. I won the Giro d'Italia because I was the best rider in the race, and I won it on top of Coppi's mountain, the Stelvio.

In some respects I'm prouder of the Giro I rode the following year. I only finished third, but I proved to people that my victory hadn't been luck. I proved that I was a proper bike rider.

I'm retiring from the bike shop soon, and I'm going to write my memoirs with a fan from Rome. He knows much more about my career than I do …

Race director Vincenzo Torriani took a huge risk in finishing the Giro atop the Stelvio, but the Giro was in urgent need of something different. The Belgian Merckx had so dominated the race that sponsors were turning away from the sport, and even the state broadcaster, RAI, had pulled the plug on live broadcasts. By now, cycling — the great human opera — had allowed itself to be shunted not only off the front pages, but also out of Italian living rooms.

RAI would come back, but cycling would never recover the pre-eminence it had been cleaving to football for the thick end of two decades. Meanwhile, such "new" spectator sports as basketball and Formula 1 were also grabbing the public's attention. Two years earlier, 140 riders (ergo 14 teams) had begun the Giro, but in 1975 only 90 participated. Suddenly, Italy, the land of Coppi and Bartali, had just eight professional cycling teams. Fausto Bertoglio won a cracking Giro d'Italia, but the public indifference that accompanied it was deafening.

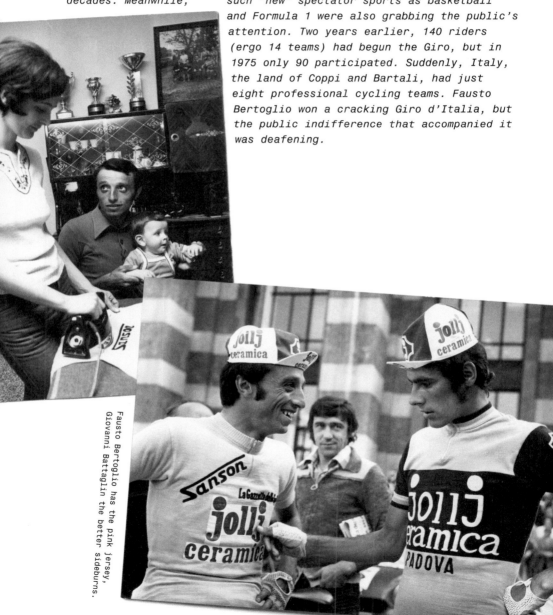

Fausto Bertoglio has the pink jersey, Giovanni Battaglin the better sideburns.

GIROTAPPA 4

I SECONDI

(SOME RUNNERS-UP)

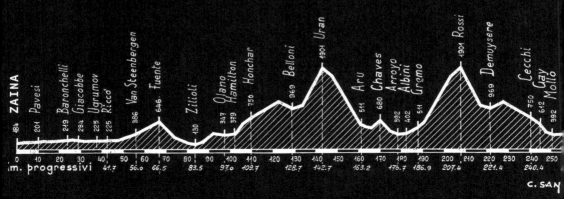

Tista would never again ride for Supermercati Brianzoli, but would sign, two weeks later, for Saronni's Del Tongo. It was his last word on the Moser–Saronni saga, and the prelude to his own cycling denouement. That autumn, he jumped out of a six-man lead group on Milan's Corso Buenos Aires to claim an extraordinary victory at the Tour of Lombardy.

On retirement, Tista – the best rider, along with Italo Zilioli, never to have won the Giro – ran a bike shop east of Milan. He's a lovely guy. Lovely, but still tortured by the Giro d'Italia.

Part of the trade-off for famous cyclists is that they become instruments. Without the journalists they wouldn't be paid, but the flip side is that the job of the journalist is to capitalize on what the cyclists do. In our case we raced against one another virtually every week, and there were very few potential winners. It was parochial, and parochialism is the source of all the best sporting rivalries. That's it; that's the way cycling always worked.

I turned professional as "the next big thing", the new star who was supposedly going to win everything. I'd been Italian junior champion, but virtually overnight I was thrown into this media world I didn't understand, and which sought to appropriate me and my career.

Journalists have to sell newspapers, and to do that they have to have stories. Rivalries are the thing that drives professional sport, and if a natural one doesn't present itself, they have to invent one. So every public utterance you make can be construed in a certain way, because however banal it is they will make it fit their agenda.

Then, as a sportsman, you have a decision to make. Either you go along with it and play the game, or you disengage. I tried to deal with it at first, but I wasn't prepared for it and I was very young. The thing that I really struggled with, though, was the way they reconfigured what I said. The character they seemed to be portraying didn't correspond with who I thought I was.

What happened was that I came along and won four races in succession in the autumn of 1963, and they were convinced I was the new Fausto Coppi. Meanwhile, Michele Dancelli was turning professional too, and he finished third at Lombardy. The following spring, Gianni Motta started, and he won a big stage at the Giro straight away. I finished runner-up behind Jacques Anquetil, and then Gianni won Lombardy that autumn. At that point the journalists started

Italo Zilioli (right) and Franco Balmamion (at the back) in his christmas jumper.

playing us off against one another, because that's the business they're in. Their editors are looking for anything they can get their teeth into, so if it isn't there, they try to induce it. Motta and I were similar riders, and we were more or less the same age. So, whether I liked it or not, that was the angle, and there wasn't much I could do to stop it.

In the end, I figured out that the best thing to say was nothing at all, because that way they'd realize that I wasn't their type. Zilioli versus Motta became Felice Gimondi versus Motta, and theirs was a rivalry that didn't need playing up because it came from within.

I wouldn't say I was the *best* descender, but I was able to do it pretty well. I crashed on Superga and somewhere on the Côte d'Azur, but I never hurt myself. I always found the descents interesting because there was a lot of psychology at play. You might suffer going up, but you're not putting yourself at risk physically. So there's talent, which you can't acquire, and also the old magic, which is worry.

Anyway, I always thought you were as well to attack a couple of kilometres before the top, because that way they couldn't see your trajectory going down …

Italo was a sensational bike rider. With the possible exception of Gianni Motta, nobody was more elegant, and certainly nobody went down mountains with such grace. One former rider I spoke to described Italo's descents as "mesmeric, like watching a snowflake".

Like many before him (Romeo Venturelli and Ercole Baldini being the most famous), Italo had been anointed "the new Fausto Coppi" by the Italian press. Then, however, he finished second at the Giro three times in succession, behind Jacques Anquetil, Vittorio Adorni and Motta.

At that point the "new Coppi" mantle passed to Felice Gimondi. Gimondi was a better cyclist than Italo — he was absolutely ruthless in pursuit of victory — but of course he wasn't the new Coppi either. Like all cyclists, Coppi was a product of the social, sporting and geopolitical context in which he existed. There was no way that Gimondi, or even Eddy Merckx, could generate the electricity that Coppi had in tandem with Gino Bartali.

I was second at the Giro in 1981, and then again the following year …

What happened was that a Swedish guy named Bernt Johansson won the 1976 Olympics. Then he moved to an Italian professional team, the Swedish media followed him a lot, and everyone got into Italian cycling.

I moved to Bergamo with another Swede, Alf Segersäll, and in 1980 we each signed two-year contracts with Bianchi. I won a stage at Paris–Nice straight away, and finished second at the Tour of Trentino. Then I won a stage at the Giro and finished fourth on GC. I won the white jersey as well, so it was quite a good start.

The following year we had a very good team for the Giro, with me, Gianbattista Baronchelli and Silvano Contini. We were three of the strongest riders, and our sports director, Giancarlo Ferretti, decided we wouldn't have one designated leader. The road would decide, and in the end it decided that Giovanni Battaglin would win instead.

I tended to get stronger in the final week, while Baronchelli and Contini struggled. So I think I could have won the Giro if the team had worked for me, but I was very young. I was a twenty-five-year-old Swedish guy living in Italy and it was all new to me. At the time, I was happy with second, but in the days that followed I started thinking about it …

There were some moments in the race that I didn't understand, but I've never spoken about it to anybody. You know that in cycling you can do a race with guys from other teams, and if there's a group of riders doing it in a certain way it can be difficult to win the race? You know the stage up to Tre Cime di Lavaredo? That was a strange day, and things happened that I couldn't understand. I was too young to understand.

I had an offer from France at the end of the season, and perhaps I should have gone. The races in France were more aggressive, while in Italy it was *piano piano* for 100 to 150 kilometres. That was no good for me because I needed it to be hard.

It was the same in 1982, with me, Baronchelli and Contini, and nobody knowing who was the leader. I was second again, behind Bernard Hinault, and afterwards Hinault told Sven-Åke Nilsson that if Bianchi had raced for me I would have won. Even Hinault had problems with me, but I wanted to help everybody.

I told Ferretti a couple of years ago that I should have won at least one Giro. I said that if he'd motivated me more to attack I'd have done it. I was *extremely* strong back then, but I was too polite and too friendly with everybody. I'd be sitting there in the group with so much more to spend, and I didn't do it. I think maybe it would have been difficult for Contini and Baronchelli if I'd have won the Giro, and maybe Ferretti wanted to avoid that.

There's another thing I want to say. The thing I'm most proud of is that I did it without taking anything. I was a clean rider throughout my career. There was a DS who came to me – I think it was after a Giro – and he asked me if I wanted to change teams. He told me they had what I needed to win the Giro, and he wasn't referring to the strength in my legs. I said, "Thanks, but I'm not interested."

There are lots of guys who have to live with the lie, and lots of guys who have decided they could no longer live with it. They've had to come out and admit everything, but I never had to deal with that. I could have won the Giro, and probably *should* have won the Giro, but I don't regret anything. I'm absolutely fine with my cycling career because I know I did it right.

Many felt that Bianchi's "tactics" in 1981 and 1982 were strange.
In 1981 Prim was easily the best equipped of the three leaders to
deal with the final-day time trial into Verona, and yet still Ferretti

Italo Zilioli has gone deep. Very.

vacillated. With no apparent strategy, he chose not to unite the team behind Prim, and nor indeed behind Contini or Baronchelli. Those two collapsed on Tre Cime, and Prim lost the Giro to Giovanni Battaglin by just 38 seconds.

The following year Hinault arrived at the Giro with a weak team, and also undercooked. He was seemingly there for the taking, but l'Unità lamented that Bianchi gave him an "armchair ride" during the first ten days. Prim later punctured, and shipped two minutes waiting for his team car to turn up. He would lose the race by 2'35".

There was no suggestion of jingoism within Bianchi, although at first glance Ferretti's inertia does seem baffling. The Giro d'Italia, however, is the tour of Italy, and Bianchi was an Italian frame-builder. Tommy Prim was a sensational bike rider and a very popular figure, but he was also … Swedish.

The age of innocence.

46

GIROTAPPA 5

LE ALTRE MAGLIE

(THE OTHER JERSEYS)

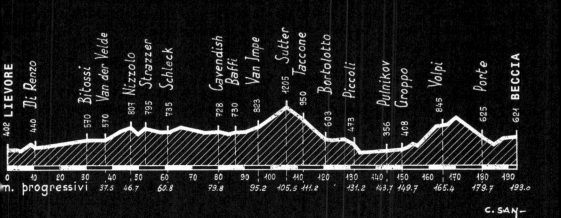

402 LIEVORE · 440 Di Renzo · 570 Bitossi · 570 Van der Velde · 807 Nizzolo · 795 Strazzer · 735 Schleck · 728 Cavendish · 730 Baffi · 823 Van Impe · 1205 Sutter · 950 Taccone · 603 Bortolotto · 473 Piccoli · 356 Pulnikov · 408 Groppo · 845 Volpi · 625 Porte · 621 BECCIA

m. progressivi

0 · 10 · 20 · 30 · 37.5 · 46.7 · 50 · 60.8 · 70 · 79.8 · 90 · 95.2 · 105.5 · 111.2 · 120 · 131.2 · 143.7 · 149.7 · 165.4 · 179.7 · 193.0

C. SAN—

In 1967 the Giro celebrated its fiftieth anniversary, so there was a lot of hype around it. The *Gazzetta* really went to town with the publicity and the festivities.

My team had neither a GC rider nor a high-class climber. In effect, the only way for us to earn any money was to get in breaks and try to win an intermediate sprint here and there. I wasn't much of a sprinter, so my chances of contributing were slim.

On the stage up in Trento, sixty-seven riders were sent home because they were over the time limit. That left me way down on GC, third to last. The last place was Tommaso de Pra, and second-last was Giuseppe Grassi. Then, two days before the finish, the *Gazzetta* made an announcement. It was going to award the last man 500,000 lire and a special *maglia nera*. They wanted to pay homage to Sante Carollo and Luigi Malabrocca, and to the golden years after the war. I would have been earning about 150,000 lire a month, so for a team like ours 500,000 lire was a lot of money.

On the final day there was a split stage. The first part rolled out of Tirano and finished at the top of the Madonna del Ghisallo. Then, in the afternoon, there was the usual cavalcade into Milan, but of course that was neutralized. So in effect there was only the morning left to try to win the *maglia nera*. My DS, Marino Fontana, told me I should try, because not only would it be good publicity for the sponsor, but also extra money for the guys to share out.

The strategy was for me to get into the break. We figured it would need five or six riders in it, because it would need to make it to the Ghisallo. So I needed to be sure it was the right one, and also to keep an eye on De Pra. It was important that he wasn't in it, because that way I'd be out of sight and out of mind. I needed for him to think I wasn't interested in the *maglia nera*, and in that respect going with the break made perfect sense.

It transpired that there were seven of us in the break. Panizza pulled, then Galdós, and a load of others I can't remember. When we reached the bottom of the Ghisallo we had eight minutes on the bunch, and half way up it Fontana appeared in the team car. He gave me the nod, and as we got near a bar I made out that I'd punctured. The rest of the break carried on while the mechanic pretended to sort the bike out, and when they were out of sight I walked straight into the bar.

Of course, all the people in there were watching the Giro, waiting for it to come past. They'd been watching me on TV a few minutes earlier, but now I was sitting among them eating a sandwich. I just sat down and waited, and eventually the peloton came into view. I hid inside until I saw De Pra come by, gave it a few more minutes just to be sure, and climbed back on to my bike. And that's how I won the *maglia nera*.

The maglia nera, *the black jersey of the last man in the race, had been extremely popular during the post-war "golden age". It had made a legend of Luigi Malabrocca, its "winner" in 1946 and 1947.*

Malabrocca owes his fame to his legendary duels with the anti-hero Sante Carollo, the 1949 black jersey, but also to the accidents of his birth.

Malabrocca was born in Tortona, a stone's throw from Fausto Coppi's Castellania. The two men had raced together as juniors, but while poor, fragile Coppi was condemned to become Il Campionissimo, Malabrocca enjoyed life as his alter ego. Malabrocca was actually a very decent rider, but in cycling-crazed post-war Italy there were any number of those. And besides, there was money — a great deal of it — to be made in finishing last.

Lucillo Lievore would finish last again in 1971.

Assisted by Ercole Baldini, Lucillo Lievore makes good his escape.

Do you remember the famous duel between Pavel Tonkov and Marco Pantani in 1998? The day Pantani broke Tonkov on Montecampione? You do? Good, because that had nothing whatsoever to do with me …

Those two were ten times stronger than me, and I never saw any of it because I was out the back as usual. When I say "out the back", I don't mean out the back of the GC group, or even the non-GC group. What I mean is out the back of the *gruppetto*, turning myself inside out to beat the time limit.

It was my second Giro. I'd finished last the previous year and I'd assumed it would be easier second time round. It wasn't, though; it was absolutely awful. I had a terrible saddle sore, and I can't begin to describe the agonies I went through. Every single minute of it was excruciatingly painful, and I had a fever as well. So each day I was finishing in a worse state than the last. I had to help Massimo Strazzer, our sprinter, but I could barely help *myself.*

Of course, I wanted to abandon, but I couldn't. My friends and family were coming up from Abruzzo, 650 kilometres away, and they had the bus booked. It was going to be the biggest party of the year, and I couldn't let them down by not getting round. They were looking forward to it, but you have no idea what it's like unless you've been there. It was a living hell …

Two days earlier there had been the big stage to Val Gardena. It was the day Pantani broke away with Giuseppe Guerini and destroyed Alex Zülle, the *maglia rosa*. That stage tends to be forgotten about because of what happened on Montecampione, but I certainly won't forget it. Pantani put forty-five riders out of the race that day, either climbed off or over the time limit. Not five or twenty-five, but *forty-five* – a third of the peloton. Bear in mind that Guerini didn't do a single turn all the way up the Sella, just came round Pantani for the win. So everybody focused on what he did to the other GC riders, and obviously that's the story of the Giro. What they tend to forget is the havoc it caused among the normal guys.

I'd be the first to get dropped each day, and all the cars would start passing me. First the team cars, then the VIP cars and the sponsors' cars. They'd offer to let me hang on to the wing mirrors, but I wasn't having that. Eventually, I'd be left on my own with just the police outriders, just in front of the broomwagon. They started giving me bottles of water, encouraging me and even offering me a tow. They could see I was suffering, and they wanted me to make it.

I'm not one of those who defines his career through having finished last at the Giro. I won a stage at the Vuelta, one at the Tour of Sardinia, and a few others. I wasn't rubbish, and when I wasn't working for my team I was a bit of a breakaway specialist. I once rode 240 kilometres alone at Milan–San Remo, so I wasn't out of my depth. It's just that when it came to the mountains, there was an abyss between Pantani and me.

So finishing last was a consequence of finishing every day. I'm very proud of being one of the ninety who did that, because there was a lot of climbing, Pantani was smashing it to pieces, and, as I said, I was right on the limits.

I can't remember the name of the journalist, but he did an experiment on the last day. We were at Lugano and he interviewed Pantani and me in parallel. He asked us the same questions – how we prepared for the Giro, the sacrifices we made, what it was like to be at the end of the journey – but obviously neither of us knew how the other was responding. The bizarre thing is that most of the answers were the same.

That said, I don't believe that Pantani suffered anything like as much as I did during that Giro. He was far too good a cyclist for that, and good cyclists make other people suffer ten times more than they suffer themselves. Take it from me: it was much easier for him to win in Milan than for me to get there three hours behind him …

The Montecampione stage of the 1998 Giro, when Pantani finally broke Tonkov's resistance, was an epoch-defining moment. Arguably more astonishing still, however, was what happened two days later.

Heading into the penultimate-day crono, a flat 34 kilometres from Mendrisio to Lugano, Pantani was leading Tonkov by 1'28". The Russian, however, had a much better pedigree against the watch. Six days earlier there had been a 40-kilometre time trial around Trieste, its topography broadly similar. It had been won by the Swiss maglia rosa Alex Zülle. He'd put 1'22" into Tonkov, and a massive 3'26" into Pantani.

Thus, Tonkov was odds-on to beat Pantani, and logic suggested it would be nip and tuck for the GC. Instead, Pantani produced an astonishing ride. He finished third on the stage, besting not only Tonkov but also — by more than a minute — the specialist Zülle.

Interviewed at the conclusion, Tonkov declared (many believe obliquely) that Pantani "ought to consider doing the hour".

Sponsors. Count 'em.

I was thirty-one and in the form of my life, but it was still incredibly demanding, both physically and mentally. People often say it's harder to win the points jersey than the GC, and that may be true. You don't ever get an easy day; you have to bury yourself to get over the climbs, and as often as not you're sprinting two or three times a day.

I'd already abandoned three times because of allergies. I used to get chronic stomach pain, and there was nothing I could do about it. I remember finishing second in a stage of the 1996 Giro, and being in such agony that I couldn't ride the following day. Thankfully, it improved from 1999 onwards, but when I was in my mid-twenties it was terrible.

I used to suffer with allergies, diarrhea, you name it. There were times when I literally shat myself from the sheer physical exertion, but I was a racing cyclist and physical exertion was what I was about. Besides, it was better to shit myself than to abandon, because to abandon was to be defeated. That was worse than any illness or physical discomfort. The thought of it was too shameful even to contemplate.

Mario Cipollini was the reference for someone like me, although I never once managed to beat him at the Giro. Danilo Hondo and Ivan Quaranta were faster than me as well. Between them, they won all the sprint stages, but I won the points and Intergiro jerseys and the new combativity prize.

I'd ridden on the same team as Quaranta in 1999. He'd won two stages at the Giro, and it had earned him a big contract at Alexia. I was left behind at Mobilvetta, a small team with a small budget, but his leaving meant that they started to build the Giro team around me. They weren't big-name riders by any means, but having them work for me gave me a chance for once. If you're going to be competitive in the points, you can't waste a drop of energy, and even more so if your rivals are faster.

Bear in mind that a sprinter who doesn't finish on the podium is actually a liability for a cycling team. His job is to hide for as long as possible, ideally until the last 500 metres. After that, the whole thing happens in the blink of an eye, so if he finishes fourth or fifth nobody sees him. Finishing fourth or fifth on a mountain finish is much more valuable, because a summit finish evolves over half an hour or so. People watching on TV have a lot of time to absorb the names of the sponsors.

People tend to associate the points jersey with speed, but I don't. For me, it was the result of an attitude, a huge physical and psychological undertaking, and sacrifice. I was an 80-kilogram sprinter, and 2001 was one of the most mountainous editions of the Giro since the war.

I don't have any photographs, I'm afraid. I've had a look around, but when I split up with my previous wife she threw a load of my stuff away. Forgive me, but unfortunately I've lost a lot of my memories …

Max Strazzer rode the Giro nine times without winning a stage. He secured his 2001 points jersey by picking up points in the hills, and by getting into the morning breakaways whenever possible. In so doing, he also claimed the inaugural combativity award.

A red points jersey had been introduced in 1967, but two years later, at the 1969 Giro, it was changed to cyclamen. Two weeks before the race, the sponsor had pulled out, leaving Vincenzo Torriani with a major headache and a significant cash shortage. He instructed Rino Negri, a Gazzetta journalist, to ring Piero Belloni. The boss of

the Termozeta domestic appliance company put up the money, and the
cyclamen jersey was born. In 2010 it reverted to red.

Introduced in 1989, the blue Intergiro jersey was abandoned after
the 2006 edition.

Santina: Orsago is a small village, maybe 3,500 people. They all know each other, and this is a big cycling area. So it was natural that everyone followed Claudio's career. He was the local hero and he made everyone proud. The parson would always ring the church bells when he won, and the whole village would have a party.

The big champions had fan clubs, but there weren't many back then. Claudio was an extremely popular rider, and I guess that's why his took off. We had T-shirts, stickers, membership cards and the like. I don't recall how many members there were, but probably about 400. There were always 300 people for the dinners, and a busload for the mountain stages of the Giro. That was the highlight of the season.

Claudio: I won my first King of the Mountains at the 1979 Giro. I could have won at least a couple prior to that, but I wasn't ambitious enough. The previous year, Ueli Sutter had pleaded with me and I'd let him win it. Afterwards I remember thinking, "Christ! How stupid must I be?"

Winning the jersey was quite easy for me. They always designed the Giro for Francesco Moser, and I was riding for him. There were no summit finishes, and such climbs as there were tended to be a long way out. The idea was that if Moser lost time on the climbs, he'd get it back on the descents, and of course my job was to stay with him. The upshot was that I was able to pick up points along the way, so that's what I did. I found it quite easy to sprint out of the group and get the points.

Santina: Everyone would come round here to watch on TV. You could see Claudio was the best climber, but he'd have to wait for Moser and it used to drive us crazy! One time my dad was here and he was bellowing at the television screen. He was shouting, "Go! Go! Leave him there! Go on your own!" He never did, though …

He'd be riding along during a mountain stage, and he'd just climb off his bike and wait! They asked Moser recently if it was true. He said it wasn't, but it was!

Claudio: During the early years there were lots of times when I could have ridden away. I remember Eddy Merckx clinging on to my wheel once. I turned to him and said, "Hang on there …"

Santina: The problem was his character. He won't have it, but he was too nice, too accommodating. The others would have rebelled, but with him it was, "OK, whatever. Who cares?"

Claudio: What can I say? I had a *gregario*'s mentality, and that's it.

Santina: He'd do anything to keep the peace, but for the rest of us – his family, his fan club, the people in the village – it was terrible. We understood that was his job, but it didn't make it any less frustrating.

Claudio: Yes, but I had a responsibility to the others as well. I was part of a team and I had to do what was best for everyone, not just Claudio Bortolotto. There were ten people in the team, and you couldn't just do as you saw fit. That wouldn't have been fair.

Guys like Sorlini or Marchetti would ride for the first 100 kilometres with Moser attached

to them. Then of course they'd abandon, but nobody saw them because their work was done before the race came on TV. They didn't get anything like the attention I did, but they were doing their job just as I was doing mine ... Anyway, I left Moser's team in 1980.
I won the King of the Mountains that year as well, and in 1981.

These days you have guys winning it who aren't real climbers. When I was riding, it was a big thing and it had real value. People like Sutter, Beat Breu and Lucien Van Impe were genuine climbers, and their objective was to win the green jersey. Nowadays, they seem to win it almost by accident ...

Claudio won the green jersey of the King of the Mountains three times. He began the Giro nine times, finished them all, and finished in the top ten three times.

When he won his first Giro stage in 1977, the press reported that he'd have won more had he not been afraid of the solitude. He was a great rider, they said, but he always allowed himself to be caught so as not to feel alone.

His second stage win, two years later, was somewhat contentious. Mario Beccia, a friend from a neighbouring village, attacked 25 kilometres from the line. Team leader Francesco Moser instructed Bortolotto to chase him down, and to sit on his wheel. He did as he was told, and came round Beccia in the sprint. Thus, simply by fulfilling his obligation to his team leader, Bortolotto was seen to pilfer the stage.

Claudio Bortolotto and friends in 1981, the year of acrylic.

MARCO GROPPO
PLAYBOY CYCLIST
PARMA, 1983

In 1982 I was a twenty-one-year-old riding for Lucien Van Impe. He was thirty-five by then, but he was still a brilliant climber. He focused on the mountains jersey, and working for him meant I was always with the best climbers. Day by day I improved my GC position, and eventually I found myself in the white jersey. I kept it to the end and finished the Giro ninth. Had it not been for the time trials and the fact that I was working for Van Impe, I'd have been in the top five, maybe even the top three …

I was hopeless against the watch and struggled on the flat, but suddenly I was the future of Italian stage racing. They gave me a new contract worth ten times what I'd been on before, and told me I was going to be the leader at the 1983 Giro and Tour de France. I had to prepare differently, so gym work, motor pacing and bigger gears to improve in the time trials. By the time the Giro started I was better on the flat, but hopeless on the climbs. I'd get halfway up them and blow up completely because I was 5 kilos heavier.

So I didn't have the condition, but my story is that a certain journalist wrote an article about me and a Giro podium girl. It became a cause célèbre, and now I'm known as the big talent who threw it all away …

I'll start by stating that there *was* a story with a podium girl, and I can confirm that we stayed together for eleven years. She was part of the Giro, and she was beautiful. She was French, but she'd married an Italian guy and she lived in Monza. She and her husband were

separated, she was five years older than me, and in simple terms I fell in love with her. Then, like an idiot, I mentioned it to one of the *soigneurs*, as you do when you're young and naive …

After the stage to Parma, she was staying in the same hotel as me. We stayed up chatting, and somebody saw us get into the lift together. I was rooming with a Dutch guy named Frits Pirard, and I admit that I was late to bed. Instead of getting in at 9, I would have arrived at about 10. I figured that Pirard would have been sleeping, and I didn't want to disturb him. So I got undressed before I got into the room, and slid straight into bed.

The next morning the *soigneur* said, "What's going on? You've been seen going into that girl's room, and Pirard says you didn't have your pyjamas."

The news spread like wildfire, and the next day I crashed and hurt my knee. At first they put me in an ambulance, but then they gave me a painkilling injection and I managed to finish the stage. I went to hospital for an X-ray, but they said there was nothing. I started the following day but the pain was too much and I had to abandon.

A story appeared in *Tutto Sport* about how I hadn't been able to concentrate because I'd spent the night with a girl, how I was a playboy, how the money had gone to my head, and how all I ever talked about was cars and women. Then Adriano De Zan, the RAI commentator, repeated it on air, and that was it, because whatever De Zan said was law. In fact, Roberto Visentini – who was a *real* cycling playboy – actually came up and thanked me because the media left him in peace for a while.

I came home from the Giro and called the girl on the phone. We started going out together like any normal young couple, but then it really started. There were threats, anonymous phone calls, people saying I'd betrayed the profession, betrayed Van Impe, betrayed my teammates, stories about how she'd been paid by Francesco Moser and Giuseppe Saronni to stop me … Believe it or not, people were comparing my story to Fausto Coppi's with the *Dama Bianca*.

I abandoned the Tour, they refused to pay me, and the whole thing finished with the lawyers. I admit that I didn't perform, but if you analyse it there were also vested interests at stake. The media likes to create that kind of story because intrigue and gossip are always good for business. Then the team had an economic interest. I was earning a lot of money – I can't deny that – and objectively I wasn't producing results. They wanted a pretext to get me off the wage bill, so the story with Mandy was ideal for them.

Marco's story is extraordinary, but also illustrative of cycling's bizarre relationship with womanhood. Following his acrimonious split with Metauro Mobili after a disastrous Tour, La Stampa *referred to Marco as a "cycling Montgomery Clift". They added that someone as*

young, handsome and charismatic as Marco
would have been the standard-bearer in almost
any other sport.

    The management and riders of Metauro Mobili
challenged Marco's version of events, but
also stated that the girl wasn't the issue
per se. They said his private life was his own,
but he was unfit, unreliable and hopelessly
unprofessional. As a consequence, his
performances were substandard, but it was he
— not they — who initiated legal proceedings.

    Marco signed a minimum-wage contract for
1984 with Dromedario, but didn't get any
results and abandoned the Giro once more.
Two years on from his staggering performance
at the 1982 Giro, he found himself working
at a petrol station.

    (The podium girls at the 1983 Giro were sponsored by Irge,
a manufacturer of pyjamas. You couldn't make it up.)

MARIO BECCIA
SEVENTH HEAVEN
SPOLETO, 1977

I remember that first win with absolute clarity. It was the first summit finish of my first Giro, and I'd never seen so many people at a bike race before.

I'd only been riding for two years when I turned pro. I was twenty-one years old, and because they didn't know me they afforded me a bit of liberty. I dropped them all, and started enjoying the moment. I won the stage by 13 seconds, but I could have won by much more. I could easily have taken the *maglia rosa* as well, but I was so busy enjoying the show that I just rolled over the line. When the GC came up, I was 8 seconds behind Francesco Moser in second place. I'm not sure he'd have been too happy had I taken the jersey – I was his *gregario* after all – but I was so immersed in the moment that it never even crossed my mind.

I won the white jersey, but in some respects it was the beginning of the end. Michel Pollentier won that Giro, and that was the last thing the Italian public wanted. From then on, Vincenzo Torriani started designing the "Giri of the Tunnels" for Moser and Giuseppe Saronni, and I was a 56-kilogram pure climber.

You'd have 140 kilometres of time trials at the Giro. You could argue that was fair enough, but the rest of the race would be one flat stage after another. I was being paid to deliver results, but I started the Giro with a 10-minute handicap. So I set about making myself the best *passista* I could be. I lost a lot on the climbs, but I had to build muscle mass to be competitive.

If there's one Giro that sums it up, I'd say 1985. Torriani wanted to give Moser the best chance of winning it, so he included four time trials and neutralized the mountain stages. The Dolomites were in the first week, and there was only one summit finish, at Val Gardena. The other "Dolomite" stage finished with an 80-kilometre descent to Vittorio Veneto.

Eventually, we reached the Apennines, and a mountain finish at Gran Sasso. Days like that were very few and far between, so I was in the front with Marino Lejarreta, Roberto

Visentini and the rest of the climbers. It was a big mountain, and the first chance for us to make an impact. I remember it well because Franco Chioccioli broke away, and we were asking ourselves why he was attacking so early. We soon found out. The stage finish was about three kilometres into the climb! Chioccioli won – he must have been tipped off – but it was the only time that the spectators had to be bussed *down* the mountain to watch a stage finish. We were just getting ready for the battle, but we rounded a corner and there was the red kite! It was literally over before it had even begun.

The same happened at Gran Paradiso, and when they interviewed me after the stage it all came out. The Giro was becoming a farce, and I said as much on live television. Two days later, the jury fined me 5 million lire.

In 1982 I was with Hoonved, and the patron was a guy from Varese named Erminio Dall'Oglio. At that time, Roberto Sassi was their athletics trainer, and they brainwashed me into accepting his brother Aldo to train me. So I followed his training methods, and he arranged for me to meet with Dr Conconi. He's become a sort of scapegoat for blood doping, but for me he was a person worthy of respect. He simply said, "Look, if you want to transfuse, that's fine, but it's entirely up to you. The only thing is that if you choose *not* to do it, the others will overtake you." I chose not to do it because I didn't trust it, and my career suffered as a consequence. Dino Zandegù, my DS, used to say, "Mario, you can't go to war with rubber bullets!" but it was my choice and I wanted it to be my career.

My attitude was, "I'll push myself to the very limits of what I can achieve, but only on my own terms." I wasn't making moral judgements about the others, but I can look in the mirror and be sure that *I* won La Flèche Wallonne and the Tour of Switzerland. My inspiration came from the fact that they said it couldn't be done. It wasn't about beating Roger De Vlaeminck, Moser and Saronni per se. It came from within, and if I'd done it with transfusions, it wouldn't have been mine ...

After the legendary Giro of 1985, Roberto Visentini put his bike in a vice and took a saw to it. He then put the pieces into a bin bag and sent them to Davide Boifava, his sports director. (Boifava persuaded Visentini to carry on, and he won the Giro the following year.)

Mario finished in the top ten six times, and won three stages. He was a talented climber, but he was in the wrong place at the right time. It was impossible for someone like him to win the Giro because the races were designed for Moser and Saronni, and, as a consequence, for Bernard Hinault. An easier route meant the Frenchman was more likely to partipate, because he was able to use the Giro as training for the Tour de France.

GIROTAPPA 6
GREGARI D.O.C.
(THE GREGARI)

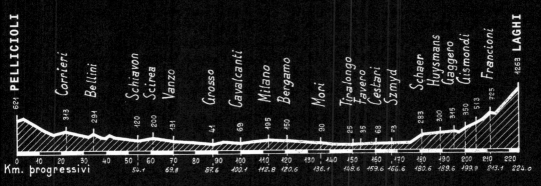

PELLICIOLI 621 · Corrieri 343 · Bellini 294 · Schiavon 420 · Scirea 200 · Vanzo 434 · Grosso 44 · Cavalcanti 69 · Milano 495 · Bergamo 450 · Mori 90 · Tiralongo 25 · Favero 35 · Cestari 68 · Szmyd 73 · Schaer 283 · Huysmans 300 · Gaggero 345 · Gismondi 350 · Francioni 513 725 · LAGHI 4263

Km. progressivi

0 10 20 30 40 50 60 70 80 90 100 110 120 130 140 150 160 170 180 190 200 210 220 224.0

54.1 69.8 87.6 100.1 112.8 120.6 136.1 148.6 159.6 166.6 180.6 189.6 199.3 213.1

C. SAN—

I suppose I'd classify myself as a mountain *gregario*. That term's out of fashion these days, but that's what I was and I didn't feel demeaned by it. Actually, quite the reverse; I felt proud to do it, and it was a true reflection of who I was. I was light, I liked going up mountains, and I liked to help others.

I'd have liked to earn a fortune, but I just wasn't fixated on the results. I tended to be happy if I'd ridden well, done my job and enjoyed myself, and the result was secondary to that. That's maybe because I have an innate lack of confidence or ambition, or something like that. What I do know is that I could never become a champion because I was neither good enough nor aggressive enough. The champions aren't generally "ordinary" people, and I think I was just a pretty simple, straightforward guy.

In 1992 I teamed up with Gianni Bugno at Gatorade. Gianni was everything I wasn't as a man and as a cyclist, and he had the sort of class the rest of us could only ever dream about. I was good at my job, but people like him and Miguel Indurain were in a different orbit altogether. So I felt honoured to ride for him, and he and I became quite close.

Aside from a pro-am stage in Mexico, I didn't win in my first four years as a professional. It didn't bother me unduly, but then just before the 1994 Giro they sent us to ride the Du Pont Tour in America and I won a stage. Nobody in Italy paid any attention because it was in America, but it reminded me what winning felt like.

The Giro started a fortnight or so later. The fourth stage was a tough mountain-top finish at Campitello Matese, the first big moment for the GC guys. We were trialling Shimano SPD pedals for the first time at that Giro, and I remember that my right pedal broke. As I was getting back on to the group, I passed Bruno Reverberi, one of the sports directors. He and I got on quite well, and he said, "Hey, Oscar! When are you going to get round to winning a bike race?" Of course, he was only joking …

When we got to the climb, Bugno said he felt OK, and I did too. So we decided I'd attack to force a selection in the *maglia rosa* group, and if they didn't come after me I might even have enough to win the stage. So that's what I did – I attacked.

I was getting really close to the finish, but then Evgeni Berzin came across to me. Gewiss had been winning everything that spring, but I didn't want to give up. In the event, though, it was hopeless; Berzin just came by me and there was nothing I could do.

I didn't really think much of it at the time, but it transpired that Berzin had taken the pink jersey as well. Obviously, both he and his DS had known he was going to get it, so in reality he ought to have been happy with that and left the stage to me. That's the way it had always worked in the Giro, and people were quite angry about it. When I realized, I was a bit upset as well, because he had no business going for the stage win. I didn't realize it at the time, but the chance would never come again. I rode the Giro eight times all told, but I never managed to win a stage.

My biggest regret would probably be 1998. I was riding for Mercatone Uno, Marco Pantani's team, and of course he won the Giro/Tour double that year. I didn't get to ride either because everything was political and I was never much good at that stuff. My wife always says I'm too soft, and I guess they just found it easy to leave me out. I never really understood how to manipulate other people …

I started as a DS in 2003, and I've lived through the evolution of cycling. It's changed dramatically, and in many respects it's much better now. You can bemoan the lack of romance all you like, but with the likes of Sky, the preparation and performance levels are incredible by comparison. That's a good thing, no?

The only thing that saddens me is that people – and, if I'm honest, it's often Anglo-Saxon people – assume that we were all doping just because we rode at a certain place at a certain time. Everybody is tarred with the same brush, guilty until proven innocent. That's wrong, and it makes finding work in cycling extremely difficult for someone like me.

Oscar won the Coppa Agostoni later in the 1994 season, his first professional victory on Italian soil. He added the Trofeo Dello Scalatore, a three-stage event organized by RCS Sport, in 1995. The race's objective was to showcase the pure climbers in a cycling paradigm increasingly dominated by passisti. *Oscar retired in 2000, and later became a sports director.*

Back then, RCS Sport ran a great many bike races, including a number of events in the south of Italy. However, globalization, allied to the doping tsunami and a host of other factors, saw the less profitable ones disappear. Races like the Trofeo Dello Scalatore folded, and so too the Trofeo Pantalica, the Tour of Reggio Calabria and the early season stage races of Sardinia and Sicily.

The Tour of Campania has recently been reintroduced, but, that aside, southern Italy has virtually no professional bike racing left. When, therefore, the Giro visits, the crowds tend to be huge. The problem for the south is that, in recent times, the Grande Partenza has taken place on foreign soil every other year. And foreign starts generally mean no Giro for the south …

Caro Oscar

anche se con notevole ritardo, desidero espri-
merti i miei più sentiti ringraziamenti
per il Tuo esemplare Comportamento con il
quale hai agito nei giorni del mondiale di
Agrigento. Un mondiale che ci ha fruttato
solo l'argento e non quella fantastica
maglia, che sarebbe stato tanto bello
vincere!.. Ma ha conforto di ciò, vale
il modo con il quale si è battuta
la squadra, impegnandosi fino al limi-
te delle proprie possibilità. So bene,
che avresti voluto gareggiare al mondiale,
anziché assumere il Ruolo di Riserva
ma credo, che sia stato altresì impor-
tante, far parte della NAZIONALE.
Complimentandomi per come hai gareg-
giato in questa stagione, formulo i
migliori auspici perché tu possa raggiun-
gere quelle soddisfazioni che meriti.
cordiali saluti
Alfredo Martini

NOVEMBRE 1994

GIANCARLO BELLINI
GRUPPO SPORTIVO MERCKX
JAFFERAU, 1972

I won the amateur Giro in 1970, so they all wanted me. Giorgio Albani told me I'd be the leader for Molteni at the stage races, so I said I'd sign with them on condition they gave me a three-year contract. That was unheard of back then, but he agreed.

I was sitting in a bar a few days later, and I picked up the paper. There was a big headline: "MERCKX TO MOLTENI!"

So Eddy was coming, and so were the rest of the Belgians from Faema. My first big race as a pro was Milan–San Remo. I was worried about the distance so I just sat on the back. My only concern was trying to finish the race, but at a certain point Eddy appeared. He said, "Is everything OK, Giancarlo? Is there a problem with your saddle? Do you need me to get you an Allen key to adjust it? Do you want me to get you a bidon from the car?" I said thanks all the same but I was just concentrating on getting round and I didn't need anything.

Then Eddy said, "I'm not sure whether you've quite realized, Giancarlo, but fifteen of your teammates didn't get to ride today. Then the other eight are all at the front. They're all doing big turns, making a contribution. I could be wrong, but my guess is that's because they understand why they're here. I also assume they're trying to help me win because they want their share of the prize money." That was when I understood …

At the end of the season all the other Italians left, so I was the only Italian rider on an Italian team. At the 1972 Giro it was me and eight Flemish guys working for Eddy.

Stage 14 was 250 kilometres. It went from Savona up to Sestriere, then dropped down to Oulx, up again to Bardonecchia, and up further still on this new road to Jafferau. It was José Manuel Fuente's big chance to catch up with Eddy, so he attacked with Vicente López Carril. I was the best climber that year, so I turned myself inside out to get Eddy across to them. I must have towed him for 30 kilometres, which was a huge satisfaction for me, as you can imagine. The problem was that I went so deep that I forgot to eat, so by the time we got to Bardonecchia I was almost out of fuel.

I kept going in the valley, then dropped Eddy off on the climb. He was only about a minute behind now, and he went across to the Spaniards and dropped them to win the stage.

I was in bits, though. I had a terrible hunger flat, and I still had five really steep kilometres to climb. I was zigzagging from side to side, just trying to keep the pedals moving, and then I saw an elegant-looking woman with a fur coat and heels. I figured I must have been hallucinating with the fatigue, because you didn't see things like that on mountain stages of the Giro d'Italia.

However, as I got closer she seemed to become real, and she was shouting encouragement at me. Then she ran alongside me and gave me a push. It was probably only a second or two of

MARCELLO BERGAMO | ITA

your own, and all the while your boss was waiting for his drink to turn up.

So it was part of the job, but also part of the hierarchy of the sport. Generally, the newer, younger riders were charged with doing it more often, and the better they did at it, the more chance they had of a renewed contract, a better contract, whatever. It was one of the ways you worked your way up the pecking order, and of course some were better at it than others.

The prevailing logic was that the owners of the shops and bars ought to have felt honoured that we "patronized" them, i.e. pilfered their stock. We were professional cyclists, and we needed sustenance to be able to do our job. That was how you crossed the moral Rubicon, but I have to admit that, at first, I found it quite difficult to get my head around it.

Anyway, on this particular stage I followed a guy named Guerrino Tosello into a bar. Like me, he was from the Veneto, but was much, much bigger than me. I'm 5 feet 5 inches tall and weighed about 63 kilos, and he was 6 feet and about 80 kilos. I was a climber, and he was a great lump of a thing who could pull like a train.

Tosello had been a professional longer than me, so he knew the game inside out. He just steamed in, grabbed the bottles as quick as a flash, and was gone. That left me standing there in the bar like a pudding, and all of a sudden the owner appeared and stood four-square in front of the door. She was a woman, but only of sorts. She was about twice my size, and was built not unlike Tosello. In that moment it became abundantly clear to me that I wouldn't be walking out of that bar with those bottles …

I was stuck in there with her, and it was one of those moments when you want the ground to open up. She told me to put the bottles back precisely where I'd found them, and so that's what I did. One by one I had to take them out of my pockets and put them back where I'd found them. She let me go eventually, but it was one of the most harrowing experiences of my life.

The worst thing was that when I got back, everyone was waiting for the drinks. I turned up empty-handed, and it's safe to say I was the butt of quite few jokes that day …

Marcello Bergamo was born into poverty near Treviso, Veneto. When he was a teenager, however, the family moved west to Lombardy. There, as Italy enjoyed its "economic boom", work was plentiful.

Marcello was an outstanding climber and an extremely popular figure. He rode professionally for ten years, five of them with brother Emanuele. He won eleven races, among them Milan–Turin and the Tour of Campania. He finished third in six separate Giro stages but somehow contrived never to win one, and was runner-up twice at the Italian championships. With the money he made from the sport, Marcello built a cycling clothing factory near Varese, and it currently employs about twenty-five people.

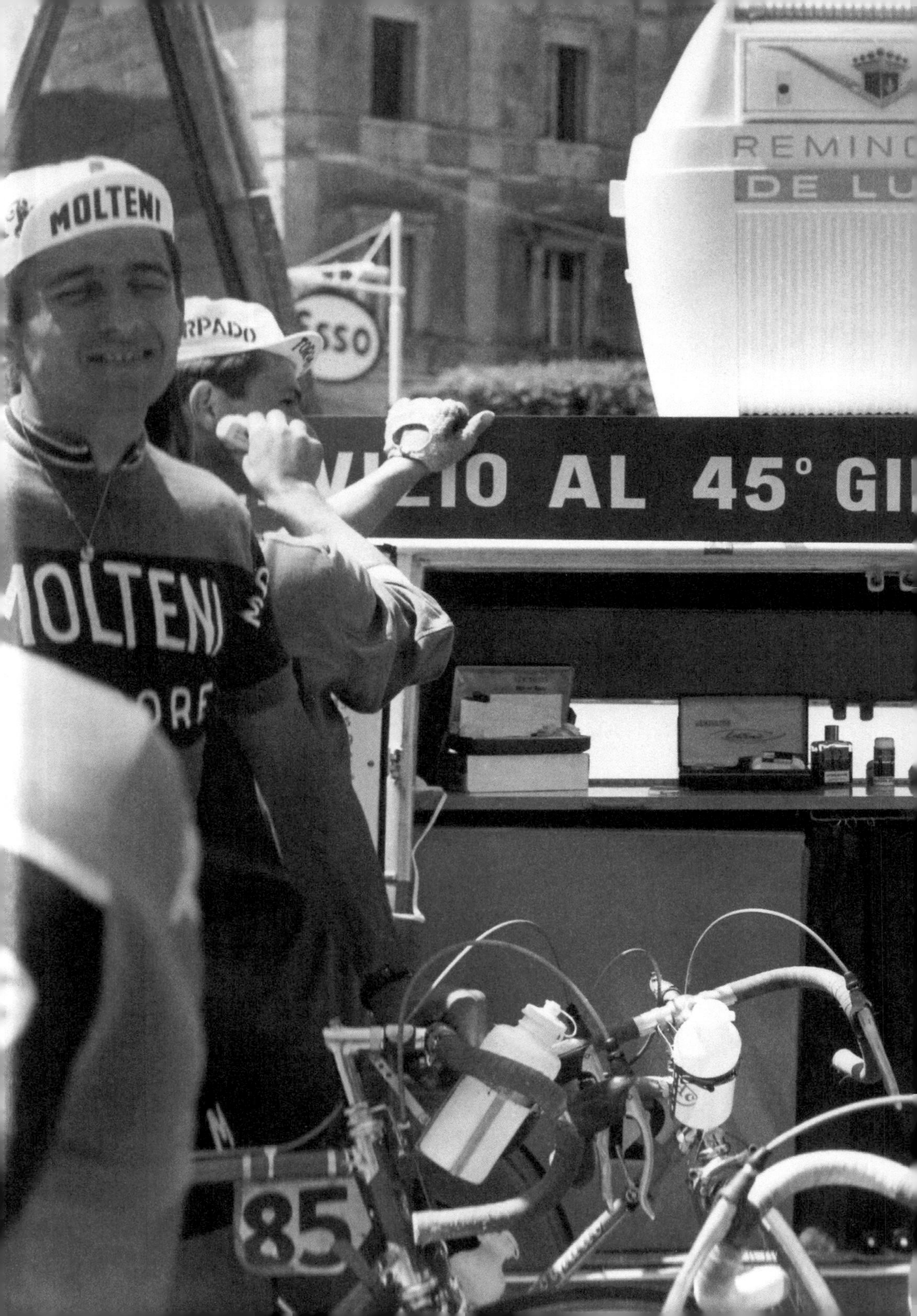
MOLTENI
REMINC
DE LU
SSO
RPADO
VIZIO AL 45° GI
MOLTENI
85

Charly Gaul had won the Giro on the Bondone the previous year, and he was in pink again heading towards the climb. The problem was that he was starting to get cocky, and the other champions didn't appreciate it. I remember that during the stage he took a policeman's helmet and put it on. He made out it was all a joke, but it was also his way of telling us that he was the boss. He'd been telling the press that he'd attack again on the Bondone and take as much time as he wanted.

Charly was the best climber I ever saw, but he had two problems: his character and his team. He hadn't any friends in the group because he was stingy with money, and his *gregari* were weak. It suited everyone for him to lose that Giro, and it suited Louison Bobet most of all. There was real needle between them, and by that stage Bobet really had it in for Charly.

What happened was that Bobet stopped for a call of nature, and so of course Charly did as well. Only Bobet didn't actually need to pee. It was a trick, and as soon as Charly started to pee, Bobet jumped back on his bike. His brother Jean gave the sign – a whistle – and at that point you knew it was full gas. Charly was left there on the side of the road, and his pink jersey disappeared into the distance. They'd decided beforehand that they were going after him by fair means or foul, and he got no help trying to get back on. Ercole Baldini and Gastone Nencini were in the lead group as well, so one way or another you had fifteen really strong Italians against Charly and Marcel Ernzer, his servant. Charly had made his name on the Bondone the previous year, but he made a fool of himself this time. He was the best rider, but he lost the Giro because he never understood that what comes around goes around …

In 1959 there was a time trial on Ischia, an island in the Gulf of Naples. It's tiny, and tourism was in its infancy. So there were very few hotels, and the ones that did exist weren't equipped to cope with something like the Giro. With short, violent efforts like that, you need to eat two or three hours beforehand so as to be almost empty by the time you begin. That meant that the riders needed to eat at different times of the day, but apparently the hotel hadn't understood that. As a consequence, there were was hardly anything to eat, and only one waiter. We were professional cyclists needing fuel, and the whole situation was just farcical.

The waiter guy was overwhelmed, and he had flat feet. Initially we were quite agitated, but after a while we'd got to a point where we'd almost abandoned all hope of getting anything to eat and it became like a scene from a comedy. The poor guy was doing his best, but what with his flat feet and all he became a figure of fun. He couldn't do right for doing wrong, there was nobody to help him, and everybody was making fun of him. He realized the futility of it all, and started mumbling to himself and cursing under his breath. He went on a sort of go-slow, and the slower he went, the more we wound him up.

There were a load of us sitting round the table, and at a certain point one of the lads pulled out a tube of liquid Simpamina. That was the amphetamine you took before a sprint, because it worked really quickly. He poured a few drops into a glass of red wine, and called the waiter guy over. He said, "Look, it's clear you're under pressure here, but don't worry because we can see it's not your fault. Let's just toast the Giro d'Italia, put it down to experience and hope that one of us wins the stage."

The waiter joined in the toast and drank the wine, and after about ten minutes he started clattering round the restaurant like a bull in a china shop. The service wasn't particularly elegant, but goodness knows it was quick. I reckon if we'd put him on a bike he'd have won that time trial himself …

The 1957 Giro remains one of the most dramatic in the post-war history of the race. Gaul and Bobet had fallen out long before the stage to Bondone, and the ambush at Ospedaletto had been pre-planned.

A triple Tour de France winner, Bobet desperately wanted to add the Giro to his palmares. However, Gaul, for all that he was beaten, was damned if he was going to sit idly by. The following day, when maglia rosa Gastone Nencini was dropped, Gaul towed him back up the Bobet group. As such, Nencini preserved his lead over Bobet, and won the Giro by 19 seconds.

Aurelio would ride for Nencini and Bobet, and later for Gaul himself. He said it was nigh on impossible to form any sort of personal relationship with Gaul. Only two of his gregari, fellow Luxembourgers Aldo Bolzan and Marcel Ernzer, enjoyed that privilege. By the time Gaul retired in 1965, speculation about the state of his mental health was rife.

Aurelio Cestari, Pierino Baffi and Miguel Poblet at play.

RENATO LAGHI
THE LONG MARCH
IL CIOCCO, 1975

I think that picture is the *cronoscalata* in 1975, but don't quote me on that. I have to admit I do look a bit rough, but believe me that was one hell of a climb …

I rode the Giro twelve times between 1968 and 1979. I finished all but two of them – I abandoned in 1969 and 1976 – but it took me ten years to win a stage. I guess in that sense my story isn't untypical for the era I rode in.

I rode my first two for Germanvox, working for Vito Taccone. He'd won five stages at the 1963 Giro, but by the time I turned pro he wasn't anything like the rider he'd been. He wasn't winning anymore, and he wasn't a particularly nice guy to ride for. A leader who doesn't get results isn't much use to a *gregario*, so in 1970 I tried my hand as a leader with Sagit. I got some decent placings, and as often as not I was in the top ten in the single-day races. I didn't have a sprint, though, and I wasn't good enough on the flat to be a GC rider. So it was clear to me that I didn't have what it took to become a champion, and that if I were to carry on, it would be as a *gregario*. From there on in I rode for Franco Bitossi.

Cyclists always complain about being fatigued, but a real bike rider is tired after four days, not fourteen. I found the first few days quite hard, but I always came out of the Giro much better, fresher and stronger than heading into it. There are effectively two kinds of cyclist: those built for stage races and those not. The more I rode, the better I felt, and 1971 would be an example of that. There was no rest day at the Giro that year, so we rode for twenty-one days solid. The Giro finished at the Vigorelli in Milan on the Thursday, and we flew to Zurich straight afterwards. The following morning we rode the first stage of the Tour de Suisse. By the time the race finished I'd ridden thirty-one days solid, and my legs were turning themselves. I was sick to death of the bike, but I had sensational form …

The problem with form was that, as a *gregario* for a champion like Bitossi, I hardly ever had a chance to use all of it. He very rarely abandoned a race, and he was a genuine warrior. He fought to the death every day, which meant we'd try to support him every day. However, in 1977 he abandoned the Giro, so we were free to try for ourselves. Six of us went away after a few kilometres of stage 19, and the GC group didn't move. We went over the Tonale together, then I was first over the top of the Presolana. The last climb was the Zambla. It's a really long, hard slog, but I was flying that day and I won by over a minute and a half. It had taken me ten years, but I'd finally won a bike race.

Tuscan Franco "Crazy Heart" Bitossi, whom Renato Laghi served for most of his career, took part in sixteen consecutive giri *from 1963. All told, he won 171 professional bike races, among them twenty-one stages of the Giro. That places him eleventh on the all-time list, but what's unusual is the fact that he was neither a sprinter nor a time trialist. Bitossi, however, was an extraordinarily good climber and an extraordinarily tough human being. He was no GC specialist either (although he finished in the top ten no less than seven times), but for the thick end of twenty years he offered his sponsors unparalleled value for money.*

Bitossi won the mountains prize three times and the points twice, and was popular with both the fans and the gregari *who served him. While many of the great champions were despotic figures, Bitossi engendered loyalty through his decency and humility. And also because, through his exploits, they earned exceptionally well …*

Renato Laghi in (unwitting) sports photograph of the year bid.

GIROTAPPA 7

QUELLI CHE NON CE L'HANNO FATTA

(THOSE WHO DIDN'T QUITE MAKE IT)

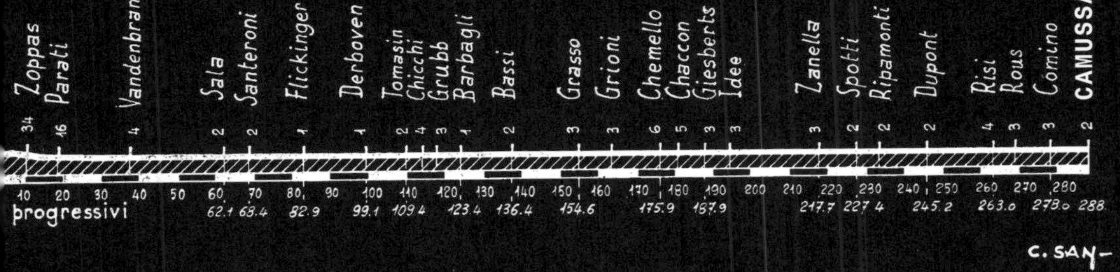

34 Zoppas
16 Parati
4 Vandenbrande
2 Sala
2 Santeroni
1 Flickinger
1 Derboven
2 Tomasin
4 Chicchi
3 Grubb
1 Barbagli
2 Bassi
3 Grasso
3 Grioni
6 Chemello
5 Chaccon
3 Giesberts
3 Idee
3 Zanella
2 Spotti
2 Ripamonti
2 Dupont
4 Risi
3 Rous
3 Comino
2 **CAMUSSA**

10 20 30 40 50 60 70 80 90 100 110 120 130 140 150 160 170 180 190 200 210 220 230 240 250 260 270 280
progressivi   62.1 63.4   82.9   99.1 109.4   123.4 136.4   154.6   175.9 187.9   217.7 227.4   245.2   263.0 273.0 288.

C. SAN-

Adriano: I remember the first two because they were the ones that conditioned my life as a cyclist and as a man.

My first pro race was the Coppa Ugo Agostoni. I was first over the Ghisallo and I finished third. They had high hopes for me as a GC rider, and I started my first Giro the following May. I was thirteenth on GC and it was the thirteenth stage, down in Sicily for a time trial from Catania to Taormina. It was the day before the rest day, and after the stage we were going to fly to Milan for the final week. I felt good, I wasn't a bad time trialist, and I was sure I would do well in the mountains.

So there I was, warming up for the time trial, and suddenly, WALLOP! Fontona, one of my own teammates, just clattered straight into me! We finished up in a big heap on the floor, and I knew straight away that it was over. I ended up flying back to Milan like everyone else, but when we got there I went straight to hospital to have my collarbone bolted back together …

Loredana: To have someone from the village riding the Giro was a major event. My dad was following him every day on the TV and in the papers, but then all of a sudden he was out of the race and lying in a hospital bed in Varese. I didn't know anything at all about cycling, but I knew he liked me. I can't remember exactly *how* I knew, but you just do. I think he'd sent me an autographed card or something. Anyway, my dad said, "*Povero Cristo!* At least go and see him in hospital."

Adriano: I remember now – a friend of mine had given me her address. When I came out of hospital I couldn't ride so I suppose I had a bit of time on my hands. You know how it is … One thing leads to another, doesn't it?

I started the following season quite well. I was fifth at Milan–San Remo and my team decided to give me a free hand at the Giro. That happened very rarely back then, but they thought I had it in me to become a GC rider. It was a sort of make or break moment, because I knew that if I did a good Giro, I'd have a chance to ride for the overall. You only really got one shot at it, and this was mine. Back then, there was very little money in cycling, and only the leaders earned well. If you weren't one of them you were a *gregario* earning not much more than a factory worker, so it was imperative that I stayed out of trouble and put three solid weeks together.

On stage 8 we were in the south again, heading for Naples. As usual down there, the crowds were huge, and as usual it was boiling. Seven of us got away, and I was virtual *maglia rosa*. You weren't allowed to get drinks from the team car like they do today, so when it was hot the fans would hose you down, give you a bottle or just throw a bucket of water on you as you rode along.

What happened was that this guy decided it would be a good idea to throw a full bucket at point-blank range. I fell straight on to a police motorbike, and that was it. My Giro was finished, and so were my chances of becoming one of the leaders …

Following his misadventures in southern Italy, Adriano became one of the best gregari *in cycling. He signed for Molteni in 1967, and*

supported previous winners Gianni Motta and Franco Balmamion at the mythical 50th Giro. He would later work for such champions as Italo Zilioli, Franco Bitossi and Roger De Vlaeminck. He completed each of the eight giri he subsequently started, but never as part of a winning team.

Adriano rode professionally for fourteen seasons, although he only won twice. In 1967 he broke away at the Tour of Ticino, and two years later he won a stage in Catalonia. He almost wore yellow at the 1968 Tour de France (he was third on GC for a time), but it wasn't to be.

He and Loredana have been married since 1969.

PIETRO ZOPPAS
THE MORNING MAN
TERMINILLO, 1960

So I signed with Gino Bartali at San Pellegrino. The idea was that Fausto Coppi would be with us for a year to show Romeo Venturelli the ropes. Coppi was the *campionissimo*, and Meo was going to be his successor. Then Fausto went and died in January, so now the tactic was that Meo would honour his memory by becoming a champion himself.

The second stage was a time trial at Sorrento, and Meo beat Jacques Anquetil to take the pink jersey. Everyone was in delirium because it was inconceivable that an Italian neo-pro might be able to beat Anquetil.

They said Meo was the new Coppi, but I knew he wasn't. He and I had ridden together as amateurs, and we'd roomed together. He was incredibly strong, but he had two major defects as a cyclist. The first was that he didn't like suffering, and second was he didn't have an actual brain.

So anyway, Meo was *maglia rosa*, and he'd beaten Anquetil to get it. Anquetil, by the way, was the nicest guy you could ever meet, a gentleman. He was a champion, and yet he treated me as if *I* were a champion. What? Coppi? He'd been a godfather to me, always offering me advice and suchlike. What advice? I can't divulge what he said because … Oh well, alright. He told me to take the bomb. I was against it, though, and I didn't take it … Actually, I can't be sure about that because it may be that Giovanni Proietti, the Italian team manager, slipped me one before the time trial at the Peace Race. I almost won a stage there, but that Russian who won the Olympics punched me in the stomach in the tunnel under the stadium.

Anyway, where were we? Meo had the jersey now, and we had to try to defend it. I remember because my uncle came to watch and he was the bishop of Nocera dei Pagani. He wasn't having it with Coppi, what with the furore over the *Dama Bianca* and what have you, so he came to see me but I never got a word in edgeways because of Bartali. I'd just said hello to my uncle when Bartali butted in. He said, "Excuse me, your excellency, may I have an audience?" Then he took him off to an anteroom and that was the last I saw of my uncle …

So that's where the problem started. Meo had the pink jersey and he demanded pickled gherkins for dinner. It's true that Meo seemed a lovely guy, but when there were pickled vegetables involved he had a tendency to become very aggressive. He was eating them like an animal that night, and there was nothing anyone could do to stop him. I used to say to him, "Meo! You need to go easy with the pickled gherkins!" but when he got it into his head that he wanted them there was no holding him. So it's no wonder he didn't sleep that night, and no wonder he was sick. If you drink champagne and overdo it with the pickled gherkins, it's obvious you're going to be sick! He managed to get dropped and lose the jersey the next day, on a pan-flat sprinters' stage.

On stage 5 we had to go up the Terminillo, and they set off at full gas. Meo was straight out the back again, and me and Pellicciari had to wait for him. It was hot, and Meo said, "I'm thirsty!" He'd already drunk everything he had, so I gave him my bottle, thinking he'd just take a few sips. Instead, he drunk every last drop, so now *I* was the one who was thirsty …

After a while Meo piped up again. He said, "I'm thirsty!" so I told him so was I, but we'd no water left because he'd drunk it all. We were in the middle of nowhere, but I took a detour into a village nearby and managed to get a bottle of champagne from a bar. I brought it back to Meo, and he started gulping it down. I said, "At least save me a bit!" but he didn't – he drank every last drop! He wasn't terribly well mannered, Meo, because he hadn't been brought up properly.

Anyway, he'd drunk the champagne now, and he set off like a train. Bartali came up alongside us and said, "Bravo Zoppa! You've saved our Giro!" but I was barely coherent because I was struggling to stay on Meo's wheel. What with the effects of the champagne and all, he was absolutely hammering it and I was clinging on for dear life …

Then after a while the effect of the champagne wore off and he collapsed again. We got him to the bottom of the Terminillo, but then I had to leave him with Pellicciari. I beat the time limit, but Meo climbed off. I was over the time limit in the time trial instead.

The following year I was one of thirteen over the time limit down in Cosenza. Six of us were from the same team, and it was all Vito Favero's fault. He'd finished second at the Tour de France, and it had gone to his head. He'd left school at eleven, like the rest of us, but after the Tour he married a schoolmistress. He thought he was better than the rest of us, and he didn't want us doing well if he couldn't. So we all had to wait for him and we all missed the time cut.

In 1962 I survived the Dolomite stage in the snow, but there were no hotels up there and I finished up sleeping on a floor. The following day I went for an intermediate sprint, but one of my pedals broke. I ended up on the floor again, only this time with concussion. They gave me someone else's bike and I got round the stage, but then they gave me a bike with a faulty rear mech'. There was no way I was going to get round on *that* …

Pietro was known as "the Morning Man" owing to his proclivity for early breakaways. In 1962 alone, he won 120 flasks of Chianti and 25 forme of Grana Padano at intermediate sprints. He says he never saw any of it, but that drunken, cheese-munching journalists, mechanics and soigneurs would often appear alongside him during the stages. They would thank him profusely for his efforts on behalf of the entire Giro caravan.

Pietro abandoned again in 1963, but somehow fell on his feet the following year. For the first time, moving cameras were able to capture the final kilometres of the stages. Prior to the ninth leg to Ravenna, however, his Cité team had been anonymous. The owner thus informed them that if they failed to animate the race again, they'd be sent home forthwith. Pietro had ridden for a team in Ravenna as an amateur, and knew the run-in well. He escaped with a Belgian, Jos Hoevenaers, and galloped to a splendid victory.

Pietro abandoned two days later to maintain his 100 per cent record. What a guy.

FIORENZO TOMASIN
HIS OWN DEVICES
VESUVIAS, 1959

We were desperately poor and often went hungry. That was a great incentive …

San Pellegrino was a mineral water company, but they also had a new product, an orangeade. They sponsored a professional team to promote it, and Gino Bartali ran it. That made sense for San Pellegrino because Bartali guaranteed them publicity and also invitations to all the big races. You got to ride Milan–San Remo, Lombardy and, above all, the Giro.

Everyone who started with San Pellegrino was hoping to get a bigger team the following season, because you couldn't make a living riding for Bartali. You signed a ten-month contract and they paid you 60,000 lire a month. It was factory wages, but at least you were in the shop window.

We all made our way to Milan for the Giro, our dreams about to come true. I was about to ride for three weeks alongside Ercole Baldini, Charly Gaul and Jacques Anquetil, the superstars.

The first stage finished at Salsomaggiore, a spa town in Emilia-Romagna. It ended with a bunch sprint, but I was one of the strongest. The following day there was a time trial around the town, and that's where my cycling career started to fall apart. I punctured, but they'd managed to load somebody else's bike on to the car. I had to finish the stage on a bike that was 10 centimetres too big for me. It was a Bartali bike, obviously, but I looked like I belonged in the circus.

Each night the other teams would take themselves off to the best hotels, but Bartali would haul us off to a convent somewhere. Bartali may have been devout, but I can assure that we weren't sleeping in monasteries in the hope of receiving some sort of divine intervention. We were there for one reason only, and that was so that he could save money. We were professional athletes, and yet we were sleeping in a monastery and eating in a canteen!

He had short arms, Bartali. If there was no convent, he'd have us in the cheapest, seediest hotels. If they were by the sea, there'd invariably be a bar or some such downstairs, and there would be music playing until five o'clock in the morning. We'd be up at six, trying to eat steak and pasta in readiness for the stage ...

We only had one masseur at the Giro, and he didn't bother with me. He'd give me a five-minute rub-down, and then tell me to take a hot bath with vinegar! Then we never had enough jerseys because Bartali used to give them to the monks. Everyone else would appear in brand-new, pristine jerseys each morning, but we'd be wearing the ones we'd worn the previous day and the day before that.

On stage 7 there was another time trial, a *cronoscalata* up Mount Vesuvius. I was a decent time trialist, but obviously I was one of the first

Romeo Venturelli needs fuel. Fiorenzo Tomasin obliges.

The mythical *ritiro spirituale*.

off because I'd lost so much time with the fiasco at Salsomaggiore. With Bartali, we always had to go to mass before the stage, and on this particular day we got to the start even later than usual. It was too late for me to warm up, and I ended up missing the time cut. That was the sum total of my Giro d'Italia …

The following year I got a contract with Atala and had another go at it. What happened was that I had a mechanical on the stage to Asti, and me and Louis Rostolan rode a four-hour pursuit to beat the time cut. I managed it, and they told me that the best way to beat the fatigue was to get in the break the following day. I did as I was told, but when we started the climb to Cervinia I had a terrible hunger flat. I started hallucinating, and I had to pack the following day.

That winter Atala told us that we had to take a course of hormones. I was already sick of it to be honest, and that was just about the final straw. I wasn't about to start messing about like that, just to be someone else's dogsbody, so at twenty-six years of age I became an ex-cyclist. I can laugh about it now, but at the time it was just humiliating …

In dominating the cronoscalata *on Mount Vesuvius, Charly Gaul put almost a minute into Jacques Anquetil. Gaul's time of 22'46" (21 kph) compelled the jury to increase the time limit from five minutes to six. Had they not, three of Anquetil's* gregari *would have been* hors delay. *Fiorenzo was one of the four who failed to make the time cut regardless, but in the normal course of events he was an outstanding tester. Later that season he would win the Gran Premio Boldrini, a two-up time trial, with teammate Ernesto Bono. It earned them a start at the Trofeo Baracchi the following week, where they finished a very creditable seventh.*

Atala's ultimatum over the hormone treatment left Fiorenzo so disillusioned that he walked away from cycling. He gave his bikes away because he "couldn't stand the sight of them", but started riding again six years later.

CLAUDIO COMINO
NEARLY MAN
CUNEO, 1977

I was twenty when I turned professional, and that was my big mistake. I'd only ridden two years as an amateur, so I wasn't mature enough – either physically or psychologically. Had I waited a couple of years, then maybe it would have been a different story, but there you go.

My situation was unusual, and the context was unusual. I started with my local club, SC Cuneo. The president was a guy named Agostino Bonetto, a local entrepreneur involved in the building trade. He loved cycling, and we'd some good riders, so he decided we ought to become a professional team. So for 1976 he put a load of money in, and a few others from the business community chipped in too. We were all going to turn professional together, and it was going to be the first professional team to represent a district, as opposed to a brand. In the end, however, only two of us turned pro, and they filled the roster with guys who didn't have a contract.

I felt under quite a lot of pressure because it was a big thing for the town and everybody was convinced that I could make it. I seemed to be the only one who doubted it, but I loved cycling and there were thousands of Italians who would have killed for the chance to be a professional. I was being offered it after only a couple of years of riding, so I couldn't turn it down.

Bonetto got us started, but the intention was for the local authority to come on board and take on the running costs. Only for some reason they didn't, and Bonetto was left holding the baby. He couldn't afford to fund a full ten-man team, and that meant we couldn't ride the Giro. So we joined up with another team and rode the Tour of Switzerland instead. I finished seventeenth, which wasn't bad for a neo-pro, but the team ran out of money at the end of the year.

I was still having doubts about turning professional, but I was offered a contract with Franco Bitossi's team. I started to suffer with pain in my legs, but I suppose I was going reasonably well. On the way back from the Tour of Tuscany, our DS, Italo Zilioli, told me to get ready for the Giro.

A few days before the Giro, I went for a medical. They did the blood tests, but then the doctor called me and told me there was too much nitrogen in my blood. My kidneys weren't working properly, and that meant I couldn't ride the Giro. I was absolutely crestfallen, and I just decided to pack it in.

I think the Giro would have been a make or break moment anyway, because I'd been struggling psychologically. It's not as if I was even close to winning races, and like most professionals, I felt as though I was just clinging on all the time. You don't mind suffering if there's a chance you can get a result, but I didn't see one coming. They persuaded me to give

Claudio Comino (right) with fellow Cunese Remo Rocchia.

it another go in the autumn, but my heart wasn't in it. I stopped altogether after the Tre Valli Varesine.

I'd like to pretend I'd have become a big star had I ridden that Giro, but I don't think I would have. They tell me I shouldn't have stopped and that I was talented. However, I'm not one of those who packs it in and then spends the rest of their life regretting it, and stopping enabled me to build a normal life. I guess it would have been nice to have ridden the Giro, but it's not something that keeps me awake at night. There's much more to life than riding a bike …

Agostino Bonetto's ill-fated SC Cuneo experiment remains unique in the history of Italian professional cycling. The intention was to retain at least ten riders under contract, enough to field a team at the Giro. However, the Australian Alan Spokes chose to return home instead, Walter Passuello decided to do another year as an amateur, and others chose not to continue.

Of the eight who did eventually sign on, only three found a team for 1977. Claudio and Remo Rocchia joined Vibor, while the New Zealander Bruce Biddle joined Francesco Moser at Sanson. They still say that Claudio Comino could have become one hell of a bike rider.

PIERGIORGIO CAMUSSA
THE FALL GUY
AREZZO, 2008

I was twenty-six in 2008. I was riding for NGC Medical, a Pro Continental team, and we were given a wild card for the Giro.

I come from Bosio, a village close to Fausto Coppi's Castellania, so I'd been brought up on stories about him, Costante Girardengo and the other great champions from these parts. I was close to Sandrino Carrea, Coppi's most famous *gregario*.

This area had once been the home of cycling. We have the museum of the *campionissimi*, Coppi's house, and there are always events celebrating the great champions. Everyone knows the stories …

We'd had nobody ride the Giro for twenty-seven years. I'd dreamed of riding it for as long as I could remember, and now, finally, it was about to happen. I was over the moon, and you can imagine the pride people felt when it was announced. I was proud as well.

All that aside, the Giro is the big shop window. It may seem absurd, but two hours in the break at the Giro are worth more than a win at races like the Gran Premio di Prato. I was never going to be a champion like Coppi, but this was my chance to make a name for myself and hopefully make a decent living from cycling.

The weekend before, there were two races down in Tuscany. On Saturday we had the GP Larciano, and on Sunday the Tour of Tuscany. So we were all set to do them, and then to take a ferry across to Sicily for the opening stage of the Giro. However, when I arrived at the hotel on the Friday, there was a strange atmosphere. One of my teammates said, "It's possible we won't be riding the Giro."

It was a pretty major shock, but nothing was official at this point and nobody really knew what was happening. So we went off, did the race, and tried to put it to the back of our minds. Then, afterwards, they told us that we were out of the Giro and that Astana were in.

They'd been excluded from both the Giro and the Tour because of all the doping scandals. However, they had Contador, and Contador is Contador. He's a big star, and so from a marketing and prestige perspective he's extremely valuable. You could argue that, by comparison, we were a bunch of nobodies, but we're all human beings and they just shattered our dreams without giving it a second thought.

The official statement was that it had been a "joint decision". They said that both the team management and Angelo Zomegnan, the race director, had felt that we weren't ready. That was strange because eight months earlier he'd decided we *were* ready, and it's inconceivable a cycling team would volunteer *not* to ride the Giro d'Italia. It was, as they say, a *very* Italian affair, but Zomegnan was the *padrone* and he did as he pleased.

I've always suspected that Astana bought their participation at that Giro, although I try not to think about it too much. It's too painful, and it still sickens me the way they were all glad-handing and slapping one another on the back.

The organizers said they'd be honoured to have us the following year, but we all knew it was nonsense. We ended up riding the GP Kranj in Slovenia instead, wondering what on earth had happened. Then, just to rub salt into the wound, they told us our sponsor was pulling the plug. We carried on, but they confirmed it was folding later that summer at Lombardy Week. By then the transfer market was done and dusted, so we were stuffed.

So I'd been on the verge of the Giro in 2008, and in 2009 I found myself riding for a lousy Continental team. I wasn't paid a cent, not even my expenses. I think my hotel bill for the pre-season training camp remains unpaid to this day.

Mine was the Giro d'Italia that never was, but life goes on and I still love to ride my bike. It's probably best if you don't mention it to my dad, though. He's been boycotting the *Gazzetta dello Sport* since May 2008 …

In accepting Astana back into the fold, race director Zomegnan explained that their original exclusion from the Giro hadn't been the result of a perceived moral deficit. Rather, he tried to convince an incredulous media, it had been because they hadn't "achieved the requisite sporting criteria".

Notwithstanding the fact that Stefano Garzelli had won the 2000 edition and helped himself to two stages in 2007, Zomegnan also saw fit to leave out his Acqua & Sapone team. Contador won the Giro, although subsequent events suggest that the 2008 peloton was one of the dirtiest in history.

Piergiorgio now works for the Michelin tyre company.

Piergiorgio Camussa and his dad, a diehard ex-Gazzetta reader.

GIROTAPPA 8
LA FAVOLA DEL GRUPPO
SPORTIVO FILCAS
(THE FAIRYTALE OF
G.S. FILCAS)

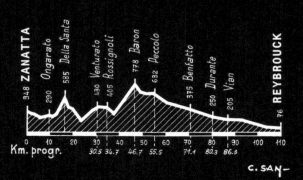

REMIGIO ZANATTA
SPORTS DIRECTOR
SAN BENEDETTO DEL
TRONTO, 1974

So I put the team together and we set off for the big league in our little minibus. Franco Ongarato got third in a stage down in Sardinia, which was a decent start for us. Then a lead group of six came in at Milan–Turin, and Fraccaro was in it with Roger De Vlaeminck, Italo Zilioli and Franco Bitossi. At Tirreno, Fraccaro finished third in the time trial and third on GC. That was our first big result, and even Eddy Merckx said he was impressed.

FRANCO ONGARATO
RACING CYCLIST
NAPLES, 1974

There were things going on in the team that I didn't really understand. There was only one masseur, young Baron, and he was just starting out. Benfatto and I would often do our own massages, and before Milan–San Remo I had the national team masseur come along. Then the mechanic was a plumber, and he knew nothing about bikes. There were continuous problems with the bikes …

When we went to the Tour of Campania, someone from Filcas had booked us into a first-category hotel right in the centre of Naples. The centre of Naples is noisy and stressful, and a cyclist needs to be calm and to sleep well. The thing was that a bottle of water there cost 10,000 lire, so Zanatta told us we had to go to the market to get water. So I said, "Remigio, this is absurd. You can't book us into a hotel like this on the one hand, and expect us to fetch our own water from the market on the other. We're professional athletes."

To infinity and beyond.

89

We had ten riders because in any given race that was all you needed. We knew we weren't going to be racing abroad, so there was no value in having a big roster. Even a big team like Bianchi would only have fifteen riders, because they were only ever doing one race at a time.

Vian had developed a heart condition, and the doctors told him he had to stop right away. So now we were left with nine, and one of them was Adriano Durante.

He'd been a good rider in the mid-sixties, but he was thirty-three or thirty-four and, to be honest, we'd only taken him for publicity and strategic reasons. He wasn't supposed to go to the Giro, but now we had a problem. We needed ten for the Giro, but we also needed a reserve.

I rang the general secretary of the cycling federation. I told him I needed a sprinter and another rider and he said he'd ask around and come back to me. There were no Italians, but he rang Vittorio Adorni because *he* knew everyone in cycling. Adorni was working as a sports director at Bianchi, and apparently he got on the phone to Guido Reybrouck in Belgium. Reybrouck had retired, but he'd been a sprinter, and he and Adorni had ridden together for years. Like a lot of the Flemish back then, he'd ridden for Italian teams, so he spoke the language.

The general secretary came back to me and said, "It seems that Reybrouck's brother is very fast. His name's Wilfried, but if you want him you'll need to speak with Adorni."

So that's what I did. I rang Vittorio Adorni ...

My brother Guido won the Belgian championships in 1966, six stages at the Tour, three at the Giro and four at the Vuelta. He also won Paris–Tours three times, so he was pretty famous. He was twelve years older than me, so of course he was my hero.

I'd win ten to twenty races a year, but I wasn't a champion like my brother. I was just an amateur riding kermesses, but at the end of the 1973 season I stopped. I met Monique and got a job as an ambulance driver, and that meant working in the evenings, on Saturday and on Sundays.

I was sitting in the pub one night, playing cards with a group of friends. Suddenly my brother walked in and said he'd had Adorni on the phone. He said there was an Italian team looking for riders, and he'd told them I was fast.

I suppose I'd *been* fast, but I was out of shape because I hadn't been on the bike at all for two months. Besides, fast riding around Flemish churches is hardly the same as fast with De Vlaeminck, Basso and Sercu, is it? Tearing around villages in West Flanders is very different from riding over Italian mountains with Merckx and José Manuel Fuente ...

Guido said they were offering a contract, and I'd nothing to lose. I spoke to Eric Serlet, an all-rounder guy I knew, and we got on a plane to Milan.

I got to the airport and waited, and sure enough these two characters appeared. Serlet looked like a normal sort of a kid but the other one looked like one of those American hippies ...

Let's just say that he couldn't have looked less like a cyclist if he'd tried. He was short, he was wearing a vest, he had long hair and he had his ear pierced. I was always pretty rigorous about the way my riders presented themselves. There

was absolutely no way any of my riders would have been allowed to race with an earring, so this didn't look terribly promising …

So now I found myself in the car with these two Flemish kids, neither of whom spoke a word of Italian. I couldn't speak Flemish, or even French. I spoke half-decent Italian, but Trevigiano dialect was my first language. However, I'd made my bed and I had to lie in it, and I'd a bike race to get to down in Tuscany. We set off late afternoon, about 5.30, headed down to Montelupo Fiorentino.

Somewhere near Modena one of the wheels fell off the car. That was a bit alarming to say the least, but eventually they turned up and we fixed everything. However, we didn't set off again until about 11 pm, so the long and the short of it was that we didn't arrive at the hotel until about two o'clock in the morning.

Romeo, the mechanic, had to cobble a bike together for each of them the following morning. He did that, but then Reybrouck turned up at the start in a pair of trainers! To be honest, it made no difference because he was dropped straight away. Within about thirty kilometres the two of them had climbed off.

Afterwards, Baron went off to buy him a new pair of cycling shoes.

RINO BARON
SOIGNEUR
TUSCANY, 1974

There was something wrong with his pedal stroke, and his muscles weren't working in harmony. I went and bought him a pair of shoes, yes. He was a size 41 like me, so I set the shoes up as I would have done for myself.

REMIGIO ZANATTA
SPORTS DIRECTOR
LECCE, 1974

After Tuscany we headed straight down to Lecce for the Tour of Puglia, a five-day stage race. We were quite lucky because Vian's old bike fitted Reybrouck pretty well.

The *percorso* was flat, and it was quite windy. It looked good for Fraccaro, and our strategy was for Benfatto to stay close to him and work for him. So that was fine, but then this Reybrouck came up to me and started waving his arms about. He said, "Me! Sprint! Sercu! De Vlaeminck! Me! Sprint! Me! Vroom! Vroom!" I thought, "God help me – the kid's absolutely crackers. What on earth am I supposed to do with him?"

Anyway, he didn't sprint because he was nowhere near, but at least he got round. The next day, Tista Baronchelli was on the front, but he ploughed straight into a bloke selling fruit on the side of the road. You know one of those wagons? He brought half the peloton off, including Reybrouck. He finished up concussed, with blood pouring down the side of his face. Baron had taken it upon himself to look after the guy, so it was him who carted him off to hospital …

FRANCO ONGARATO
RACING CYCLIST
MARTINA FRANCA, 1974

By the time we got to the Tour of Puglia, I could feel my legs coming back. I was sixth on the second stage and I fancied my chances on the last day. I spoke to the mechanic, the plumber guy, and said, "Look, I need a new chain, but make sure you change the block as well. You can't change one without the other, OK?"

He said that was fine, and when we got to the sprint I was convinced I was going to win. When I started my sprint, though, the chain started jumping, and I ended up finishing fifth because the plumber hadn't changed the block.

Della Santa, the boss of Filcas, was at the finish. He said, "How did it go?" I was livid and I said, "I was third 200 metres out and I'd have won if I'd had a bike that actually worked!" I showed him the problem with the chain. All this took place just beyond the finishing line, in front of the spectators.

REMIGIO ZANATTA
SPORTS DIRECTOR
MARTINA FRANCA, 1974

Motta won the stage, and Della Santa accused Ongarato of having sold it. They had a blazing row right there in front of everybody, and neither of them would back down. This was five days before the start of the Giro. It wasn't good.

Afterwards, Sercu came up to me. He said, "Look, I'm going home for three days, so I'll take Wilfried with me. That way he's not going to be left here with a hole in his head, feeling sorry for himself. I'll take him, and I'll be sure to bring him back for the Giro."

Sercu was a really straight guy so I had no problem with that.

FRANCO ONGARATO
RACING CYCLIST
CASTELFRANCO VENETO, 1974

So we all went to dinner at Fior before setting off for the Giro. Everyone was grumbling about the way things were being organized, but my feeling was that it was pointless chittering among ourselves. I wasn't interested in being politic so I stood up and said, "Look, last year I did the Giro with two masseurs and two mechanics, and it still wasn't enough. There's too much to do even for good mechanics, and as riders we shouldn't be worrying about whether or not they're up to the job."

It could be that I called the mechanic "the Plumber", which probably wouldn't have gone down very well, but the long and the short of it was that we were heading off to the Giro totally unprepared.

At that point Della Santa stood up and said, "You, Ongarato, are a liar, and you've always got an excuse for everything. The other day at Martina Franca you told me you'd been third 200 metres from the line, but you weren't; you were thirteenth or fourteenth. What's more, if you were really passionate about being a cyclist you'd gladly ride the Giro with one masseur and one mechanic."

He was wrong, and what's more I'd showed him the problem with the chain. The secretary grabbed hold of my jacket to try to keep me calm, but I wasn't having it. I got up and said, "It was *Fraccaro* who was thirteenth, not me, and if you're saying that I just make excuses then it's *you* who's a liar! You saw the problem with the chain with your own eyes, so at this point you can pay me my wages for May, and I'm off. There's no way I'm riding the Giro for this team!"

And that was the last I ever saw of Filcas ...

WILFRIED REYBROUCK
RACING CYCLIST
DAMME, WEST
FLANDERS, 1974

My brother told me that if De Vlaeminck came to talk to me, I just had to answer him directly, and not to feel intimidated by him.

One of my teeth fell out at the airport.

REMIGIO ZANATTA
SPORTS DIRECTOR
VATICAN CITY, 1974

So there we all are on the eve of the Giro, our big moment. We all go to see the Pope, and Reybrouck's still banging on about sprinting. He's telling me how he's going to beat De Vlaeminck and Basso, Van Linden and Sercu – all that old nonsense. So far he's done three days' "racing" with us, and all he's accomplished is to make himself look like a pillock. He's turned up looking like I don't know what, then climbed off, then hospitalized himself. Fact is, though, that we've lost both Vian *and* Ongarato.

For all we know he might be worse than useless, but we've no choice in the matter. He says he's a hot-shot sprinter, and we have to take his word for it. He's all we've got left ...

REMIGIO ZANATTA
SPORTS DIRECTOR
FORMIA, 1974

So now we're in the team car, there's going to be the sprint, and at least this time Reybrouck's still in the group. Fraccaro and Luciano Rossignoli have volunteered to pull for him, and we're about to see what he's made of. To be honest, we're not holding our breath, but suddenly the speaker starts shouting, "Number 44 has won! Number 44!" I can't actually believe what I'm hearing, but then he starts going on about a great victory for Filcas!

RINO BARON
SOIGNEUR
FORMIA, 1974

He's only gone and done it! He's actually beaten Sercu, Basso and De Vlaeminck, and he's on the podium pulling on the *maglia rosa*!

The *maglia rosa* shows his teeth. (Most of his teeth.)

WILFRIED REYBROUCK
RACING CYCLIST
POMPEII, 1974

The following day we went to Pompeii and there was another sprint. I was following Bitossi's wheel, and I was sure I was going to win again. I saw a gap, but then suddenly two riders from De Vlaeminck's team had hold of my shorts …

LUIGI VENTURATO
RACING CYCLIST
SORRENTO, 1974

It seemed that everyone around the Giro was pleased for us, and we were enjoying our fifteen minutes of fame. It was all a bit of a fairy tale, and everyone loves a fairy tale, don't they?

When we set off the next day we didn't really have a strategy for defending the jersey. We were just looking forward to reading about ourselves in the papers again, and trying to get ourselves on TV again.

It was a summit finish at Monte Faito, but there were more sprints to come and Reybrouck had proved that he was some sort of phenomenon.

The stage itself wasn't that long, and nor was it particularly hard. To be honest with you, we weren't organized at all, and I have to accept my share of the responsibility for that. I wasn't in the *gruppetto* and I probably ought to have been.

Then Remigio probably should have had half the team stay with Reybrouck, but he was new to it all as well. As I say, everyone was quite naive ...

The stage was only 130 kilometres. It split on the first climb, the Agerola, and I stayed in the lead group with the climbers. I left the old boy driving the second car with the *gruppetto*, because I figured Durante would look after Reybrouck, and maybe Benfatto. Obviously, Basso, Sercu and the other sprinters would be there as well, so all Reybrouck had to do was to stay with them. There was no radio communication back then, but I didn't see any particular danger. The problem was that I hadn't reckoned on Fuente attacking like that, and blowing the whole race to bits.

What can I say? Durante clearly decided he wasn't going to take care of Reybrouck. Like all the other old hands he would have grabbed the first car or motorbike he could get his hands on, and been towed to the finish. He left Reybrouck and Serlet to their own devices, and obviously none of the other sprinters' teams were going to give them a hand. The likes of Basso would have been towed, no question, and they'd have accepted the fines as part of the game.

Reybrouck was just a kid who'd never seen a mountain before, and he had no idea what he was getting into. As I said, none of us really knew what we were doing ...

Wilfried finished over the time limit.

By mid-season, the new stars, Claudio Bortolotto and Simone Fraccaro, were being courted by bigger, wealthier teams, and Filcas didn't have the budget to match the offers. The whole thing started to unravel, and on 28 July the entire team abandoned the Trofeo Matteotti, a brute of a race in the Abruzzo.

The Matteotti was one of the three events that, collectively, constituted the Italian team championships, and Della Santa was incensed by what he'd seen. That evening, he stated that he'd had enough, and that he was pulling out of cycling forthwith. In the event, the mythical Filcas cycling team made it to the end of the season, but never won another race.

Remigio Zanatta was never paid for his work at Filcas; rather, he did it for the love of the sport. He had another brief sojourn into professional cycling in the early 1990s, working for two years with Gianni Savio's ZG Mobili team, but didn't like it one little bit. Over the years, however, Remigio nurtured dozens of riders into the professional ranks. Among them was his son Stefano, who would win the Giro as a gregario for Gianni Bugno, and twice as a DS for Ivan Basso.

Following the row with Della Santa, Franco Ongarato decided to take three months off and enjoy life. He was minded to look for a new team

97

in 1975, but a freak diving accident left him paralysed on the right of his body. He recovered, but never cycled again. Two of his nephews, Alberto and Rodolfo, would ride the Giro d'Italia.

Rino Baron would win the 1975 Giro with Fausto Bertoglio's Jolly Ceramica, and would work with such champions as Francesco Moser, Moreno Argentin and Freddy Maertens. His greatest contribution to the sport, however, probably lies in the biological passport. He developed the prototype for the riders of his amateur team, and the rest is history. His son Ronny is currently a World Tour mechanic with Lampre.

Luigi Venturato joined Zonca at the conclusion of the 1974 season, and did two more years as a professional. He never won a race, but finished the 1976 Giro d'Italia in sixty-third place. He went back to construction work, and didn't touch a bike for forty years. When we met, he'd just started riding again at the age of sixty-seven.

Attilio Benfatto carried on until 1976. On the track, he won World Championship bronze as a stayer, and silver in the team pursuit. On the road, he won bronze in the 100-kilometre team time trial. With the money he made from cycling, he built a family house close to Venice and started a metallurgy business. He also trained junior cyclists.

Wilfried Reybrouck rode a single post-Giro sprint crit' — and that was it. He says Filcas paid him three months' wages, but failed to honour the rest of his contract. He returned to the Giro the following year with the Dutch outfit Frisol—GBC, but the entire team abandoned. He only won one more significant race, a stage at the Tour of Holland, but later became a DS himself. He's never seen the film of his Giro stage win, and nothing of the two stages he spent in the maglia rosa.

Filcas at the 1974 Giro. Wilfried Reybrouck is on the right.

GIROTAPPA 9

È UN PO' ... COMPLICATA
(IT'S A BIT ... COMPLICATED)

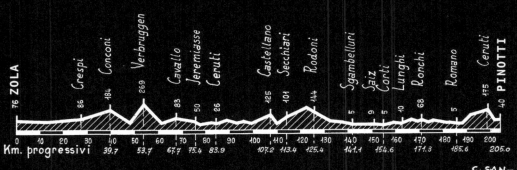

I signed a professional contract in 1980, but then I got a fever and had to abandon the Tour of the Aosta Valley. Afterwards, I got a call from the boss of the team, and he said they'd had a change of heart. He said they were taking one of my teammates instead, Moreno Argentin. I said, "Yes, but I've signed a contract!" He just said that, in reality, those contracts weren't worth the paper they were written on.

I stopped cycling and got a job, but then Italo Zilioli came to see me. He was running the Fiat amateur team and he said, "Look, we'll give you a new car and 10 million lire a year." My dad was on 8 million, so eventually I agreed. I did two more years as an amateur, and then I got a call from Argentin. He said, "Do you want to turn professional with Sammontana?" I turned professional with them on a two-year contract.

By that time, Argentin had become a champion. It was like meeting a soldier you'd once known and all of a sudden he's a general. I knew straight away that it was going to be difficult, and from there on in he and I barely spoke. I was stuck there, though, because I had to fulfil my contract.

I joined Supermercati Brianzoli in 1985, and I rode the Vuelta and the Giro that year. The Giro was really hard for the first ten days, but I remember the Vuelta better. Robert Millar had the jersey, but Peugeot let Pedro Delgado escape. I was born in France and I speak French well, so I went up to Gilbert Duclos-Lassalle and told him we were prepared to ride. He just waved me away for some reason, and the gap kept growing. Everyone could see they weren't going to bring it back on their own, so I asked him again and he waved me away again. It was one of the strangest things that ever happened, because the Vuelta was disappearing up the road. Eventually, he came up and said they wanted us to ride, but by then it was way too late …

Francesco Moser joined us for the following season, and he bought the medical avant-garde with him. You knew that with Francesco you were going to be 100 per cent *gregario*, but that was fine because you earned a lot of money. Seeing him outside the top ten of a bike race was like seeing four days of rain in the Sahara. He was the strongest human being I'd ever met, no question.

Anyway, they told us we had to go to the Passo Tonale for some tests a few days before Christmas, but I'd barely touched the bike for three months because I'd been hunting. So I wasn't ready and I *certainly* wasn't fit. Damn!

They fitted us with these strange heart-rate monitor things, and told us we were going to be doing something called FRS. They were tests developed by Professor Conconi, and apparently they measured all sorts of parameters. We rode off and did the Val di Non, then started up the Passo Tonale. They would stop us from time to time and take the data from the heart-rate monitor. Believe it or not I felt OK, and I must have gone reasonably well. The following morning at the hotel, Dr Michele Ferrari came up to me. He started using this strange terminology, but it was all a riddle to me. He said, "I've looked over your numbers and I can see you've been training really well. *Bravissimo!* Really exceptional …"

The thing with those tests was that you had to have a really light recovery ride the following day, but instead I went and did a big climb near where I live. I felt the tendon go straight away, like elastic snapping. When I got home I had a lump like a small apple, so I knew there was something seriously wrong.

Moser won Tirreno, and then we did Roubaix. They'd signed a crazy Austrian named Harald Maier – they liked Austrians and Swiss for tax reasons – but this guy just took it upon himself to break away. Without asking Moser! I pulled a lot that day, but when Francesco

the TV and press, almost forgetting the Giro itself, focused almost entirely on these issues …

The Giro was in trouble, and it was getting worse by the day. We had Zakhirov and Sgambelluri positive for NESP, a new-generation EPO, and Chesini was actually placed under house arrest during the race. That evening, I spoke with some of the sports directors. We had a meeting, and at one o'clock in the morning we made our minds up. We decided to move firmly, and at seven o'clock I rang Verbruggen. Then I spoke with Manolo Saiz and Francesco Moser, presidents respectively of the teams' association and the riders' union. I told them we were going to ask Corti to have Simoni leave the race. If he refused, I'd call off the stage, then hold a press conference and explain why. I then issued the same request to Manuela Ronchi of Mercatone Uno, because Sgambelluri was in the same situation, waiting for the counter-analysis. After an hour, Corti called me, and informed me that Simoni was already on his way home to Trento …

The 2002 Giro represented a watershed moment in Italy's relationship with the Giro. It followed on from the Festina affair at the 1998 Tour de France, Marco Pantani's catastrophic expulsion in 1999, and the San Remo blitz of 2001. For a century, the professional cyclist had been a reverential figure, but by now the wider public was convinced that the sport's doping culture was intractable. The expulsions of Garzelli, Simoni et al. seemed merely to confirm it, and the sport faced ridicule in the mainstream media.

In the event, Simoni, positive again for cocaine during the Giro, would return to racing in August. He was able to prove that the cough sweets he'd ingested did contain traces of the substance, and would win a stage at the Vuelta that autumn. Garzelli, who always maintained his innocence, now works for RAI as an expert summarizer.

DENIS LUNGHI
RIGHT PLACE, WRONG TIME
VALKENBURG, 1998
CHIETI, 2002

My fourth year as an amateur, the first race was Monte Carlo–Alassio. I was second behind Ivan Basso – the usual cock-up in the sprint. Next was the Trofeo Strazzi. Terrible weather, rain all day, and I won by two minutes. Basso was second …

After that I was never out of the first five. Third, fourth, second, fifth. I wasn't very good at getting to 110 per cent, but I could ride at 90 per cent all year round, understand? To be honest, that probably wasn't the best way, but that's the way I was. My body was intact, I trained well and ate well, and I was a clean cyclist.

Five of us were selected for the Worlds in Valkenburg. Fusi, the manager, didn't really want me there, but I was one of the best in Italy so he had no choice. The five were me, my teammate Ruggero Marzoli, Basso, Danilo Di Luca and Rinaldo Nocentini.

When the race started, Marzoli and I were told to go with the break. I had the strength to do two races that day, but we weren't allowed to pull. In reality, Fusi sent us because he wanted one of the others to win. They all rode Pinarello bikes and we didn't, but whatever … Anyway, there were about ten of us in the break, and I promise you that had we been allowed to pull it would have stayed away …

So now there were only three of us left: me, Marzoli and Matthias Kessler. They caught us on the penultimate lap, but I could hardly feel the chain. I was ready to start racing properly, but then Basso attacked and of course I couldn't move. I was on the wheel of a Dutch guy, praying, praying, praying that he would make the junction. Basso was there, four metres away from us, but the guy couldn't quite get across and Basso rode away. When I got home and watched it on TV I cried, and it still breaks my heart even now. Watch it on YouTube and you'll see. That was it. That was the moment …

So Basso was world champion, with Di Luca and Nocentini second and third. At the end of the season I won the Prestigio Bicisport, though. It was the points classification for the best amateur in Italy, and the prize was a holiday in Zanzibar.

I signed as a pro with Polti, and I remember the first training camp down in Calabria vividly. Every time there was a climb, I was at the front with guys like Ivan Gotti, Richard Virenque, Mirko Celestino and Davide Rebellin. I was going well, but as we got deeper into the season … Well, let's just say that when the important races started, you needed to prepare differently.

What I mean is that I turned professional just as they introduced the 50 per cent haematocrit rule. They basically legalized EPO use, and that was a problem for me because my natural haematocrit was always between 47 and 49. So, even if I'd wanted to do something … I'm really not interested in spitting in the soup, but it's just that … Ask anyone you like. They'll all tell you I rode at the wrong time.

It's difficult for a neo-pro to have any freedom in a team like that. So I did my work as a *gregario*, looking and learning and trying to grow. I had a two-year contract with them, but then Antonio Bevilacqua told me that Colpack wanted to sponsor a professional team and he was going to be managing it. He was going to take some of the young riders from Polti, and run the team in parallel. I was happy about that because they were like family to me. When I'd ridden for Antonio as an amateur, I'd had other teams offering me three times the salary, but I hadn't gone and I was right not to have gone. Why? Well, you know … the environment.

So I went from struggling to get rides at a big team to being the captain of a small one. In some respects it was a step back, but it was also two forward because I had some freedom. We didn't ride the Giro, but I won the GP di Carnago. Then I got second behind Jan Ullrich at the Coppa Agostoni, third at the Bernocchi, lots of top-ten finishes and what have you.

The next year I rode the Giro and did OK, then I won the Giro del Friuli, lots more placements. They selected me for the Worlds in Lisbon, but only as a reserve this time.

In 2002 we only found out we were in the Giro ten days before it started. We didn't have the money for a GC rider or a good sprinter, so it was all on me. Stanga, the manager, called us into the motorhome on the eve of the race, and I'll never forget what he said: "The bike isn't a toy, and the Giro d'Italia isn't a game. This is a serious thing, and you need to produce."

I think that in some respects the blitz of the previous year was helpful because people were worried about being caught. I think it perhaps levelled the playing field a little bit, you know? Each day I was trying, and the stage to Chieti – what was it, the twelfth? – looked good. It was 200 kilometres, up and down all day, not a metre of flat but no really big mountains. It was ideal for me, and I liked it when it rained. I think there were six of us in the break initially, and then four. There were three circuits of Chieti, and I rode away on the second. So I'd have done about thirty kilometres on my own. Indescribable …

The thing is it's a numbers game, and someone like me has very few chances. There were probably ten sprints that year, then two time trials and seven GC stages. So in reality almost every road stage was won by either a GC rider, a sprinter or by Pérez Cuapio, the Mexican climber guy.

There were about two hundred guys in that Giro, and 190 of them never had a hope in hell of winning a stage …

Following his masterpiece at Chieti, Denis decided to ride the queen stage of the Giro with the GC group. He actually led them for a while and, after having climbed the Pordoi, Fedaia and Campolongo, finished fifth atop the Passo Coe. He says he began that Giro with a haematocrit of 47, and finished it with 47.

In 2003 Denis signed for Alessio, a much bigger team. He finished both the Giro and the Vuelta ("insanely fast") and won stages at the Tour of Abruzzo and in China. However, a routine test revealed a heart anomaly, and his professional career finished at the age of twenty-seven.

Denis said that, while life goes on, having to stop crippled him emotionally. He says he's probably been on the bike "fifteen times" since, and completely disappeared from the cycling world. However, each year he would go for the tests anyway. He would do so in the hope that he'd be given the green light to return, and didn't resign himself to the fact that it was over until he was thirty-five.

Ivan Basso won the Giro twice, Danilo Di Luca once.

MARCO PINOTTI
CRONOMAN
OSIO SOTTO, 1995

When I turned amateur, the club's sports director said I needed to take iron, vitamins and amino acids to recover. I think I paid about 50,000 lire for the amino acid tablets, and took them home.

When my dad saw them he said, "What are they?" and I said, "They're amino acid tablets. I need them to help me recover." He said, "How many are you supposed to take?" and I told him it was ten a day, or whatever it was. He said, "So you're doing sport because it's healthy, but you're telling me you need to take ten of these a day? If you need these to ride a bike there must be something wrong with you. You must be ill!"

I told him the sports director had told me I needed to take them. He said, "So you're telling me you're taking medicine because a *cycling coach* told you? That's funny, because I always thought that doctors were qualified to dispense medicine, and that cycling coaches were qualified to coach cycling …"

Then he made an appointment with a cardiologist, a guy who'd looked after him and my grandfather. I didn't know it at the time, but he was also the regional president of the Italian National Olympic Committee. He said, "OK, so the first thing to remember is that I'm a medic, not a sports director. The second thing is that you don't need amino acids. You need regular sleep and a good, varied diet with eggs, milk …"

The problem is that at that age you're so malleable that you don't believe what the doctor says; you believe what the coach says. Anyway, between

them they convinced me that I *didn't* need them, so I gave them to one of my teammates. That was one of the reasons I started to have problems with the DS. He didn't like the fact that I wanted to carry on studying for my degree, didn't like the way I rode for myself, and he *certainly* didn't like the fact that I'd disobeyed him over the tablets.

In May I won a race, and that proved I could do it without amino acids. The DS said, "You'll never be a rider." Then they stopped paying my expenses – lack of discipline …

When the Festina scandal happened at the 1998 Tour, I was about to turn professional, and I saw it as a positive thing for me. I kept on seeing it as a positive thing, because I figured that each time they drummed a cheat out of the sport it became cleaner. I thought, "The more they write about this in the papers, the better it is." I wasn't thinking about the long-term consequences of it, and I never felt ashamed to be a professional bike rider.

The riders had *suspicions* about who was clean and who wasn't, although it tended to be based on their public declarations. A lot of it was supposition, but you get a feel for these things … So – back to the medical analogy – I saw it as a kind of illness. Each time someone tested positive it got a little bit better, and each time there was a raid and they rooted someone out I was all for it. In retrospect, though, I have to admit that I was only partly right. Why? Well, because they cut so much out that the patient – Italian cycling – is almost dead. It's on life support …

Over time people started believing that it was impossible to ride these distances without doping. *That* was the real issue, possibly even more than the doping itself. It wasn't true, but it was one of the main reasons the sponsors walked away and the money was sucked out of the sport.

So I'd say that there *was* a lot of doping, but also that it was exaggerated. One way or another, everybody arranged themselves around it. Some cheated, others used it as an excuse to explain why they didn't win, some did both, and others just got on with being the best rider they could.

My dad? He was quite a simple man, but by no means a stupid one. He was quite linear, but I think also quite intelligent.

Marco Pinotti's career arc is in some ways a reflection of the times. Although blessed with an exceptional engine, he struggled to compete against the very best during the EPO years. Instead, he found a niche as a champion time trialist, and as an advocate of clean sport. As cycling gradually cleaned itself up — and he maintains that, despite the naysayers, it has significantly cleaned itself up — his results improved exponentially. Many of the chemically enhanced "champions" who beat him were ostracized, while he continued to find employment in a changing cycling paradigm.

When Marco captured the maglia rosa for a second time at the 2011 Giro, he gave an extremely forthright post-stage interview on RAI. He stated that his was a victory not only for the anti-doping principles and practices of his HTC-Highroad team, but also for clean cycling as a whole. It was a seminal moment and, notwithstanding the fact that he was no great champion, his remains a seminal career. On his retirement, his morality unimpeachable, Marco found work as a sports director for the BMC professional team.

GIROTAPPA 10
L'ORGANIZZAZIONE
(THE ORGANIZATION)

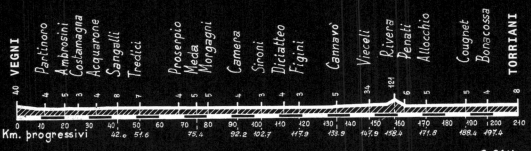

VEGNI · Partinoro · Ambrosini · Costamagna · Acquarone · Sangalli · Tredici · Proserpio · Meda · Morgagni · Camera · Sironi · Diciatteo · Figini · Cannavò · Vieceli · Rivera · Penati · Allocchio · Cougnet · Bonacossa · TORRIANI

40 · 4 · 5 · 3 · 4 · 8 · 7 · 4 · 5 · 5 · 4 · 3 · 4 · 3 · 5 · 34 · 121 · 6 · 5 · 5 · 4 · 8

Km. progressivi
0 · 10 · 20 · 30 · 40 · 50 · 60 · 70 · 80 · 90 · 100 · 110 · 120 · 130 · 140 · 150 · 160 · 170 · 180 · 190 · 200 · 210

42.0 · 51.6 · 75.4 · 92.2 · 102.7 · 117.9 · 133.9 · 147.9 · 158.4 · 171.8 · 188.4 · 197.4

C. SAN-

Organizing the Giro, for all that it's a big responsibility and a historical responsibility, could never be as tough as the journey I undertook to get here …

I grew up in Rome, and I was working for Franco Mealli. I'd started in 1976, and my first race was Tirreno–Adriatico. Then came the Baby Giro, the World Championships in Ostuni, and so on and so forth. There were about twenty to twenty-five days' racing in our stable each year, events like the Tour of Lazio, Tirreno, the Tour of Puglia. Then Etna, Umbria, Friuli … They were important races but I knew in my heart of hearts that I was playing in Serie B. They weren't the Giro d'Italia.

By the early nineties Vincenzo Torriani's health was deteriorating, and Carmine Castellano had come on board full-time to replace him. Meanwhile, Mealli had smoked himself almost to death, and there was a discussion about the *Gazzetta* buying our races. Eventually, Castellano said, "We'll take the races, but only on condition that Mauro comes with them."

The big test was the 1994 World Championships in Sicily. The Mafia had murdered Falcone and Borsellino, the two judges, in 1992, and Sicily needed to demonstrate to the world that there was more to it than the Mafia. The Worlds were a major part of that, but Mealli was too ill to come so the whole event fell upon me to organize.

The problem was that the inauguration was 15 August, and I didn't start working on it until after Tirreno. People work for years to prepare a Worlds, but I had four months to put it together and there were *four* sites. It was the first with an individual time trial, and the last with a 100-kilometre team time trial. We had to close the A29 motorway – in effect, to close *Palermo*. The date is actually seared into my mind. Zen Velodrome. 15 August 1994. 5 pm. The opening ceremony …

Cavenaghi, the managing director of RCS Sport, came to Sicily and shadowed me to see whether or not I was up to the job. I'd say an average of three hours' sleep a night, up with the bakers and to bed with the *barristi*. Then I was dealing with vast sums of public money, 28 billion lire. You might think there's nothing unusual about that, but this wasn't Rome or Milan, this was Sicily in the 1990s. The first visit I had from the Carabinieri was in April. We were less than a fortnight in, and they'd already sequestered all the documents.

I lost 15 kilos, and the morning of the opening ceremony I wasn't able to tie my own tie. I had to ask my wife to do it, but somehow we made it. I'd passed the test, and I reached an agreement with Cavenaghi to start working under Castellano. I sold my house in Rome, moved my family up to Milan, and, just as I did so, Cavenaghi was replaced.

The new MD offered me less than a third of what we'd agreed. I told him I couldn't accept it, but he said, "Have you got anything in writing from Cavenaghi?" I told him I hadn't, because I'd been about to begin a working relationship with the guy, and without trust relationships are groundless. That taught me a valuable lesson, but it didn't alter the fact that I was living in a rented house in Milan, and I was unemployed. I was contemplating moving everything back to Rome, but a couple of days later they called me back. Eventually, we came to an agreement.

I'd never had any intention of supplanting Castellano, but it was kind of implicit that when he retired I might assume his position. It didn't work out that way, though, because Angelo Zomegnan came on board instead. So one way or another, I had to wait until 2011 to take on my current role.

I often think how fortunate my predecessors were to have predated social media. Back in the day, there was the *Gazzetta dello Sport*, and it was the Bible. If it wasn't in the *Gazzetta*, it hadn't happened, whereas these days the scrutiny is 24/7 and instantaneous. The phone is extraordinarily powerful, and extremely dangerous in the wrong hands. It's no longer just the means by which people communicate; it's become the *reason* people communicate.

People criticize me without understanding my remit. They say I'm out of my mind because I take the Giro abroad, but they've no idea why we do it. They don't understand, for example, that when I go to the south I get no financial return, but that the Giro belongs to all of Italy. In order for me to take the race down there, I need to find the money from somewhere, don't I?

I often wish the job was more passion and less business, because the more business there is, the less heart there is … I'd also like to be more ambitious, but there are certain structural and economic limits that perhaps my friends at the Tour don't have to deal with.

Mauro Vegni. Matter of fact.

In 2005 RCS Sport was in advanced negotiations with the Franco family, owners of the Vuelta a España. The lawyers had signed it off, and the deal seemed imminent. At the eleventh hour, however, the Francos ceased to communicate, and shortly afterwards it was announced that ownership had passed to Antenna 3. Three years later ASO acquired a 49 per cent shareholding in the race, and so the trajectory of twenty-first-century cycling was set.

In 2016 Cairo Communications acquired a 59 per cent shareholding in RCS Media Group, the parent company of the Giro. The majority shareholder, Urbano Cairo, is the president of Torino FC. He publically declared that he found it "illogical" that the Giro turned over €25 million, the Tour de France €110 million. He stated that the Giro accounted for 15 per cent of the Italian TV audience in May, a very important month for advertisers. Meanwhile, across the border, the Tour harvested 20 per cent, but in the "dead" month of July. He added that he found it unfathomable that RAI were paying RCS Sport €5 million (he called it "una miseria"), while Euro Media France was paying the Tour €44 million. Watch this PAY-TV space …

ANNA PORTINARO
MISS GIRO D'ITALIA
CASALE MONFERRATO, 1962

What I most remember is blind panic! I was just an eighteen-year-old girl, and I wasn't used to being on stage in front of people. To be honest, the thought of it absolutely terrified me.

My grandfather owned Café Rossignoli, a very big bar here in the centre of town. It was always extremely busy, particularly when the livestock market was on. My daily routine was quite simple. I went to school in the day, and in the evenings I worked in the bar. One of my jobs there was the *Totocalcio*, the football pools. Obviously, a lot of sports fans used to come in to bet and talk sports, and the big sports back then were cycling and football.

One of the men who used to come in was named Guaschino. He was a good friend of my grandfather, and he used to sell tractors, combine harvesters and suchlike. He was a big cycling fan, and he'd been part of the organizing committee responsible for bringing the stage finish to Casale. One day he was in the bar and he said to my father and grandfather, "You know we've got the Giro d'Italia coming? Why don't you get Anna to be Miss Tappa?"

Why me? I don't know to be honest! I suppose I wasn't ugly, but nor was I the best looking girl in town. Maybe it was just convenient! At first I begged them to find someone else to do it, but it was the first time my father had ever asked anything of me. So I couldn't really say no and he was proud that his girl had been chosen for such a big occasion.

The days prior to the stage were a living hell. It seems ridiculous now, but I was petrified. I'd say to my mum, "I don't even know what I'm supposed to do! I don't know how to behave in front of all those people!" Then I'd be trying different outfits on, taking them off, getting myself in a terrible state. In the end, I settled on something I thought was quite classical, but the agonies I went through choosing that outfit …

When the big day arrived it was terribly hot, and I was sweating with worry *and* the heat. I was standing below the stage, waiting, but there wasn't anyone there to tell me what to do. Eventually, they just shoved me up on to the stage, and I kissed the cyclists, smiled as best I could for the cameras and gave out the flowers. If you watch the film of it you can see I don't really know what to do with myself. I keep fidgeting and fiddling with my hair …

And that was that – weeks of stress and anxiety for those five minutes as "Miss Tappa"! Did it go well? I think so. Everyone seemed happy enough, and my dad was proud of me.

It may seem anachronistic in the twenty-first century, but the Giro still sets great stall by its podium girls. As recently as 2011, former race director Michele Acquarone described them as one of the cardinal points of the race. These days, four are chosen (one for each of the jerseys) and they accompany the race the length and breadth of the peninsular for the duration.

In addition, RCS Sport chooses a madrina, a high-profile "godmother". The incumbent is invariably drawn from Italy's bloated TV game-show circuit, although, on occasion, mid-ranking (but presumably "between jobs") actresses have also been appointed. Stories of guileless, big-eared bike riders "liaising" with beautiful podium girls are legion.

Anna Portinoro and her gravity-defying, B-52s-style hair. It's 1962.

CESARE SANGALLI
CARTOGRAPHER
PASSO DELLO STELVIO, 1953
PASSO DI GAVIA, 1960

The cyclists needed to know the length of the climbs, the gradient and the state of the roads, and the fans needed to know where to go to watch the race. So I played my part, because everything was decided according to the drawings I did, the timetables I drew up and the architecture of the stages we put together.

Someone worked out that I did more than 200,000 kilometres, five times round the equator. I was the cartographer of the Giro d'Italia for over fifty years …

The first one I did was 1953, when they went over the Stelvio for the first time. I'll never forget watching poor Hugo Koblet shell down the mountain in pursuit of Fausto Coppi.

The Gavia in 1960? Vincenzo Torriani had a call from Achille Compagnoni, the mountaineer who conquered K2. He lived at Santa Caterina di Valfurva, at the bottom of the climb, and he implored Torriani to take the Giro over it. It had been an old dirt track used by shepherds and farmers, but then they'd developed it into a military dirt road during the Great War. That was all it was, but Compagnoni saw no reason they couldn't go up it and they sent me to do a preliminary inspection …

It was 3–4 metres wide at most, and, when I went up there, there was 4 metres of snow. It was terribly steep, up to 20 per cent in parts. We transported tonnes of sand and gravel up there, truck after truck after truck. Legend has it that they had the local shepherds divert their animals elsewhere so as not to damage the carriageway while they were working to make it passable.

I realized that going up it would be terrible for the riders, but that it ought to be possible. Going down the other side was something else entirely, though. For that you needed skill *and* courage. You know, on the descent there are some sharp bends with no protection whatsoever, so we decided we'd take the precaution of stationing some guys there, just in case. We couldn't afford for anyone to go over the edge …

So we had this new discovery, and everyone was working day and night to try to ensure that it would happen. Two days before the stage, Torriani sent me up to do a final inspection. Truth be told, everyone was a bit worried, not least Giuseppe Ambrosini, the editor of the *Gazzetta*. I went up there with a journalist, Guido Giardini. I spent two days going up and down it, double-checking with the various people involved in the works.

On the eve of the race we were all there in the hotel lobby, awaiting the final decision. There was the mayor of Bormio, the parson, local dignitaries, Compagnoni himself and the famous skier Marco Confortola. When I took the call from Torriani, there was dead silence. Then, when he confirmed that it was on, there was this great round of applause. I'll never forget that moment. I kept a stone from the Gavia for forty years, but then in 2000 I donated it to the Museum of Dreams at Feltre. They organized an event to honour my work, so it was the least I could do …

I used to consult the maps from the Geographic Military Institution, work out the gradients according to the coordinates, and check the feasibility of taking the race wherever it needed to go. That was always the easy part – the length, the height, the steepness. The timetables were mainly just laborious work. I didn't much enjoy spending autumn evenings drawing them up, but it was necessary so I did it.

It's not easy to reduce a 200-kilometre stage into 30 centimetres, and still less so when you consider it was going to be printed half the size again in the *Garibaldi* or the *Gazzetta*. First I drew them with a pencil, then with ink. When you see the designs in the *Garibaldi*, or in the *Gazzetta*, they might look like pure geometry, but actually they're not. I'd try to be faithful to the altimetry, and to include

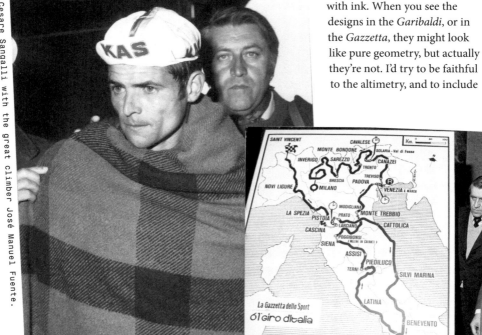

the key points along the route. Then population centres so people knew where to go, intermediate sprints and climbs, but also to render the *nature* of the stage. That was the biggest challenge.

Torriani would tell me where the stage started and finished, and give me the key points in between. So if a stage needed to pass over this mountain, or through this town – whatever – I'd go and study it, and offer advice on the route. Maybe we'd want to avoid a certain town centre, or a stretch of road that wasn't suitable, and so on. Torriani wasn't a cyclist, and, to be honest, he was much more interested in the show than in the technical and sporting elements. Castellano was much more interested in that, because he came from a cycling background.

These days it's all done on a computer, but don't ask me how because I haven't got the faintest idea. My daughter has a computer, but I wouldn't even know how you turn it on.

Cesare Sangalli was born in Milan in 1923. A quiet, modest, unassuming man, he has been a true giant of the Giro d'Italia.

Cesare grew up close to the headquarters of the Gazzetta dello Sport, and as a boy he would watch the great champions at the punzonatura, the sign-on before the Tour of Lombardy. He loved cycling, although his own great sporting passion was rugby.

In 1951 the Gazzetta dello Sport had need of someone with excellent calligraphy to compile diplomas for the finalists of the sporting events it organized. Luciano Andreini, a boyhood friend, recommended Cesare. The following year, the Gazzetta's cartographer left to do illustrations at the Corriere della Sera, and Cesare was invited to work on a freelance basis.

The 1960 stage over the Passo di Gavia remains one of the greatest, most dramatic day's racing in the history of the Giro d'Italia. It would be twenty-eight years before the Giro would return, and here again the stage is writ large into the legend of the race.

SERGIO MEDA
BUSINESS BEFORE PLEASURE
APELDOORN, HOLLAND, 2016

The Giro exists in its context. Sport is business, and it can't be otherwise. So when we talk about the idealism of sport – Olympian principles like loyalty and respect – it's difficult for them to emerge within the context of sport as a marketplace.

Do you want to know how the Giro is born? Usually, it's delivered in a night, after a certain quantity of cigarettes and many months of thoughts, discussions and compromises. Some of the compromises are good, some really bad. Nowadays, there are just so many people involved in the decision. Lots of them are marketing people, some are advertising, and one knows about cycling and about stage races. What I'm saying is that the person who understands sport has the *penultimate* word, not the last.

Armando Cougnet and Vincenzo Torriani, the first two patrons of the Giro, were blessed. Between 1909 and 1990 they were the architects of the race, and they were able to build it in perfect autonomy after having consulted the country, politics, institutions, companies, regional development agencies and local tourist boards. The Giro was built around the sales potential of the *Gazzetta*.

Nowadays, the only thing that matters is the economic element, because the bills need to be paid. This also applies when the Giro starts abroad – in effect, every other year. A foreign start usually means something like a 60 per cent increase in television costs, because RAI sends too many people and too much equipment. When Mediaset televised cycling for four years, they did so with half the staff.

RCS Sport has first and foremost to fulfil a financial obligation. Therefore, if the Giro takes cycling abroad, you can be certain it's not simply as a mechanism to honour the local Italian population. The days in Ireland were worth millions (they say €6 million), and the Dutch, who aren't noted for their philanthropy, clearly judged that it was an investment worth making. They'd be earning €1 million without too much difficulty.

In Italy the Giro is rigorously free of charge, but elsewhere it's a gold mine. They sell tickets to the finishing line, and local merchandising delivers excellent returns. Meanwhile, at home, the crisis leaves local, provincial and regional governmental bodies unable to meet their financial commitments. Those able allocate a tidy sum (€80,000 for a stage start, €150,000 for a finish), but feel put out by the fact that there's no return. Rather, the monies serve simply to cover the emergencies, the day-to-day.

Like the Tour and the Vuelta, today's Giro is a question of televisual visibility and of the sponsorship that is its immediate consequence. The higher the audience, the higher the price for the rights the following year, and the higher the value to the brands.

The TV executives are comics; they tear their hair out because of the quantity of people who tackle the climbs on foot

in order to applaud their heroes. The executives want nothing more than for those people to sit themselves in front of their TV screens, notwithstanding the fact that it would signal the death knell for cycling. It's a show for the people and *of* the people. They gather by the roadside wherever they are, because they want to breathe in the toil of those who ride.

Angelo Zomegnan took my place when I left the *Gazzetta* in 1980. Had I stayed, a lot of things would have been different, and probably better.

When Zomegnan arrived, there was a sense of mystification. He maintains that he was charged with replacing Carmine Castellano, and that's why he accompanied him in his final Giro in 2005. During the time when he demonstrated his true character, he always gave the impression of being a decision-maker, someone who never seemed to have doubts. He would never say, "Let me think", but obviously even intelligent people don't always have the truth in their pocket. Sometimes, you need half an hour or a day to come up with the right answer, but he was a man who resolved everything in an instant. So with this "I'm in command" way of his, he fascinated the top brass at RCS.

The problem was that when Zomegnan spoke, he had a sacred mountain behind him, the *Gazzetta*. So people believed what he said, because the paper and the position bestowed legitimacy and authority. So, by definition, he became credible.

I don't know what happened to the €12.8 million, but I don't believe for one minute that Michele Acquarone is a crook. He's not a person capable of organizing something like that …

Sergio Meda returned to RCS as press officer in 1995. He stayed on until his retirement in 2009, his final Giro the centenary edition. His son, Federico, now produces the Garibaldi *(Road Book).*

Sergio has published a number of books about cycling. The most recent is Il Giro in Vetrina *(2016), an examination of the race as a cultural, commercial and institutional phenomenon. The work details Fiorenzo Magni's perspicacity in attracting the non-cycling sponsor Nivea, back in 1954. In persuading cycling's institutions to accept "third-party" sponsors, Magni ushered in a genuine revolution in the sport. The book explores the Giro's subsequent trajectory, and its evolution as a marketing and PR entity.*

STEFANO DICIATTEO
PRESS OFFICER
CUNEO, 2009

People often ask why I've stayed so long in the same job, but I don't really understand the question. I can't imagine a better job than the one I have.

Everything I feel about the Giro you can find in this article by Marco Pastonesi. It refers to the death of Fabio Saccani, a *moto* rider who died during the 2009 race. I keep it in my wallet, because for me it says it all:

"We're a circus, a great orchestra, an ambulatory spectacular. We too are a peloton. We're riders who don't turn the pedals, but rather we spin photos, words and images, push railings and crash barriers. Then tables and chairs, cables and connectors, telephones and microphones. Ours is a moving city which is born, miraculously, every 24 hours, appropriating and then abandoning. We're enthusiasts and lovers; seduced and spellbound. We're workers and hired hands, full-time and temporary, amateur and yet professional. We'd gladly do it all for free.

"We're numbers, names, surnames and nicknames. We're faces and signatures, eyes and glances. We're men and women who've broken away, and for three weeks we ask ourselves whether the break isn't, in fact, the very best form of pursuit. And, in our own unique way, we care a great deal about one another.

"Ciao Fabio. You're already missed."

My first Giro was 1994. I'd just finished university, and I'd started writing for a couple of local papers. A family friend had a son who was supposed to work for RCS Sport during the Giro, but then he was called up for military service. His mum and dad knew I was a big sports fan and they asked whether I fancied it. Obviously I did, and that was the beginning.

At the time it was photocopying, stapling documents, stuff like that. Then there was a thing where the journalists predicted who was going to do what in each of the stages. I got involved in that, and I started to get to know some of the journalists. I couldn't believe my luck, because here I was at the Giro d'Italia. I felt like the cat that got the cream …

They called me again the following year, and from 1996 I started working with the press officers. Initially, I was

117

freelance, but I've been staff since 2001. Of course there are always issues to deal with. However, if you knew what was going to happen it would be pretty dull, and the Giro is very seldom dull!

The busiest time for me is the two hours post-stage. There's a lot of protocol involved at that time, but you learn how to deal with it. Problems? I had a bit of a rough time when Zomegnan decided I wasn't cut out for the job and moved me sideways. However, I found an ally in Mauro Vegni, and he helped me to come through that period.

I've done the Giro twenty-three times, and I've only ever had one day off. It was 22 May 2010, the day Nibali won his first stage. He attacked on Monte Grappa and won on the descent, but I was off "sick". Actually, I was in Madrid watching Inter Milan win the Champions League Final, but I was back at Malpensa by eight o'clock the following morning, and at the top of the Zoncolan by midday …

Until recent times, French was the official language of cycling. However, English has become the sport's lingua franca, and the Giro has moved to keep step. The development of the Garibaldi, *the Giro road book, is indicative of the evolution. First created in 1949, it was published exclusively in Italian. That's because 89 of the 102 starters were home-grown, and all of the teams were sponsored by Italian bike and component manufacturers. The demographic of the peloton evolved over time, but it wasn't until 1997 that RCS Sport saw fit to produce the* Garibaldi *as an Italo-French bilingual publication.*

By the 2011 Giro only 30 per cent of the peloton was Italian, and Italian cycling was struggling to attract sponsors prepared to make World Tour-sized investments. By now, the sport was a truly global affair, and RCS replaced French with English. Recent Garibaldi *have even been made available to the public, downloadable on www.gazzetta. it. Elsewhere, press releases are published in English, and so too the race's prodigious social media output.*

ANTONIO PENATI
VOLUNTEER
NIBBIONO, 1988

I was a Giro commissar seven times. The first was in 1989, and I'll never forget the day the designation notice arrived. It's like the football referee when he's told he's going to officiate at the biggest match of the season, isn't it? It's the *Giro d'Italia* …

In 1971 I was asked to drive a commissar in a race a few kilometres from here. I enjoyed doing it, and I realized it was the only way to watch a bike race close-up. I said to the guy, "What should I do?" and he said you needed to take a course. So that's what I did: I went to Milan on Sundays and qualified as a judge. Then, in 1973, I started doing regional amateur races, and in 1977 I became a national-level commissar. Pretty soon I was doing the biggest races on the Italian professional circuit.

The designation for the Giro would generally arrive in December or January. That was a tense time, because you were waiting and hoping. I was selected again in 1990, then 1993, 1994, 1997 and 1998. I did it again in 2007 when I reached sixty, but by then the riders had transponders so it was much less intense and much less interesting.

I was the finishing-line judge, so it was a big responsibility. In a day-to-day sense, I did the sign-on, and after that I'd go on ahead so as to be ready for the intermediate sprints and then

the finish itself. Most of the work was done before the race, though. I studied the route, the rule book, the jerseys, the sprinters themselves. If you do something for passion, you're always more concentrated on doing a good job, aren't you?

The objective was simple enough – to establish the classification without equivocation or problems. You hoped the photo-finish camera worked 100 per cent, but in a bunch sprint it can't pick up all the numbers of all the riders. You needed to know cycling, and to know cyclists. It was like any other job. The better you were at it, the better your chances were of being promoted, and being promoted meant doing the biggest races with the biggest riders.

I planned my annual leave around the races. My great fortune has been to have work colleagues who understood, and above all a wife who understood. She was never jealous of my cycling life, and she never resented the fact that we were never able to go on holiday. The Giro is three weeks, so what with all the other races as well …

There are dozens of stories. Cipollini's first stage win in 1989, the way the public responded to him and to Pantani, the Zoncolan, the Fedaia, the avalanche in 1994. In 1993 there was a stage in Agrigento, Sicily. I was in the car with the air conditioning on, and when I got out to go to the finish it was 42 degrees.

I'm a natural-born collector, and I've never been able to stop. What you see in this room is probably about 10 per cent of what I have. The spare room is full, the cellar is full and every cupboard is full. My dad's old house is 100 metres from here, and it's full. Hundreds of cycling books, magazines, photographs, programmes, cigarette cards, postcards, chewing-gum cards, autographs. Then every edition of the *Gazzetta*, magazines, stamps, medals, pennants, documents, badges and gadgets. I'm trying to collect a medal from every world championship. You have to check all the eBay sites every day, travel around to the fairs and markets, keep in touch with other collectors around the world …

The problem with a collection like this is what to do with it when I die. I don't have kids who are interested, and you need at least one house to store it all. You also need the financial commitment and resources to improve it, and a hell of a lot time and passion to curate it.

So I've no idea. It's my life, so I guess it ought to die with me. The easiest thing would probably be to hire a couple of trucks and take it all to the incinerator …

The look of love. With Evgeni Berzin in 1994.

The modern-day Giro is a commercial and organizational juggernaut, but it's still held together by disparate and yet totally committed volunteers like Antonio.

The race jury has grown exponentially over the decades. In 1951 it was comprised of three elements, but these days ten individuals are involved. The jury president co-ordinates three componenti *— jury members assigned tasks according to circumstance — while four judges circulate the race on motorbikes. In Antonio's day, there were two finishing-line judges, but with recent developments in technology only one is necessary.*

There are cycling devotees all over Italy, and a great many cycling collectors. There is nobody quite like Antonio Penati, however, and no cycling collection remotely like the one he husbands …

THE TORRIANI BROTHERS, SONS OF THE FATHER, SAN GIOVANNI ROTONDO, 1947

Gianni: The Giro was 24 hours a day in our house, 11 months of the year. It conditioned our childhoods 100 per cent, for better or for worse. The best way to describe it would be as a kind of pregnancy. The closer to the birthing we got, the more stressful and anxious our father became, and as such we became. The birthing wasn't actually the moment at which the race began, but the day before. That was when our mum packed his bags and he readied himself to go.

At that point he changed completely, because all the stress of the preceding months dissipated. For ten months he'd been building the boat, and now, finally, he got to set sail on it. He got to be the captain …

Marco: He was extremely devoted to Padre Pio, a very prophetic priest who was well known because he always displayed stigmata. So one day while the Giro was down in Puglia, our father and Gino Bartali went to San Giovanni Rotondo, where Padre Pio had his priesthood. They didn't have an appointment, but what with Bartali being *maglia rosa*, they assumed they might have a chance to meet with him.

They went to the sacristy and one of the monks recognized them straight away. He was enthusiastic, but he said, "The problem is you can't really just turn up where he's concerned. You never know how he'll respond, and if the moment's wrong he might take umbrage and send you on your way. He has mass in an hour, though, so wait in the corridor between the sacristy and the church. He's bound to see you and you might have a chance to meet him."

So they went and waited, and at a certain point they saw Padre Pio walking along the corridor. He looked upon them and said, "You two! Never at home!" He wasn't interested in their fame, but he had the ability to look into souls. He instinctively understood what kind of lives they had, and he reproached them for neglecting their family lives and for always being on the road.

Marco and Gianni Torriani at the seaside.

Gianni: That "never at home" became a kind of mantra for our mother, a standing joke. Our father's work was his mission, and his office was 50 metres from the house. He had to take two lifts to get to here from there, and he found that terribly frustrating because it was time lost. His working day started at six in the morning, and he finished when he was exhausted. That was usually around midnight. Our mother was a saint ...

Marco: He was criticized endlessly. If the wrong guy won the Giro, it was his fault; if the stages weren't to the liking of certain riders, it was his fault ... He was quite resolute, though, because he felt he knew his job and the determining factors were unchanging: the position of the climbs in relation to the stage finishes, the distribution of the harder stages, the placement, type and distance of the time trials ...

The notion that he'd prepare the Giro for a certain rider is factually incorrect. He prepared it in the hope that it would be spectacular, yes, because that way the public was more engaged. So of course, as the race organizer he had to be mindful of who the protagonists were likely to be, but not because he favoured any particular rider. He understood that the public wanted to see the great champions perform, and he wanted the Giro to have a winner worthy of its heritage and significance. Then again, so did everyone else, but ultimately it was the riders who determined what kind of show it became, not him.

So in answer to your question, he probably wouldn't have chosen for Michel Pollentier to beat Francesco Moser in 1977, but that would apply to 100 per cent of Italians, not just Vincenzo Torriani. Pollentier won because he deserved to, but the most important thing for our father was that it worked operationally and that the competition was fair and balanced.

He tried to keep his distance from the riders themselves. He was often accused of being aloof for that, but he viewed it as an intrinsic part of the job. To do otherwise was to lose not only objectivity, but also the wider view of the Giro in its totality. That was fundamental to him.

Vincenzo Torriani, Gino Bartali, Pope Paul VI and others.

When the riders retired they would become his friends – we'd often have Fiorenzo Magni, Alfredo Martini or Gino Bartali here – but not while they were active. He was friends with people like Teofilo Sanson, Ernesto Colnago and lots of other industrialists and sponsors, but not with the riders themselves.

Gianni: Our mother made it her business for she and our father to socialize with people from outside the sports world. She needed that balance in her relationships, and she needed for *him* to have it.

Was he a genius? Objectively, yes. He could have been anything he wanted, but the Giro was his calling and his being.

An immensely charismatic man, Giro patron Vincenzo Torriani was arguably the sport's greatest ever mind. He understood implicitly that sport was above all entertainment, and that it needed to be marketed as such. In the early 1960s he was one of the architects of the success of Sergio Zavoli's legendary Processo alla Tappa, *Italy's first talk show. Later, he broke the mould in negotiating TV rights with private broadcasters.*

In 1982 Torriani was knighted. He became a Cavaliere di Gran Croce, one of the highest honours the Italian Republic can bestow.

Torriani died in April 1996, and six months later a monument was built in his honour at Madonna del Ghisallo, the spiritual home of cycling. The Giro currently awards the Trofeo Vincenzo Torriani to the winner of the stage featuring the Cima Coppi, the highest peak in the race.

From left: Marco Torriani, Gianni Savio, Giovanni Michelotti, Gianni Torriani, Aldo Zambrini, Bruno Raschi and Vincenzo Torriani. The Giro's brains trust.

GIROTAPPA 11

QUELLI CHE RACCONTANO

(THE STORYTELLERS)

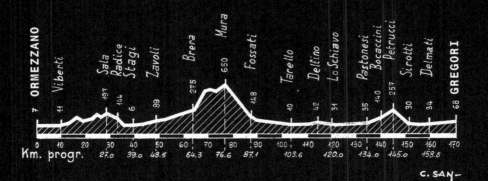

ORMEZZANO — Vibenti — Sala — Radice — Stagi — Zavoli — Brena — Mura 650 — Fossati — Tarello — Deltino — Lo Schiavo — Pastonesi — Bocaccini — Petrucci — Sirotti — Delmati — GREGORI

7   44   497   114   6   89   275   448   40   42   31   35   440   257   30   34   68

Km. progr.   0   10   20   30   40   50   60   70   80   90   100   110   120   130   140   150   160   170

27.0   39.0   48.5   64.3   76.6   87.1   103.6   120.0   134.0   145.0   153.8

C. SAN—

There are three ways to write about cycling. They represent the three ages of cycling journalism, and they're a mirror on the evolution of the sport. When I began, you had what I call the "cantors", the lovers. They venerated cycling, and for them it was almost liturgical. They were the people who founded the sport, and they wrote psalms to it. Most of what they produced was a paean, because, for them, the riders were celestial figures. They lived in a cycling context that saw Fausto Coppi and Gino Bartali as the heirs to Alfredo Binda, Costante Girardengo and Learco Guerra, the champions who rode between the wars. A lot of these cantors were only semi-literate, which was just as well because so were their readers. You didn't need to be a literary giant to write a psalm, and they had no pretensions in that respect.

Then you move on to what I call the eroticists, people like me. Gianni Brera was our prince, and we were people who were no longer simply enamoured of cycling. For us, it was more conditional, and we studied the love – including the love act – itself. We cared about it deeply, but we wanted to try to understand it as a phenomenon. We were interested in the things that influenced it, and the things over which it had influence. We tried to understand the impact it had on its constituents, and to view it in a much wider context.

Then you have the final age, ergo the final group. It's the age of pornography, and of the pornographers. They operate in the age of decadence, and their ideas about how they present the sport are a reflection of that fact. There is very little that's erotic about the way they represent the sport, but they are explicit to the point of obscenity.

Gianpaolo Ormezzano holding court.

The perception of the sport, and above all of the cyclists themselves, has changed beyond recognition. That's the story of cycling journalism in the fifty-seven years that I've lived it.

I wanted to be a sports journalist when I was eight years old. When I was ten, my father took me to the first stage of the 1946 Giro, Milan to Turin. I wasn't there to see the cyclists, though. My father was a friend of Raro Radice, the famous cycling journalist of *Tuttosport*, and he wanted me to see him. By the time I was sixteen I was pestering the editor to let me write for the paper, and I started covering cycling full-time in the autumn of 1958. I've been writing about it ever since …

I was so prolific in the sixties because there was no alternative. I slept very little and wrote extremely quickly, and it was my job to fill the paper. I had some cultural understanding of the race and of Italy, so I was able to provide the colour around the race itself.

There were three or four of us working on the race back then, but I produced the most. I'd be up at seven, devour the papers, then write as we drove. Obviously, it was a portable typewriter, not a computer … Then interviews, then ring it through – the paper was so poor that we didn't even have a telex. I didn't see the bike race, but then journalists never did. These days, they can watch it on TV or on a telephone, but so can everyone else. Any time, any place, anywhere.

The sport is fine; it just doesn't belong to the France–Italy–Belgium axis anymore. We're almost irrelevant now, because while we venerate our past, it moves on regardless. It's a corporation, and it conquers new frontiers all the time. They race all over the world, all year round. The evolution of women's cycling is incredible, and the bicycle is winning again in towns and cities. The technological advancements are astonishing.

Thanks to doping – and I *mean* doping, not *anti-doping* – we've discovered incredible health benefits. Other sports are only just beginning to recognize them, but ridiculously, clumsily and with all its stupid gaffes, cycling has been way ahead of the game.

My own doping experience? I wanted to understand what it was like for the riders, no more and no less. I did it shortly after the anti-doping laws had come into force and just before Tom Simpson died. One of the sports directors – a very famous former cyclist himself – told me precisely what they took, and I ingested thirteen different tablets in one day. As best as I could determine, the net result was nothing: I went about my work as normal but I didn't feel a thing. Maybe I wasn't supposed to. Maybe that was the whole point …

The Gazzetta dello Sport *is widely held to be Italy's cycling newspaper. It organizes the Giro, Lombardy, Milan–San Remo and a host of others, but back in the day its cycling output wasn't, per se, more prolific than that of the competition. It was one of four national sports dailies (now three), and their respective customer bases were conditioned first and foremost by geography. That always was the major determinant of a newspaper's editorial policy, and sport didn't exist in a vacuum.*

Traditionally, Rome's Corriere dello Sport *was widely read in the capital and all points south.* Tuttosport, *the Torinese daily, focused on Turin's two great football teams, and proliferated in Piedmont and Liguria. The now defunct* Stadio *was based in Bologna, and its readership was drawn from the Adriatic seaboard and the north-east. Given cycling's popularity there (and the absence of a giant footballing team in that part of the peninsular), it generally covered the sport more extensively even than the* Gazzetta.

These days, Tuttosport *and* Corriere *cover cycling hardly at all, while a normal day sees* Gazzetta *dedicate a single page to the sport it helped to create. That increases for the Tour de France, the Giro and the monuments, but, in general terms, Moto GP, Formula One and basketball are deemed more newsworthy. The decent cycling writers that remain, guys like Ormezzano, work for such specialist websites as tuttobiciweb.it.*

I'd have been eight. The caretaker at my primary school was mad about cycling, and he had this encyclopedic knowledge of it. I told him I was a cycling fan too, and at first he thought I was making it up. Then, when I told him the names of every member of every team in the Giro, he started to take me seriously.

One of my heroes was a local rider, a *gregario* named Adriano Pella. He rode eight seasons as a professional, but he only ever won once, a stage at Paris–Nice. As fate would have it, I finished up writing his biography. Adriano died in 2013, but he told me a story about what happened to him at the 1973 Giro. It's a nice anecdote, but it's also illustrative of the humility of the *gregari*. It's about the magic of the Giro and, I think, about what it is to be a cyclist …

Adriano had been struggling, struggling, struggling for two weeks, and finally he managed to get in the break. It was a Sunday and the stage finished down on the Tuscan coast, so the crowds would have been big. Anyway, ten kilometres or so from the finish he punctured. The group caught him, so another day had gone by and still nothing doing. He finished the stage eighteenth.

First communion, Borgo d'Ale.

Adriano started riding back towards the hotel, feeling a bit sorry for himself. It had been years since he'd won a race, and neither he nor anyone else in his team had earned any money at that Giro. He was riding along, lost in his own thoughts, when he heard a female voice from behind the guard rail. It was a young woman, and she had a little girl with her. She said she wanted to give her daughter a souvenir, and asked him if he could spare his cycling cap. Adriano felt a little embarrassed because he'd ridden hard for four hot hours and the cap was sweaty and a bit worse for wear. However, he gave it to the little girl, and it took his mind off things for a few minutes. It had been, when all was said and done, just another day at the coal face.

After dinner, Adriano was thinking how he'd have liked to have Piera, his wife, with him. Forte Dei Marmi is beautiful, and she'd have loved the beach and the bars. Then, just as he was enjoying his revelry, his DS turned up. He seemed quite agitated, and he told Adriano there was a guy in reception who wanted to see him. Adriano thought he must have done something wrong, but he couldn't figure out what it was.

When Adriano got to reception, the guy told him that his wife had been at the finish with their little girl. He then asked Adriano if he was rider number 136, and he confirmed to the guy that yes, he was. Adriano was wondering what was going to happen next, and he was a bit fearful. Instead, the guy told him that his daughter was really, really happy, and he wanted to thank him. He asked him if he was married and Adriano said he was, to Piera. The guy said he was the owner of a nightclub and a deluxe hotel. Then he offered Adriano a week's holiday for two in Forte Dei Marmi.

There's another story about the noble *gregario* as well. You can't print his name, but he was famous for not being particularly polished …

OCT • 72

The race started at Verviers, in Belgium. There was a great deal of symbolism involved, because the Giro was starting abroad, and they were going to ride through all the nation states of the new European Union. With Eddy Merckx being both Belgian and Eddy Merckx, the crowds were massive, and one of the dignitaries was Princess Paola of Belgium. She was a beautiful, elegant Tuscan woman, and she'd married Prince Albert of Belgium. So all things considered, it was an important moment for the Giro, for Belgium, for Merckx and for her.

There was a lot of pomp and ceremony, and finally everything was set. Princess Paola was given the honour of sending the Giro on its way with the specially made flag they'd had prepared. Just as she was about to drop the flag, the *gregario* guy, who probably had not the faintest idea who she was, turned to Merckx and said, "What do you reckon, Eddy? Do you think she's wearing any knickers under that skirt?"

Giovanni Tarello belongs to the great tradition of Italian sportswriters. He's written a number of extremely eloquent books about cycling, among them biographies of the 1931 Giro winner Francesco Camusso and the great 1950s climber Giancarlo Astrua.

Vincenzo Torriani's 1973 Giro was a masterpiece conceptually, but it would be a week before an Italian won a stage. In the final analysis, Merckx claimed six of them and, by a huge margin, the GC. He spent the entire race in the pink jersey, and also won the points, as the Belgians helped themselves to thirteen of the twenty stages.

Martín Emilio "Cochise" Rodríguez secured Colombia's first ever Grand Tour stage win, while the Spanish climber José Manuel Fuente triumphed at Auronzo di Cadore and carried off the King of the Mountains. The Italians managed a poultry five stages, and but for a courageous display by the debutant Giovanni Battaglin their Giro would have been a washout.

My first Giro was in 1982. I knew nothing about cycling, but I have to say the choice I made that day conditioned not only my career, but also my entire life. I've lived extreme situations, seen the most extraordinary natural beauty, spoken with unique individuals, and taken what a close friend of mine called "the best medicine known to man" – suffering.

My marriage broke up when my daughter Rebecca was two and a half, in November 1992. Her mother went to live elsewhere, and at that time it was sacrosanct that the kids stayed with their mum. In addition, I was a sports journalist, and most sport happens at the weekend. So I was hardly seeing my daughter, and I was very close to a nervous breakdown. I couldn't sleep at night, and the doctor said, "If you want to retain your psychic well-being, you need to do a lot of sport. You need to get to eleven o'clock at night physically exhausted because that way your brain, for at least four or five hours, has more urgent things to contend with: rest."

So having written about cycling for ten years, I started doing it myself. Having followed the champions, I started trying to emulate them, riding all the big mountains of the Tour and the Giro. It was salvation, and moreover it helped me to become a better journalist. Finally, I understood something of what they were living. I don't think you can really be a cycling journalist unless you've ridden a bike …

Moments? Too many. Being in Laurent Fignon's room at the end of the 1984 Giro when he was convinced that Francesco Moser had stolen it from him. Then the Gavia in 1988, watching Franco Chioccioli in the pink jersey. I've never seen a rider so close to … not to *death* but to … ruin. He was like a leaf, shaking. Stefano Del Tongo, the sponsor, was actually crying for him. "Get a doctor!" he was shouting. "The boy will die!" It took him twenty minutes to come round.

Gianni Bugno, for me the greatest gentleman of all. His first son, Alessio, was born in May 1990, twenty-five days before my Rebecca. Then we each separated at around the same time, and from that point onwards he and I probably talked more about our kids than about cycling. We were quite close by then, and of course we were going through the same thing.

It was 1994, I think, a summit finish at the Giro. Gianni didn't get into the team motorhome. Instead, I watched him get into one of the team cars with a woman by his side. Obviously, I understood that she was his new love. Her name was Angela Maria and she was from Trentino. Everyone knew Gianni was separated, but I had an obligation as a journalist to write what I saw. I tried to be sensitive about how I wrote it, but then the following morning the headline on the front page was, "BUGNO, ESCAPE FOR LOVE!"

Gianni came down for the start, and called me over. I'm thinking, "Here we go. He's going to have nothing more to do with me." So I said, "Well, Gianni?" and he said, "What you've written is perfect, but let me ask you a question. If you were me and this morning your little girl read

"VIBERTI, ESCAPE FOR LOVE!" what might that do to the relationship you have with her? Now think of the damage this could do to my relationship with Alessio."

I asked Gianni to forgive me, and he did. From that point on, our friendship was strengthened, and we're still friends to this day. Why? Because he understood that I'd been in a difficult situation. I'd been practising journalism, I'd attempted to do it correctly, and had I not done so I'd have compromised my professional integrity.

One more on Bugno. You know he was rooming with Emilio Ravasio in 1986, when he crashed and died? You know Ravasio would have survived if there had been a helicopter that day? You know that Gianni became a helicopter pilot? You know he's never spoken about it publicly, and probably never will? Well then, you know the kind of man Gianni Bugno is …

Paolo Viberti covered cycling for Tuttosport *for more than thirty years, while twin brother Giorgio wrote about the sport for* La Stampa.

The story with Gianni Bugno underscores the complex nature of Italian cycling journalists' relationship with the riders. The two parties have always been interdependent, for obvious reasons, and as with all relationships there's an element of confidence and of compromise. Without access to the stars, the journalist is unemployable, and most riders perfectly understand the correlation between their ability to generate content and their wages.

In broad terms, Italian cycling journalists are more tolerant than, say, their Anglo-Saxon counterparts. Their reporting tends to be much less critical, but also less driven by personal or editorial agendas. Its focus has always been on the physical and technical elements of the sport, and much less on the political, economic and ethical issues surrounding it. It's generally much less judgemental and less accusatory, and in that sense it's a mirror on Italian society. It also largely explains why it has struggled to adapt to the Anglicization of cycling …

**FABRIZIO DELMATI
PHOTOGRAPHER
PASSO DELLO STELVIO, 7 JUNE 1975**

I went to photography school, and when I was twenty I took courage and rang Vito Liverani at the Olympia agency. They took me on in September 1971, and of course they did all the cycling. I'd just started and they said, "You've to go to Canonica. We need you to photograph Eddy Merckx."

The first time I did the Giro was 1973, but the first one I did in full was 1975. I was following Enervit, the "Giroclinica" as it was known back then. I saw them taking blood samples from the riders during the race. They would drive alongside, withdraw the blood and then the rider would carry on; I guess they were just beginning to study it. I don't think I've ever seen such a quantity of people as I saw on the Stelvio on the last day. It was a mountain full of humanity, and that was when I truly understood the love that people had for this sport.

As a photographer you live the race in a unique way. You're privileged because you see it at close hand, but you have to produce work. You know you're in the presence of these champions, you're totally focused on it, and you're aware of what's happening. However, it's not gratuitous in the way it is for a fan, because the more dramatic the event, the more the work itself becomes immersive. It's something I struggle to explain, but the experience is totally different.

The best example, cycling aside, is something like the 100 metres hurdles finals I did at the Olympics and the World Championships. The stadium, the sense of theatre, these great athletes … It's absolutely fantastic and I wouldn't change it for the world, but I'm there to get the best photographs I possibly can. If I start enjoying the occasion I'm not doing my job. You're in it, but you only really *enjoy* it afterwards.

The Giro changed a lot over the years, largely as a result of the technology. First, the stages began earlier and finished sooner. When I started, a typical stage finish was between three and four o'clock, but progressively they finished later and later. I'm guessing it was because of television. They need to get the sponsors on as many screens as possible, and that conditions everything.

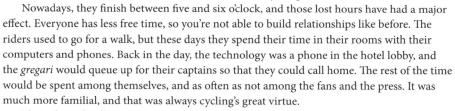

Nowadays, they finish between five and six o'clock, and those lost hours have had a major effect. Everyone has less free time, so you're not able to build relationships like before. The riders used to go for a walk, but these days they spend their time in their rooms with their computers and phones. Back in the day, the technology was a phone in the hotel lobby, and the *gregari* would queue up for their captains so that they could call home. The rest of the time would be spent among themselves, and as often as not among the fans and the press. It was much more familial, and that was always cycling's great virtue.

These days, there's just too much distance, and I also think the agents have had a major effect on things. If I said to Gianni Bugno, "Gianni, can I come round to yours and do some photos on Tuesday?" he'd say, "Yes, just give me call on Monday and we'll sort it out." Try doing that with a world champion today! It would be impossible because there are so many filters in the way. It would be a real shame if it becomes like football. Cycling's beauty has always been its proximity and its accessibility. I worry that we're losing that.

If there's a bike race round here, of whatever sort, I'll go and watch it. It could be an amateur race or even cadets, but I go and watch regardless. So you have kids racing, but 80 per cent of the people watching are my age. There doesn't seem to be that renewal of fans, and that's a real shame.

Fabrizio left Olympia for ANSA in 1976. Between 1982 and 2009 he covered the Giro, among other sports, for RCS. When he started photographing the Giro, there were less than ten accredited photographers. The Italian agencies would each send one, RCS Sport would send a team, and the local papers would be present according to the stage. As the Giro became a global event, so the demography of both the press corps and the peloton changed. The number of photographers and journalists increased, and the behaviour of the teams evolved accordingly.

Giro stages traditionally began early in the morning because, quite simply, they were much longer. Between the wars, the distances decreased, training programmes became more sophisticated, and the bikes improved dramatically. The speeds increased exponentially, and as such they were generally done by late afternoon.

In 1954 the Catanzaro–Bari stage, 352 kilometres and 11 hours under a broiling sun, provoked outrage among the riders. A go-slow ensued, and never again would a Giro stage exceed 300 kilometres. The longest stage of the ninety-ninth Giro d'Italia was 240 kilometres.

**CLAUDIO GREGORI
JOURNALIST AND PURIST
FRANCE, JULY 1923**

I'm working on a biography of Ottavio Bottecchia, researching the 1923 Tour de France. The French hadn't won for twelve years, and Bottecchia's captain was Henri Pélissier. So the team did everything in their power to ensure that Bottecchia finished second. The financial return was ten times what it would have been had he won, but I maintain that the race itself was devalued …

In 2016 we had Steven Kruijswijk in the pink jersey, then Esteban Chaves. Then Vincenzo Nibali took it and went on to win. That's fine, but his having won doesn't alter the value of the race or the values that inform it. I don't actually care who wins the Giro, only that the values are respected and upheld. As a journalist, I've always tried to defend that idea.

For me, the Giro itself is the issue, not the individuals within it. What I mean is that it's not just a bike race; it has to aspire to be much more than that. It has to be a set of ideas, an expression of Italy and its culture. The problem is that, by definition, it's a business as well, and therein lies the contradiction.

I have a different perception of sport, because I fail to see it as a business. Sport is desire, intelligence, effort, physical aptitude. I'm extremely militant in this, and I probably appear still more so in the current paradigm. I remember a heated discussion with a famous TV presenter. My position was that if Marco Pantani was cheating, he needed to be sent home. The presenter said, "But Pantani gives us a viewing figure of 7 million!"

The ongoing celebration of Pantani … I'm all for recalling Pantani, but objectively. His haematocrit values were 41 in the winter and 60 when he crashed at Milan–Turin. We can't lose sight of that, because his having cheated is hugely instructive, not only in terms of what happened to him, but also in terms of what has happened to our sport.

The thing that hurts me most was – and is – the capacity to forget. There's an ongoing contextual shift, and little by little it's less about sport and more about commerce. When I see someone like Cipollini as the big protagonist at the Giro presentation, I don't like it. I understand that he's cycling's Pavarotti, but the fact remains that he went to Fuentes and he doped. The Giro should aspire to more than that.

Then there's this idea that serving a suspension wipes the slate clean. Well, it doesn't wash with me. I know Ivan Basso well. I've had dinner at his house, met his wife, his lovely kids and his dog, Birillo. They're nice, but it doesn't change what he did, and what he did doesn't vanish when the suspension finishes. He made a strategic choice to dope, another to deny it, and another to write a book reaffirming the lie. That had consequences for the sport, and for lots of people in and around it. His having come back and won the Giro again doesn't absolve him, and it certainly doesn't make it all right.

I had a colleague at the *Gazzetta* who was a specialist in anti-doping. He was based in Rome, and his work was concentrated in and around Rome. Professor Conconi was at Rome, the Football Association was in Rome, so lots of things were going on there. He and I were of a similar mindset, and by and by he started to work in cycling. He found it extremely difficult, and at a certain point he said he couldn't stay around it. He'd started to feel co-responsible, so he left.

I understood why, but then he came to me and said, "How can you stay in this environment, Greg?" and I said, "Because if I'm out of it I can't affect it, and I can't shame those who do it. By being inside I can break their balls, and inform people about what they're doing." That, within the limits of what I could achieve, was always my attitude. I love the sport too much to have watched it destroy itself.

Cycling always had more attention than other sports, so obviously the damage was greater. Then the fight against doping in cycling was ferocious, and it was played out in public. Football, for example, never had that, because it chose not to engage. Ask yourself why Maradona was found positive when he washed up as a player. Why was he positive at the World Cup and not while he was playing for Napoli?

Obviously, the *Gazzetta* has a commercial interest. By the same token there's a journalistic imperative, and you have to respect that at all costs. I can't speak for the paper as a whole, because it isn't any one thing or any one human voice. The director of the paper has an editorial view, and the content is conditioned by that and by the prevailing winds.

What I would say is that the cycling journalism that *I* practised wasn't compromised by commercial interests. The necessity to sell newspapers never informed it, and the journalist shouldn't concern himself with that anyway. I think I reported the sport objectively and fairly, and nobody ever suggested I should do otherwise. Over the piece, I think the journalism took precedence over any notion of protectionism as regards the company's properties.

The future? Bleak, frankly. Italy doesn't have a World Tour team, and Sassuolo are near the top of Serie A. Who's paid for them to be there? Giorgio Squinzi, the owner of Mapei …

Claudio Gregori has always been one of Italian cycling's more informed voices. He began his working life as a PE teacher before turning to journalism in 1974. He joined the staff at the Gazzetta *in 1986, and has written principally about cycling. He's produced compelling biographies of (among others) Toni Bevilacqua, Giovanni Cuniolo, Luigi Ganna and, most recently, Eddy Merckx.*

The Pantani issue is complex. In the 1990s his popularity transcended mere sport. When, therefore, his EPO use was exposed, the public was convinced that all cyclists were "cheating". Of course, he didn't dope in a vacuum, so technically they weren't far wrong.

RCS Sport still judge the veneration of Pantani to be commercially expedient. It may be good for their shareholders in the here and now, but its medium-term consequences have been catastrophic. The groundswell he created has long since disappeared, but he remains ubiquitous. He was a sensational rider, but his legacy is as tragic as his death in 2004. The man in the Italian street remains convinced that cycling is filthy, and the sponsors have been irretrievably lost.

GIROTAPPA 12

I NOSTRI AMICI

STRANIERI

(OUR FOREIGN FRIENDS)

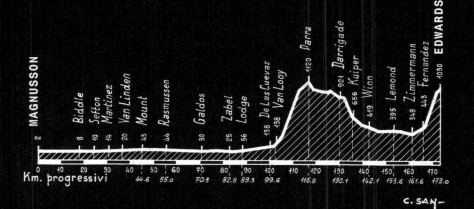

"Cyclist Glenn is to ride for the national team…"

When I was a kid, Tommy Prim was a big star, and watching him at the 1982 Giro was one of my first cycling memories. So when I started cycling, the dream was always to ride for an Italian team. Everyone in Sweden was much more interested in the Giro than the Tour de France.

In cycling terms, ours was a very small country, so it took me a long time. I was twenty-six when I got the chance to turn pro with Amore & Vita, Ivano Fanini's team. I moved to Tuscany with my wife and two children, but I had no idea whether I'd be any good as a professional.

I was a sprinter, and people like Mario Cipollini were my idols, you know? At the beginning, I never even got anywhere *near* the sprints. I was never in the first hundred, let alone the first ten. Initially, we didn't get a place at the Giro, but at that point I wasn't good enough anyway.

I was in America riding the Tour du Pont, and it was the first time that I felt like I was able to compete with the professionals. I finished third in the points, and straight after the race they told me we were riding the Giro and I was in! I, Glenn Magnusson, was actually going to ride it!

The first stage was in Athens. I was really pleased with myself because I got sixth, but I noticed that Cipollini had an 11 sprocket on his bike. I'd never seen one before, but that evening I told them I wanted an 11 as well. I must have asked them ten times before they agreed, and the following day I used 53 x 11 for the first time in my life. I couldn't believe it when I won the stage, and, to be honest, neither could anybody else …

Ours was a tiny team, so to win a Giro stage was huge. They said, "We're going to support you so that you can try to win a stage every year." They really weren't bothered about the smaller races because the only people watching them were Italian cycling fans. The Giro had a global TV audience, so that became my objective. There would be seven or eight stages for the sprinters each year, and the aim was to try to win one of them. Winning the GC at the Tour of Puglia was the best thing I ever did on a bike, but, whether you liked it or not, the Giro is just a hundred times more important.

In 1997 we had Silvio Berlusconi as a sub-sponsor. The jersey changed to the red and black stripes of AC Milan, and we had "Forza Arcore" written on it. Berlusconi's political party was called Forza Italia, but political parties weren't allowed to sponsor cycling teams. Everyone knew he lived in a huge villa in Arcore, so it was pretty obvious what it meant. There was a big reception in Lucca, and it was pretty cool to meet him. Fanini was very smart, and getting Berlusconi involved was a clever thing to do. He was the most powerful guy in Italy, he owned the TV channel that broadcast the race, and he dominated public life.

We had a great team at the 1997 Giro, but Cipo was

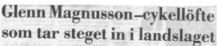

Glenn Magnusson–cykellöfte som tar steget in i landslaget

Oskarshamns Cykelklubbe duktiga Glenn Magnusson har blivit uttagen till ungdomslaget. Han fick beskedet i onsdags att han tillsammans med åtta andra killar ska representera Sverige vid "Hökens ungdoms sexdagars".

Glenn är enom representant från Smålland i ungdomslandslaget. Han har kvalificerat sig då genom att åka bara i de observationstävlingar han deltagit i under våren.

Mellan 2 och 5 juli går täninlagen av stapeln i Hjo och Tidaholm. Glenn tävlar en av de åtta killar fött de 46 och 48 som blivit uttagna att spela med danska och norska landslagens juniorer som deltagar.

Förväntad

Uttagningen till landslaget är inte…

Brinkonsbn bycker Glenn:
– Eftersom jag är förstaårs-cyklist i min åskrigningsago, blev jag överraskad att de tagit ut mig. Det är alltid ovåntat att man försa-åringen blir ett blir uttagen. Det nar så jag bara riktigt

Glenn, som hittills i år tränat varje dag, tror inte att han kommer att någon speciellt extra inför landslags-debuten.

Fem mil i veckan

– Just nu tränar jag lyt timmar varje kväll. Kör cirka fem mil på cykel om man räknar all slags träning. Kanske kräver jag lite extra innan tåvlningen, men då tränar jag på åt att jag har tid till det.

Om "Hökenda sexdagars" säger Glenn:
– Det är en stor tävling med ett hundratal deltagare. Det tyska det teknologier, som är förbundet. Norge och Sverige är mer jämna, men även Norge blir underlägset.

Om sin egna kraft säger han:
– Det blir svårt att göra något. Jag lyckas försvara mig bandtags-cykla då man stälde sig åt.
LISELOTTE LINDEN

Tomas slog till i Krönloppet

Tomas Pettersson, Oskarshamns CK, slog till igår i Vimmerby. Han vann juniorklassen i Krönloppet, som arrangerades av CK Vimer.

I Arbkners lkkr det sin egna uppgjordha, Gerry Sundkvist, Emeling och Roberta Vaesli, följde gott tatte drugli låta och bads en bättergande ledning 10 vare före starta. Men just i Vattentandacken några vare fikte state hoppats ledjas av för Vaesli och han försvunnen bli sekunder. Därmed var Emeling vann tillkomste nad de sista varven.

Oskarshamns hade en stor flura i juniorklassen. Tomas Pettersson meu fira Niklas Jacobsson, Ekeji CK. Orli Oskarshamn hade dess framstigstende placeringar i ollas klasserna fom här.

Glenn Magnusson vare två, i Mikael Jacobsson var trejde, i och Vaesli vann.

Resultat

Klass FS &cLå: Tomas Karlsson, CK Vimer, 2) Ulrik Lessing, CK Hjner, 3) Tomas Knd, Jönköping.
Klass FB &cLå: 1) Rolf Andersson …

Klass FA &cLå: 1) Cerudin Ahh, Linn-Lotte Ivansson, Oskarn

OCK: premiär:

Glenn slagen i spurten – Lotta vann som vanligt

Oskarshamns Cykelklubb stora lädte Glenn Magnusson blev att räkna med även i vår – trots att han är ryggd i sin klass den här skrongen!

Det berinade Glenn vid premiärtävlingen i Norrköping under helgen.
– Han blev nämligen treka – med samma tid som segraren.

Ändå går förste varvet av det kilometer långa loppet gick Stefan Andersson, Motala, tres. Glenn tog dock sömnderdt uppe jaknen på nedåtvägligheten och var fastad renstrak från och jämnt i sin tråg-de-slunge som led han för att nolan Glenn och Stefan mile mel-blas om en vinnare och här tar de sitt varven.

Stefan Andersson visste de vore en lite satisker. Han lät rödaligter Glenn skriva precisleker. Därför fin de matvärdestaleder bättre krafter

basically unbeatable. He had the strongest team, and there was no way you could come round him. So by the time we got to the Cuneo stage, time was running out. We'd had twelve stages, he'd won everything, and we had the Alps and the Dolomites to come.

We had a really strong young guy named Dario Andriotto. I said to him, "Look, I can't beat Cipo if I try to come from behind him. He's too powerful, so the only way for me to have a chance is to go early." We decided we'd try to surprise them and then try to hang on. It was a small chance, but it was the only chance we had.

So the plan was that I'd get on Andriotto's wheel about a kilometre from the finish. He'd then give it everything for about six hundred metres, and try to get to the front of Cipo's train. That's what he did. He got me to about four hundred metres, and I took off from there. It was way, way too early, but what else could I do?

Cipo was taken by surprise, and for a split second they didn't know what to do. It was actually Serguei Outschakov, the Russian guy from Polti, who tried to jump on to my wheel, but then he crashed. I won easily in the end, and I was really happy because the gap was so big that they gave me a second on GC!

So Cuneo was the best sprint I ever did. I lost to Cipollini many, many times, but that time I beat him with my brain as well as my legs. I beat him again the following year in Vasto. Afterwards, he said he was "Father Christmas", but I can assure you that he was *extremely* pissed off that day. Cipo never gave anything away. Not ever …

Glenn Magnusson's three stage wins — and the split seconds that separated him from the runner-up — justified his salary for an entire season's racing. That's indicative not only of the difference between the Giro and the others races, but also of Mario Cipollini's pre-eminence. For the velocisti it's all about winning, but for a Swedish rider to turn pro aged twenty-six and defeat Cipo at three successive giri was a remarkable achievement.

Glenn joined Lance Armstrong's US Postal Service team in 1999, but didn't much enjoy it there. He signed for Farm Frites after a single season, and rode the Tour and the Vuelta in the service of other, more famous riders. He never again participated in the Giro, but like many non-Italian ex-pros he still rides his bike here each summer.

GEORGE MOUNT
ALL THE WAY FROM AMERICA
CENTRAL ITALY, 1982

So here I am in my second Giro, humping up a hill towards a mountain spring and I decide to try for a few points. It's early on, and if you start getting a few points every day you never know where you could wind up. I'm not a bad climber, I'm feeling frisky and the only other guy going for it is some little guy. 'Shit,' I think to myself, "That's freakin' Van Impe! How the hell did this happen to me of all people?"

How did this guy from California wind up in the hardest bike race in the world, sprinting for a mountain top with one of his biggest heroes? Where I came from it wasn't considered possible to go "over there" and race with the big guys. I was told so much crazy stuff by people who all acted like they had an idea of what it was like to be a pro bike racer. My bones were too big, Americans can't hold a wheel like the Europeans, you're insane, no American could ever do that, etc. etc. Fortunately,

Tulio Bertacco — Hans Oersted — Raniero Gradi — Alessandro Pozzi — Pierangelo Bincoletto — Roberto Visentini — Moreno Argentin — Gianni Giacomini — Salvatore Maccali — Maurizio Bertini — Claudio Corti — George Mount

SAMMONTANA gelati all'italiana

I figured out early on that they really had no clue. Plus I had a passion that wouldn't be denied.

I took up racing bikes at seventeen to get out of an abusive household. I loved riding long and hard, and when I took up racing it came naturally to me. With a little coaching and more detailed training, I started to win. Still, we were thousands of kilometres from Europe. A couple of guys had gone and failed, and if you met them they talked as if it was simply out of the question for an American. We occasionally had copies of Euro cycling mags to pass round at races, and these stories from beat-up riders who had gone and failed at the lowest level of the sport.

And yet here I was in 1982, having started racing eight years earlier, battling with one of my heroes. His talent was way beyond mine, but I was still giving it a go. I almost bust out laughing at myself and how ludicrous this all was. During my early years of racing, I worshipped guys like Eddy, Freddy, Roger, Felice, and the rest. Then, when I finally "passed" to a professional team in 1980, it was a good one, and we had Maertens on the team for a while. When I met him, I was almost dumbstruck. The thought of being on a team with one of my heroes was simply too much.

When I tried to talk to people back in the States about what was happening, I got the distinct impression that no one believed me, or at least that they couldn't comprehend what was happening in my racing career. I think to some degree that's still true. Nothing I did in Europe had any media coverage in the US at the time, so little is known of what was happening. Still, it wasn't a piece of cake getting there. In 1980 there were not many foreigners riding on Italian teams, and no Americans anywhere.

I went to Italy in 1977, rode the Baby Giro with the US team and did well. However, nothing prepares you for the big tours, and at the time the Giro was the hardest. The depth of talent on the Italian teams was astonishing, and every finish had a local hero. Most of the teams didn't bother with the races in France. Their sponsors didn't care, so the Giro was where you made your name. The passion and aggression in the races and the emotion of the riders and fans is a big part of the Giro. No *"sang froid"* like in France …

No, I didn't beat Van Impe. I didn't try too hard because that wasn't the point. He was going for the mountains jersey and I still had a slew of days lugging water to my captain and getting him over the mountains.

Racing in the Giro? As good as it got. There wasn't anything better …

The Giro's first English speaker had been the Londoner Harry Grubb. He abandoned the biblical 1914 edition. The 1924 winner, Giuseppe Enrici, had been born in the United States, but was raised in the Canavese. A team of Australians abandoned the 1952 edition, but it would be 1960 before the Irishman Shay Elliott won a stage. Six years later, England's Vin Denson won at Campobasso, and the South African Alan van Heerden triumphed in Perugia in 1979.

"Smiling" George Mount was the first American to ride the Giro. When he made his debut in 1981, he was one of only two non-Europeans (and two native English speakers) in the gruppo. *The other was an Australian, John Trevorrow.*

Ron Kiefel became the first American Grand Tour stage winner in 1985, as Greg LeMond finished third behind Bernard Hinault and Francesco Moser. When Andy Hampsten captured the maglia rosa *in 1988, the* Gazzetta *heralded the "dawn of the yuppies". Predictably enough …*

MICHAEL RASMUSSEN
SELF-TAUGHT CLIMBER
BOLZANO, 1990

I was fifteen or sixteen, racing in Denmark. Obviously, our country is full of flat, windy roads, and I was just getting my ass kicked. Then I went to Italy with the local cycling club, the first time I'd been away on holiday without my mum and dad. We stayed on a campsite near Bolzano, and we started doing the Dolomite climbs. That was when I discovered that I had a special talent. I could ride away from the people who had been killing me on the flat, and right there and then I decided that this was where I was going to live my adult life. I was going to be a cyclist, and I was going to live in Italy and train on those very climbs …

After that I went there as often as I could. Each time I had some free days, I'd get on a train to Italy, check into a small hotel and spend fourteen days, or whatever, training by myself in the mountains. So Italy – and specifically the Dolomites – was where I discovered myself as a cyclist, and it conditioned my life and the trajectory of my career.

The first Grand Tour I rode was the 2002 Giro, and all told I did it four times. It was very relaxing because there was no pressure to deliver results, just to lay the groundwork for the Tour de France. There was no media fuss, nobody much cared, and I just found it … *enjoyable.* I would come out of it with the kilometres I needed, and then I'd start my Tour training. I only ever targeted a stage win once, but I didn't get it. The weather was miserable that day, and Iban Mayo won instead. It was on the last Friday, and I remember speaking to a guy two days later as we rode into Milan. He said, "I'm going to have a week off the bike now – I'm off to the beach!" I said, "I'm going to have a day off and then I'm going to start training for the Tour …"

The Giro is easily the most beautiful and easily the most romantic of all the big races, but it just wasn't compatible with me as a cyclist. All riders have natural cycles, and I needed the heat. I was extremely sensitive to the cold, and in practical terms it conditioned my season; I was just much better in July than in May.

When I'd switched from mountain-bike to road cycling, the objective had been to test myself against the best. I wanted to know exactly how good I was compared to them, and of course they were at the Tour. As much as I loved the Giro, it was inconceivable that I might be competitive there. I lived in Italy and I love Italy, but the Tour is much bigger and much more important.

I see it from the other side now, because I'm working as a journalist. There are Danish guys riding the Giro as well as the Tour, but 90 per cent of my newspaper's cycling budget is spent in July. You can apply that to other newspapers, and to pretty much all the countries outside of Italy and maybe Belgium.

I was a GC rider and a climber, so obviously I didn't win that often. When I did, they tended to be important ones, and of course I won stages at both the Tour and the Vuelta. It would be really nice to say I'd won at the Giro as well, because that's quite a select club, isn't it? However, the fact is that there's no Giro stage on my *palmares*, and that's a shame ...

Many Danes have animated the Giro, but none has even so much as podiumed. Between 1968 and 1974, Eddy Merckx delivered five wins for the Belgians, before Michel Pollentier and Johan De Muynck triumphed in 1977 and 1978. The great French riders Jacques Anquetil (twice), Bernard Hinault (three times) and Laurent Fignon account for six, while the Swiss Hugo Koblet became the first foreign winner in 1950. His countrymen Carlo Clerici and Tony Rominger also have a maglia rosa apiece. The Russians Evgeni Berzin, Pavel Tonkov and Denis Menchov have each won one edition.

Spain's Miguel Induráin and Alberto Contador have two each, while Luxembourg's Charly Gaul won miraculously in 1956 and 1959. The English speakers Stephen Roche (Ireland) and Andrew Hampsten (USA) confounded expectation in 1987 and 1988, as did Canada's Ryder Hesjedal in 2012. Gösta Pettersson began Sweden's love affair with the Giro by winning in 1971, and the Colombian climbing specialist Nairo Quintana prevailed in 2015.

As of 2017, the Dutch, the Brits, the Germans and the Australians are still without a pink jersey.

The Giro struggles with protracted periods of foreign domination. The all-foreign podium of 1972 was a catastrophic indictment of Italian stage racing, that of 1995 the consequence of three turgid weeks. Likewise, when the gutsy Ryder Hesjedal preceded a Spaniard and a Belgian, he did so amid general indifference.

I was riding for a Belgian team that year, Tulip. I'd done all the early season Italian races, though, because the Giro was always the objective. I'd finished fourth in the Trofeo Pantalica, gone reasonably well at Tirreno, the Tour of Sicily … I was top twenty at the Tour of Trentino. I reckon I did half of my season in Italy that year.

The Giro itself? I remember a bunch sprint at Aversa, near Naples. They'd warned us about Italian sprints, so we all had those ribbon helmets, for what they were worth. It was an absolute war – totally merciless. There must have been about twenty crashes that day. I think I came down in about the ninth one …

Then Terminillo when Franco Chioccioli cracked, and Allan Peiper having a really bad day. He didn't eat meat, only fish, so every night at dinner we had this performance over his fish. This particular stage he had a hunger knock and he said to the masseur, "Get me something to eat!" The guy said, "Sorry, but it's got ham in it." Peiper went, "I don't care – just get me something to eat *now*!"

Then I remember another day climbing with Peiper. We weren't in the *gruppetto*, but we were out the back of the front group. The race had gone away from us, but I was young and full of enthusiasm. I was on the front, pulling, but then Peiper, the old pro, turned round to me. He said, "You see that ravine down there? If you put your wheel so much as half an inch in front of mine, you're going down it …"

I came from a cycling family, and I'd been to see the 1982 World Championships at Goodwood when I was fourteen. I was already riding, but at that point I decided I wanted to be a professional. There wasn't a career path for a young British rider, though. I was working for the Ministry of Defence in 1988, and I asked them for six months unpaid leave to ride the Seoul Olympics. They refused, so I'd no choice but to resign and live on my savings. Then I took myself off to Belgium to ride as an amateur. That was the only way to do it back then, but I'm not bitter about it. Think of the British guys who went across post-Second World War, the sacrifices they had to make …

Our GC guy for the Giro crashed out after ten days or so. I was in the top twenty for the first week, but I finished up forty-eighth. I suppose that wasn't bad for my first Grand Tour, but it's neither here nor there if you're not in the first twenty-five.

There was no rest day and the final week was the Alps. What happened was that they replaced the cranks on my bike without telling me. I used 172.5 mm, but because I was tall they decided 175 mm would be good for me in the mountains. The net result was that I was on my knees, and I slipped a long way on GC. Don't get me wrong: I'd have slipped anyway, but I finished up with a strained tendon. Had there been another mountain stage, I'd have been out, no question …

I was supposed to do the Tour de France as well, but what with the tendon … Shame, really, because as fate would have it I never got another chance.

Wiltshire's Harry Lodge was one of two Brits to compete at the 1992 Giro, the other being Sean Yates. That was two more than the previous edition, and two more than would take part in 1993. Such was the paucity of British cycling back then.

Harry met his future wife at Linate Airport (she was working there) and would ride for an Italian team, Amore & Vita, in 1994 and 1995. He did the Vuelta for them, but never again the Giro. He lived briefly in Tuscany before relocating to Varese, in the Italian cycling heartlands north of Milan.

The 1992 Giro was won with consummate ease by Miguel Induráin. He took the jersey on stage 3, cemented it the following day in the time trial, and never once looked in any danger whatsoever. In truth, the GC "contest" was a procession. Previous winners Franco Chioccioli and Andy Hampsten were utterly outclassed, and climber Claudio Chiappucci, twice a podium finisher at the Tour, never once dropped Induráin.

The Spaniard saved the best for the final-day time trial. Over 66 flat kilometres from Vigevano to Milan, he put three minutes into Chiappucci, four into Chioccioli, five into Hampsten. He would add the Tour in July, and would complete the double-double the following year.

My mum was from Treviso, and she'd met my father there after the war. They got married, and she came to live in England, and so did my grandmother. We never spoke Italian at home, but via a very circuitous route I finished up riding for a good amateur team down in Tuscany. That was the start of it; I was the first British cyclist to ride professionally for an Italian team.

My first Giro was 1976, when Felice Gimondi won. I was twenty-six, but I was at a disadvantage because I'd spent too long racing in England. I'd won a lot of races at home, ridden the Olympics, and I'd done two good years on the Italian amateur circuit. I'd won the Tour of Friuli-Venezia, which was a big race. So I'd earned a pro contract with Sanson, Francesco Moser's team, and that was no mean feat for an Englishman. The *gruppo* back then was 90 per cent Italian, and Italian cycling was extremely provincial. It didn't have a European perspective, never mind a global one. It wasn't like they were suddenly going to sell more ice creams in Milan because they had a bloke from Bristol in the team …

I'd picked up the language pretty well, and I think I was strong. I was focused and extremely committed, and I knew what was at stake. I was determined that I wasn't going to fail, because the thought of going home with my tail between my legs was terrible. I didn't want to give the "told you so" merchants that satisfaction, you know?

That was all fine, but nothing I'd done before had prepared me in any way for the sheer physicality of those three weeks. I had to learn to cope with the distance and the heat, and then of course you had to ride over big mountains. I was able to absorb that pretty well; I could pull on the flat all day and I could cope with hills up to six or seven kilometres. What I found extremely difficult were the changes in rhythm, and just the speed these people rode at. Sometimes, the intensity of the racing knocked you for six. It was like being punched in the face day after day, and at times I felt totally out of my depth. I felt like I needed to learn to ride all over again.

I became a good *gregario* for Francesco, and we won a hell of a lot of races together. I got round every Giro I rode, and I really enjoyed the life. I was riding for a super champion, earning a decent wage and living the dream in Italy. Then, in 1980, Bernard Hinault came to the Giro …

I think Roberto Visentini had the jersey, but it was tight. We were coming back up from the south, one of those brutal Apennine stages somewhere in the Abruzzo. We knew it was going to be a day for strong guys, as opposed to pure climbers. Anyway, we did the first couple of climbs – I think one of them was the Macerone – and then Hinault went to the front. I'll never forget it because he had this look in his eye that was actually quite scary. It's an old cliché, I know, but he did actually look like a man possessed.

Suddenly, there was mass panic in the peloton, as if the earthquake we'd been frightened of had finally arrived. Hinault just wound it up and wound it up, and within a few minutes the whole thing fell to pieces. He just rode everyone, Moser and Giuseppe Saronni included, off his wheel. I'd been a professional cyclist for five years, but I'd never experienced anything as devastating as that. It was carnage.

The Foggia to Roccaraso stage of the 1980 Giro has assumed mythic status for myriad reasons. The first and most obvious is that it was Bernard Hinault's first Giro, ergo the first statement of his murderous intent. The ferocity of his attack visited utter desolation on the other GC "contenders", with maglia rosa Visentini shipping six minutes, Silvano Contini seven, and so on.

It's also remembered because, while the rest capsized, a thirty-four-year-old gregario riding his thirteenth Giro somehow managed to cling on. Wladimiro Panizza was an immensely popular figure, and his miraculous performance that day represented the apotheosis of a career spent clinging to the shadows of the champions. As he tearfully pulled on his first ever maglia rosa, the entire cycling community wept for him and with him.

Panizza retained it for six dreamy days before Hinault destroyed him — and everyone else — on the Stelvio.

GIROTAPPA 13

GRAZIE A DIO ...

(THERE BUT FOR
THE GRACE OF GOD)

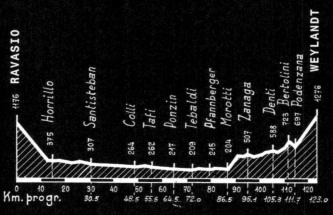

C. SAN—

Our dad had died three years earlier, hit by a car while he was out on his scooter. Our mum had become progressively more apprehensive, and she fretted about Milo and I constantly.

He'd ridden the Giro the previous year, but when we dropped him at Linate, our mum was in a state. He said, "Stop worrying, mum, it's absolutely fine. I'm only going to ride the Giro. Anyone would think I was heading for my own funeral …" That was one of the last things he said to her before he caught the flight down to Palermo.

His team's sprinter, Urs Freuler, won the prologue. That meant they had to try to protect the jersey on the opening stage, so Milo would be busy chasing down the breaks. I went off to work as normal, and when I got home my mum told me she'd watched it with a friend of hers as usual. She said a break had gone and they'd lost the jersey. There'd been some sort of a crash, but everyone had ridden to the finish and they hadn't mentioned Milo.

He was rooming with Gianni Bugno, and apparently, when they got back to the hotel, Milo told Gianni that he'd been held up in the crash. He said he was fine, but then after he showered he started complaining of a headache.

At first they just assumed it was the heat, but then he started to become incoherent. His speech became slurred, and he didn't seem to know what he was saying. Gianni started to worry so he called Vescovi, the team doctor. They decided to send Milo to the hospital, and that would have been at about six o'clock.

At the hospital they were treating a few guys who'd come down in the crash. Milo had no visible injuries, so they probably just assumed he was suffering from sunstroke and dealt with the more pressing cases first.

Carlo Menicagli, the sports director from Selle Italia, was there with one of his riders. He was sat with Milo when he noticed that he was making strange, involuntary movements. He seemed to be going into spasm, and Menicagli could tell something was badly wrong. He alerted the staff, and they decided they needed to do a CT scan as soon as possible.

The problem was that the hospital at Sciacca didn't have a machine, which meant they had to transfer him to Palermo, 130 kilometres away. For some reason the helicopter wasn't available, so they bundled him into an ambulance and drove him there instead. It took the best part of two hours so it would have been almost eight o'clock by the time they got there.

When they arrived, the CT scanner was faulty. This wouldn't have happened in the north, but they weren't in the north. They were in Sicily in the mid-1980s, and it was a different world …

So they transferred him *again*, this time to a private clinic. They did the scan, and obviously there was a hematoma. However, they couldn't treat it because they didn't have a specialist, so they took him back to the other hospital in Palermo.

Of course, I didn't know any of this. I had my dinner as normal, and sat down with my mum to watch the Giro highlights on RAI. If memory serves, they were on after the news, so it would have been about 10.30. Just as they were about to start, the phone rang and it was Franco Cribiori, Milo's sports director. He told me to pack some things and to get the next flight down there …

It's probable that Emilio Ravasio hit his head on the stem of his bike, but nobody really knows. No images exist of the crash, and the only physical evidence was a tiny nick on the shoulder of his jersey.

It would be midnight before they operated on him, but by then the hematoma was "the size of an orange". He would remain in a coma for fifteen terrible days, before passing away on 27 May 1986.

Ten years earlier, the Spanish rider Juan Manuel Santisteban had also died following a Giro crash in Sicily. He hit a guard rail and died instantly. On hearing of Milo's death, his widow, Mercedes Crespo, wrote a letter of condolence to Giro d'Italia patron Vincenzo Torriani. Via Emilio Ravasio, inaugurated by Gino Bartali, is a residential street on the eastern fringes of Sciacca.

Two other riders have lost their lives at the Giro. Orfeo Ponzin died when he hit a tree at the 1952 edition, and Wouter Weylandt crashed while descending the Passo del Bocco in 2011.

FEDERAZIONE CICLISTICA ITALIANA
ROMA

PROFESSIONISTA   LICENZA N.   3489

Cognome MOROTTI
Nome OLIVIERO   valevole fino al   1969
Nato il 1. 3.44   31 dicembre
Indirizzo MEMBRO
VIA TALPINO 21
Società G.S.SAGIT

TREGASIO TR. M
IL PRESIDENTE   FIRMA DEL TITOLARE

1969

Oliviero: I was a good descender, but this was new. It was an old military road that none of us had ever ridden before. It was twisty, narrow and pretty dangerous.

The GC group was up ahead, and I think I was in a small second group. What happened was that I misjudged a left-hand curve and there was no guard rail. It was just a few planks nailed together and I was heading straight for them. I knew immediately that I was in big trouble. You have time to process thoughts, but not to do anything about them.

They say your life flashes before you, and it's true. I still see every detail of it with absolute clarity. I saw my dad asking me why I wanted to give up a decent job to become a cyclist, my brothers praying before eating – they were priests – and my poor mum up in heaven. I thought, "I wonder if I'm coming to join you?" Then I thought about what the journalists would write about me, about my girlfriend, who always said I should do something else. She's my wife now …

I landed in a field and just kept rolling. I hurt my head and my leg a bit in the summersaults, but nothing more. It's just as well there was grass on the mountain, because otherwise I wouldn't have lived to tell the tale.

The bike was destroyed, but they came to get me and put me straight onto one of the spares. By the time I got on it I was at the next curve, so I must have rolled 50 metres. I tried to get going but I had to stop because I was too shaken up. I tried again but my head still wasn't clear. Eventually I got going though, and after a while I was fine.

The next day we rode around Lake Garda, then did the climb to Polsa. The descent was terrible, one of those dreadful gravel roads. I punctured three times on it, but it never bothered me and I never felt unnerved by what had happened. I just got on with riding my bike and never really thought anything of it. I suppose I was just one of the lucky ones...

Mino: It was about a year before I was walking again under my own steam …

A breakaway of four was away, then the pink jersey group and then us. There would have been ten or eleven of us, and we weren't far behind the GC bunch.

The road was *extremely* narrow. It wasn't wide enough for two cars, so there were passing places along the way. As we came down it, a sponsor's car pulled out of one of them, but he misjudged the speed we were descending at. He came out right in front of us just as we reached a left-hand bend, and at that point I was second wheel behind a Spanish guy. He hit the brakes to try to avoid the car, and my instinct was to try to avoid him. I knew straight away that I was in trouble …

There were no railings, so I just carried on over the precipice. I only fell about twelve metres – I went back to see it later – but I finished up with eighteen separate fractures. I landed on the rocks and I guess I was breaking different bones with each summersault.

When I stopped, I was in a mountain stream, in a sort of cove. I remember that my left shoulder was hanging in front of my chest, that neither of my legs worked and that one of them seemed to have burst. I assumed someone would come for me, but nobody did. After a couple of minutes, I realized that I was stuck, because the only functioning limb I had was my right arm. So I couldn't actually move, and I was thinking, "I don't know what to do now. I think I'm done for …"

I propped myself up on the working arm as best I could, and I saw a herdsman with his cattle. He had a wooden yoke on his shoulders with a bucket on either end. I started yelling at him, and he started coming towards me. He wanted to carry me back up but I said, "No, don't do that – it'll just make it worse. Go and stand in the middle of the road instead, and make them stop. Get the bike first, though, and hold it up in the air. Otherwise they'll think you're some sort of cretin." It's strange, but I was thinking clearly the whole time, even as they carried me up into the ambulance.

I broke the shoulder, but the real problem was that I'd smashed both of my tibias and both of my fibulas. The right leg wasn't *broken* in the traditional sense. It was more … shattered. There was grass in there, splintered bone, goodness knows what. It went black at the hospital, and I figured that that probably wasn't a good sign.

After four or five days, I had five doctors visit me all at once. That usually means something's not working, and the consultant said, "Well, we're a bit worried about this leg. Obviously, the bone has exploded and it's badly infected. We've tried to clean it but it doesn't seem to be healing and it's poisoning you." Then he turned to the others and said, "OK, so double the dose of medicine, and let's see how his body reacts. If there's no improvement, we'll have to see about removing the leg."

I started shaking then, and I couldn't stop. They gave me an injection, but every time I closed my eyes I saw the rocks coming straight towards me. I didn't see me heading into them, you understand; instead, they were coming at *me*! Apparently, that's quite normal.

The first three months I was in traction, then a month at home, then another three months in hospital. It was pretty demoralizing, but eventually they let me go home. By then I weighed 47 kilograms. I started going to physio, and spending time in the gym to build myself up again. Slowly but surely I got better, but I knew I was never going to be able to ride competitively again.

When I was well enough, I went back to the mountain and asked around for the herdsman. I wanted to thank him, so I went to the local town hall. I described what had happened and where it had happened because I assumed they'd know who it would have been. I told them he must have been taking his animals down for milking, but nobody seemed to have the faintest idea. I went back again later, but still I couldn't find him and I never have.

He was just an ordinary old herdsman, but I often wonder if he remembers the day he saved my life. He was my guardian angel …

As an amateur, Mino had won the Tour de l'Avenir and the World Championships as part of the 100-kilometre time-trial team. He only won once as a professional rider, at the Tour of Veneto.

With his professional career over almost before it had begun, Mino started selling frames — he was the first to experiment with curved tubing — and also cycling clothing. He still runs Cicli Denti, just west of Brescia. His mum invented overshoes (Mino and his Faema

teammates had freezing feet during a winter training camp in Liguria)
and his son Paolo "won" Olympic gold as Elia Viviani's masseur in Rio.

Oliviero had finished his debut Giro (see the Virginio Levati story
elsewhere) and, following his enormous slice of good fortune on the
Croce Domini, would get round this one too. He signed for Dreher the
following season, and completed his third and final Giro. He never
won as a pro, although he did achieve a handful of top-ten finishes.

Oliviero opened a bike shop too. It's in Nembro, an hour or so from
Cicli Denti. When we met, his three kids were taking care of the day-
to-day stuff, but he was still in every morning. So too was Ramona,
the girlfriend who was worried he'd fall off his bike and hurt himself.

ELKE WEYLANDT
IN BED, WAITING
GHENT, BELGIUM, 1984

The day my brother was born is my first real memory ...

I was five, and it would have been around six o'clock in the evening. I was in
bed at my grandparents' house – I was always a big sleeper – and I heard the
phone ring. It was one of those moments when you're between asleep and full
consciousness, you know? Then my grandmother came up. She said, "You'd best get
out of bed straight away. We're going to the hospital to meet your new brother!"

I'd been on my own for five years, so I was really proud to have a baby brother.
I remember that I got to take chocolates to school.

My dad was a fireman. He really loved sport, though, and eventually he took up
cycling. It's more of a folklore thing – firemen racing in their uniforms – but it was a serious
business. You know what we're like about cycling in Belgium ...

Anyway, Dad really got into bike racing, and Wouter said he wanted to try it too. Initially,
Dad said, "You're too young," but by the time Wouter turned fifteen he was riding more and
more. He was a very smart kid, but studying didn't really interest
him. He got his high-school diploma, but for the most part he
was focused on sports. I was the studious one in our family ...

Elke Weylandt and Wouter having a ball ...

I remember the day we went to his first race vividly. It was
a kermesse in a village somewhere near Antwerp, and we made
a family day of it. The problem was they needed ten to start the
race, but only about eight turned up. So his first race wasn't his
first race at all – it was a non-race! He was a skinny kid, but by
the fifth or sixth race he was able to finish them.

Our parents worked during the weekends, but by then I had
a driving licence. I was at university, but during the summer I'd
often take Wouter to the races. I was the taxi driver and he was
the DJ. He needed just the right music to be ready for the races,
and it had to be up-tempo, dance-type stuff. One of them was
a cover of *Désenchantée* by a Belgian singer named Kate Ryan. He really liked that song, and
we had it on repeat.

So I was one of those weekend *soigneur* people, the ones who stand by the side of the road
with bottles, spare wheels, stuff like that. I generally used to walk a lap of the circuit, then sit

and read, then stand up with my *bidon* and my wheel each time they came round. So that was me – big sister driving my kid brother to the races. I loved cycling and I loved reading my books, so I was happy to do it.

Wouter was no different from thousands of other kids in Belgium. Every one of them dreams of turning professional, but at the beginning he was really small compared to a lot of the others. Then he got better and better, and I think that at a certain point we all started to share the dream with him.

One day he came to the study and said, "OK, I'm off to the race now." I said, "OK! Good luck and … er … be careful!" Then he went and won the race.

The next week he came to me and said, "I'm off." I said, "Oh, OK," and he said, "Maybe you should repeat what you said last week. You know, for luck?" So from that point on, I always said the same thing or texted him the same thing. It was always, "Good luck and … er … be careful!"

When he was a second-year *espoir* he did an internship at Quick Step as a *stagiare*. He was only nineteen at the time, so it would have been 2004. He did well, and I think they signed him right away. I'd left home by then, and I remember when my mum rang me. I could tell she was thrilled and she said, "You're only talking to the mother of a pro cyclist!" Bear in mind we're talking about Belgium, and it wasn't just any old cycling team. It was *Quick Step* … I was lost for words. It was overwhelming, really.

You know, the thing with the 108 that I find really special is that it was spontaneous. Maybe the Italian people did it because they didn't know how to write his name, but it wasn't something that was orchestrated. I think it came from within, and that's really something, isn't it?

I have a clock in the kitchen, and if I'm at home I always find myself in front of it just before 21:08. Don't ask me why it started happening to me, because it just did.

I see An-Sophie every week, and she's doing great. Of course, I see my niece every week as well. Alizée has just had her fifth birthday. She's lovely.

Elke Weylandt is a freelance press officer. When we met, she was working for the Trek-Segafredo professional cycling team. Her company is named Centotto Communications. The number 108 is retired from the Giro d'Italia.

"Good luck and … er … be careful!"

148

GIROTAPPA 14

IL CLIMA

(THE WEATHER)

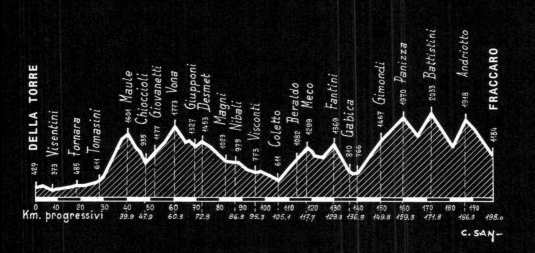

ALBERTO DELLA TORRE
FORMER CYCLIST, CONFLICTED
BORMIO, 1988

I rode the Giro five times, and worked on it for twenty-four years. Vincenzo Torriani approached me in 1982, and asked me to start taking care of the stage arrivals. I finished when Carmine Castellano did, after the 2005 race.

Torriani's biggest shortcoming was in his dealings with the Italian press. He had progressively less time for them, and the less he gave them, the more hostile they became. I remember that he had a big falling-out with a very influential journalist from *l'Unita*, the communist newspaper. Torriani was a Christian democrat, so the two of them were never going to get along. By the end, I think even he was just worn down by the whole thing.

Torriani wasn't a rider, and it's the riders who determine whether the Giro is a good race or not. When it went well – which is to say, when an Italian won – it was thanks to the riders, to the glorious Italian cycling movement, to our wonderful trainers and suchlike. Then, when it didn't, everybody blamed Torriani because he was a soft target.

When I started, the Giro was built to favour Saronni and Moser, because everyone in Italy was supporting one or the other. I think Torriani probably went too far, but it was a natural reaction. He'd been heavily criticized after Michel Pollentier and Johan De Muynck had won in 1977 and 1978, and it was in everyone's interest that Italians had a chance to win.

If there's a single stage that sticks in the mind, I would say Gavia in 1988, the one with the blizzard. I remember it because we had Moser in the car with us and he was saying, "You have to call this off, Vincenzo!" Torriani had been forty years in the job, though, and he had a feeling for these things. He understood that the Giro needs epic days, and he had a sense that something important was unfolding.

Johan van der Velde attacked at the bottom, but for some reason he didn't ask for a cape. His team car wasn't with him, so he ended up doing the whole climb in just the jersey. He started the descent without a jacket as well, but I gave him one. I think in the end he stopped in a motorhome and lost 45 minutes.

After the stage, there were the usual *polemiche,* but riders and sports directors only ever see things from their own perspective. That's perfectly understandable, but our job was different. We were charged with taking care of the Giro d'Italia as a whole. That's what we did, and the fact is that nobody got hurt.

In the final analysis, it's come to be regarded as one of the greatest days in the history of the race. The following year, they said that Torriani cancelled the stage because he wanted to favour Fignon, a Frenchman. They said that the riders could have gone up the Gavia, and technically they were probably right: the riders probably *could* have got up it on their bikes, but it was the regional safety officer that pulled the plug on the stage, not us. Besides, even if the riders *had* gone up, they'd have been stuck up there on their own. There was no way of getting trucks up and off that mountain, so there would have been no caravan, no RAI, no media centre, no jury and no anything else.

We weren't in the business of cancelling stages willy-nilly. Aside from the sporting perspective, cancelled stages were a financial calamity for us …

Calamitous or not, cancelled stages have always been part and parcel of the Giro experience, and not always due to the weather. As early as 1911, the third edition, the stage to Napoli was interrupted because of the dire state of the roads and apparent public-order issues. The stage concluded in Pompeii instead, but such was the outrage of the local population that the Gazzetta felt compelled to organize a single-day race, the Tour of Campania, in its stead.

Stages were annulled in 1912 (Rome) and 1920 (Milan), before the mythical 1946 leg to Trieste saw warring Italian and Slav factions threaten the safety of the riders. In 1956 Salerno—Frascati was called off because the police were busy ensuring that local elections passed off legally and without incident. Vietnam War protesters did for the 1967 prologue, while a metalworkers' strike in Brescia put paid to another prologue in 1983. Five years later, a demonstration by environmentalists wrote off a visit to Castelnuovo Don Bosco, and the 2001 riders' strike saw the mountain stage to Santa Anna di Vinadio cancelled.

ALDO BERALDO
A JAM SANDWICH, A PULLOVER,
200,000 LIRE
PASSO ROLLE, 1962

I was one of eight kids, but my parents couldn't afford to bring us all up. Five of my siblings were sent off to Canada, but I stayed and worked the land with my dad. Then I did seasonal work at Christmas, and bred rabbits to sell. Eventually, I saved 25,000 lire and took it to the bike shop. The guy said a racing bike would cost 35,000, but one of my brothers sent the difference from Canada.

The Dolomite stage in 1962? We left Belluno in the rain, and climbed the Passo Duran. Then it started snowing on the Staulanza, and it snowed on the descent of the Santa Lucia. I had to stop between Alleghe and Cencenighe because I was just too cold. There were some people watching from outside their house and I asked them if they would help me because my hands were too frozen to get the food out of my pockets. The guy gave me a jam sandwich, and then he took his pullover off and put it on me.

We climbed the Aurine, which was mainly tarmac, and the Cereda, which was mainly dirt. Then I found myself at the bottom of the Passo Rolle, freezing cold and completely alone. It was dark and totally silent, and I remember thinking, "What if nobody comes? What if they've all packed up and they just leave me here all alone?"

The stage was annulled at the top of the Rolle. We were supposed to do the San Pellegrino and the Valles as well, but the roads were impassable. The stage had started with 109 riders and finished with 55. If they hadn't called it off there, they would have been left with no more than 20. You were right on the limits of what the human body can cope with.

That pullover had saved me, so I thought the least I could do was give it back to its owner. I put it with the rest of the kit to be washed, and decided I'd go and see him after the Giro.

On the stage to Saint Vincent I broke away with Sartore. His team, Carpano, had the jersey with Balmamion, so he couldn't work and I had to tow him for 100 kilometres. He dropped me on the final climb and I finished second. Then, at the end of the Giro, Carpano gave us 200,000 lire. Carpano were a rich team, and that was a huge amount of money. I never understood why they gave it to us, though …

I went to the mechanics and asked for the pullover, but they didn't have it. They said, "We didn't know who it belonged to so we threw it away."

I'd just turned twenty-one when I rode my first Giro. Stage 11 was 304 kilometres, with an intermediate sprint close to my village. I won it because I knew the roads well, and I earned

Three young, hard bodies
make for the beach.

Aldo Beraldo being chatted up by the beautiful
Valeria Ciangottini, star of La Dolce Vita.

myself a cow. The mechanics sold it back to the farmer, but you know what farmers are like. That cow would have been worth 60,000 lire, but he bought it back for 35,000.

In 1963 I was doing military service but they gave me leave to ride the Giro for Lygie. Vito Taccone was our leader, and he won five stages and the King of the Mountains. I never saw any of the money, though, because I abandoned in the first week.

The last one was 1965. I double punctured on a stage down in Abruzzo, but I only had one spare. I had to wait for neutral service and ended up riding it on my own. By the time I got to the final climb, it was nip and tuck whether I'd make it, and there were thousands of fans streaming down the hill on their way home. It took me forever to fight my way through them, and by the time I managed it I was over the time limit …

According to Franco Balmamion, Carpano paid Beraldo's team, Torpado, 300,000 lire not 200,000. They did so because Neri and Pellicciari, Beraldo's teammates, had worked for Balmamion on the final Alpine stage.

The 1962 Giro was the second longest in the history of the race, and one of the hardest. Two years previously, winner Jacques Anquetil had completed 3,480 kilometres at 37 kph. Now, as the Giro sought to favour the Italian climbers Imerio Massignan and Vito Taccone, the percorso was devoid of time trials and 700 mountainous kilometres longer. Thus, winner Balmamion averaged a shade under 34 kph.

Although Charly Gaul's 1956 stage to Bondone is hewn into the legend of the Giro, the 1962 Dolomite stage was much worse. For all that Gaul's stage was biblical, the number of abandons was a consequence not only of the weather, but also of the fact that it took place two days before the conclusion of the race. Here, 60 per cent of the peloton abandoned with a week remaining and the Giro all to play for.

DARIO ANDRIOTTO
A FREEZING DOLOMITE
DESCENT TO CORVARA, 2007

The worst would be the one to Lienz in 2007. It began with the Campolongo, a climb of 20 kilometres, but it was already snowing heavily so we went to Zomegnan and asked him to let us start the stage in the valley. He told us he wasn't prepared to do it, because there were mountain points at stake and the sponsor wouldn't put up with it.

We tried to do the climb slowly, but a climb's a climb. By the time you got to the top, you were sweating, and you'd a 30-kilometre descent to do in the freezing cold. So we started the descent but there were people in tears because of the cold. I admit that I was one of them. If you can't feel your hands it becomes dangerous, so I went and spoke to our captain, Stefano Garzelli. I told him to speak with Paolo Bettini, who was sort of the shop steward. The idea was to stop the race in a tunnel where nobody could see. They went to Zomegnan and told him we were stopping come what may, and that's what we did. We were able to put some dry clothes on and warm our hands, and the sun came out later on. It turned out well in the end because Garzelli won the stage …

The most difficult part was – and is – the finishing. It's been five years since I stopped, and if I'm honest I'm still coming to terms with it. I was a pro for sixteen years, so I'd known nothing but cycling and being on the move. I'd spent my entire life cycling and resting, and being waited on in hotels. If I wasn't racing I was between races, thinking about the next one. Then suddenly everything changed in 2010. I had to try to come to terms with being at home, and to learn how to be a "normal" husband and father. That wasn't easy, and it soon dawned on me that I didn't know how to do simple, everyday things. My wife would say, "Are you going to cut the grass?" and I'd be thinking, "Cut the grass? Me?"

Cycling is chemical. When I retired I had to come to terms with a sedentary life, and I found that really hard. I had to start a normal job, with all of the stresses and strains that normal working people have to deal with. As a bike rider I was being paid not to think, and avoiding everyday stress had actually been considered *part* of my job.

I rode for a lot of leaders, and I like to think I gave 100 per cent most of the time. I spent the last eight years of my career with Garzelli, though, and with him it was different. I know they don't like the term "*gregario*" anymore, but that's what I was. With him, I would find an extra 10 per cent from somewhere, because the relationship I had with him was different. Wherever he went I went as well, and he took care of the salary stuff. I remember when

I finished with Acqua & Sapone, because Masciarelli said, "To be honest, I only took you because Garzelli insisted, but I'm glad I did."

My son races as well. Stefano's ten, but I see a lot of myself in him. It should be a game at their age, but at the end of the day racing a bike is just instinct. I go to watch him and I feel it happening to me all over again. I wish it were different, but I was born with that devil inside me. What can you do? It's who I am, and he's my boy …

Dario Andriotto was twenty-five when he turned pro. He failed to finish his first three Giri, but finally manged it at the ripe old age of twenty-eight. Two years later he completed all three Grand Tours, and thereafter he remained an integral part of Stefano Garzelli's team.

As team leader and winner of the 2000 Giro, Garzelli always began the Giro rooming alone. Andriotto would invariably share with Massimo Codol, another of the Garzelli entourage. By the early 2000s, however, the money was being sucked out of Italian cycling in the wake of the Pantani affair and other doping scandals. Thus, when the first of his domestiques abandoned, the champion Garzelli would move over to share with Andriotto in order for the team to save money.

SIMONE FRACCARO
BEYOND CARING
PASSO VALLES, 1978

The one that still frightens me is the stage to Canazei in 1978. It was snow, sleet and freezing rain all day, and I was in a shocking state. I'd say it was the most terrible suffering I ever experienced …

I was determined to get round but I already had bronchitis. I was riding for Moser, and he asked me for my gloves. I gave them to him, but I couldn't get another pair from the car. So I had to do the descent without any, and I can only describe my mental state as one of delirium. I remember thinking, "If I make it down here, all well and good. But if I don't, then so be it." I wouldn't say I was at a point where I didn't *care* whether I died, no. I was way, way beyond that. I was almost willing it …

I'd turned pro in 1974, and straight away I finished third at Tirreno–Adriatico. Eddy Merckx was there, and he became a fan of mine. He started telling people I was the future of Italian cycling. Bianchi offered me a contract for the following year, and I went because they were a big team. That was the biggest mistake I ever made.

I'd been used to riding for myself, and I'd always had a winning mentality. When I signed with Bianchi, they told me I'd have some liberty, but in reality I just became a slave for Felice Gimondi and his group. After a year working for them, I'd become almost a nobody, because they had a vested interest in my not developing.

Pushing your leader on the climbs was part of the job. In our case, it was even worse because in addition to Gimondi we had a sprinter, Rik Van Linden. On a stage of the 1975 Giro, Van Linden had the points jersey and we had to push him on the climbs as well. On this particular stage I pushed Gimondi, but I was feeling really strong. I stayed with the lead group because I wanted to try to do something for myself, but then Gimondi told me, in that way of his, that I had to stop and wait for Van Linden.

I was sick of it to be honest. I sat down by the side of the road and waited, but then after a while I thought, "Fuck this!" I got back on the bike and started riding *down* the mountain, towards Van Linden. Given that the whole situation was ridiculous anyway, I thought I might as well render it even more so. Ferretti, our DS, nearly sent me home that night. Maybe I shouldn't have done what I did, but I was a young, talented, ambitious rider. It was probably the most demeaning thing that ever happened to me as a cyclist, but that was the way the team worked. It served their purpose to keep you down, because that way you were no threat to the hierarchy.

If I'm honest, I never really recovered the enthusiasm I'd had after that, and I always harboured a sense of injustice. I always felt that cycling had let me down.

My best moment was the stage win at Longarone in 1976. Gimondi had the pink jersey, but he crashed early in the stage. It looked serious, and everyone sat up. In the event, it was nothing much, but when one of the champions crashes there's a different code. That said, I don't know whether Gimondi would have sat up had it been one of his rivals. He'd have said, "One less to worry about" and attacked. I saw him do things like that a few times ...

Eddy Merckx was a gentleman. There was an uphill finish one day, and Fabrizio Fabbri had been pushing Gimondi for ages. Fabbri was suffering terribly, and Merckx took pity on him. He was the greatest champion of all, and yet he went up to Fabbri and started pushing *him*. Afterwards, Eddy looked at me and said, "How can he treat people like that?" And that was the difference between Eddy Merckx and Felice Gimondi.

In 1977 I was riding the Giro for Jolly, and our leader was Fausto Bertoglio. On the stage to Isernia, the heat was unbearable. Two Spanish guys abandoned after 50 kilometres, and I was about to climb off as well because I'd no water left. Then somebody gave me a drop, and I ended up winning the stage.

So I was going really well, and on the stage to Forlì I was in a break with Moser and Freddy Maertens. A kilometre from the top of the climb, Fontana, my DS, came up. He said, "You need to sit up and wait for Bertoglio. He'll be here in twenty seconds." I waited two minutes, and when Bertoglio finally turned up he said, "It's pointless you waiting for me. I'm absolutely knackered!" Moser won the stage, and we lost six minutes ...

Simone Fraccaro rode ten editions of the Giro. He won two stages, but many believed he had the God-given talent to have won a lot more. Like many great champions, Felice Gimondi's public persona was at variance with his profile within the peloton. He fought splendidly against Merckx's Giro hegemony for almost a decade, but by all accounts he was an extremely demanding leader.

The pushing and towing of leaders was an accepted practice in the 1970s. However, at the 1979 World Championships in the Netherlands,

eventual winner Jan Raas was filmed being towed up the Cauberg. Ironically enough, it was Italian journalists who cried foul. Laughably, they claimed that Francesco Moser — probably the greatest beneficiary of the "tactic" — had been cheated out of the rainbow jersey by the Dutch team's antics. From there on in, the UCI increased the use of motorbike commissars, and the pushing became far less commonplace.

GIROTAPPA 15

I VINCITORI DEL 85° GIRO D'ITALIA

(THE WINNERS OF THE 85TH GIRO D'ITALIA)

SAVOLDELLI G.
BELINGHERI
MARIMONI
LOCATELLI
PELLEGRINI
RUI
ARGENTIN
MANZONI M.
FONDRIEST
CORTI
AGNELLI
PEDRUZZI
SARONNI
FIDANZA
BETTINESCHI
BRUYNEEL
CARRETTA
MANZONI S.
TERNI
DOMINGUEZ
HAMBURGER
SERRI
ZINETTI
CHIESA
GARZELLI, SIMONI, BELLI, CASAGRANDE, PELLIZOTTI, CAUCCHIOLI
QUARANTA
POPOVYCH
ANDRIOTTO
COSTA
VERBRUGGHE
RIGHI
RUSSO
PEREZ CUAPIO
VANOTTI
TONKOV
EVANS, FRIGO, GONZALEZ
DE GERONIMO
SAVOLDELLI P.

C. SAN-

'Beppe: The cycling was on my mum's side, not my dad's. They were knife-makers, and it was an itinerant life, travelling from market to market. They'd fill a rucksack with knives, and cycle from town to town selling them.

They rode huge distances – over the mountains to Switzerland, wherever. Then one of my uncles was an Italian veterans champion in the 1920s, so cycling was passed down through the generations. I wasn't particularly good because I didn't train, but I raced. It's part of our DNA.

Paolo was born in 1973, and he was cycling almost before he was walking.

Attilia: This is one of Paolo's schoolbooks from his third year at primary school. Read what it says …

"My bike used to be broken and I couldn't use it but now it's fixed. I sit on the saddle and pedal and I take the bend at full speed. I ride through the puddles, the water splashes up and I get wet. I ride on the ice but I manage to stay upright. The back wheel slips but I keep pedalling and I'm through the ice. I'm off balance two or three times but I don't crash because I'm a real cyclist. I set of at full-tilt. The bike rears up and it's difficult to keep it under control but I'm a professional. Whatever the obstacle, even if it's hard, I overcome it.

"With my bike I'll be formidable and unbeatable. When they see me, the others won't dare race me because there are no other professionals like me in the entire world. Although I'm only a kid, I can even beat Moser if I try really hard …"

He'd have been eight or nine when he wrote that.

'Beppe: We used to go out riding, but by the time Paolo was thirteen I couldn't keep up. It was hopeless. Another of my uncles was 'Beppe Marinoni. He'd been amateur champion of Lombardy, but he'd emigrated to Canada in the fifties and built a bike factory. Paolo's first racing bike came from him. It was winter 1987, so he'd have been fourteen.

We went to the airport to get it, and brought it home. We live in Rovetta, at the bottom of the Passo della Presolana, but we've a house at Colere, in the next valley. We go at weekends or when it's too hot, and Paolo really liked going there so he decided he was going to ride there on his new bike. It's a long, hard climb, the Presolana, 12 kilometres.

Attilia: We overtook him in the car and carried on. We got to the house and waited for him to turn up on his new bike.

'Beppe: It was starting to get dark and he hadn't turned up. I figured he must have crashed, so I got in the car and went back to look for him. I checked the verges, the ditches, everywhere. Not a trace, and so now there's a search party. Everyone's out looking, but there's no sign …

Attilia: I was at my wit's end. Eventually, he emerged from one of the fields with his bike over his shoulder. My daughter said, "Mum, please don't start yelling at him. At least he's alive!"

He'd reached the pass, and decided to go off exploring instead of coming straight home. The problem was the road he'd taken had two metres of snow. Actually, it wasn't even a proper road. I could have killed him …

'Beppe: He joined the cycling club, and it was all he was bothered about. He'd be off training, and he'd neither the time nor the inclination to study.

Attilia: After three years at middle school, we had to decide. He was fourteen, and he'd a decent brain. He was good at maths, so we sent him to a specialist secondary school. Problem was that the first-term results were just dreadful. He didn't like studying, and he said his training came first.

'Beppe: I went to talk with his teacher. He said, "He's a bright boy, but it's impossible to keep him sitting down for five hours."

It still is to be honest …

Attilia: He'd made up his mind. He wanted to train, and to work with his father. I was thinking it over but then he went to the school himself and picked up all his belongings! He said, "Well, it's only a matter of time before they throw me out anyway, so at least this way I won't lose all my stuff!"

In reality, he was resigning from school himself, because that way we couldn't send him back. He said, "You'll see, mum. You'll see that I was right all along …"

'Beppe: A lot of boys his age were full-time cyclists, but he wanted to work as well. I was a builder, and he became my apprentice. There were times when it would be dark and I'd say, "That's enough for today; we'll finish it in the morning." He didn't like that, though, so he'd insist on finishing whatever it was we were doing. He just really enjoyed hard work.

AUG • 73

in piedi, la ruota di
dietro slittano, ma a forza
di pedalare esco dal ghiaccio,
però mi sono sbilanciato due
o tre volte ma non sono
caduto perché io sono un
vero ciclista. Parto a tutta
birra, impennò la bici, è diffi-
cile tenerla in piedi ma
io sono un professionista.

ed ad ogni ostacolo, anche se
è impossibile, io con il mio
coraggio riesco a superarlo,
io con la mia   bicicletta
sarò formidabile e imbattibile
e tutti quando mi vedranno
non …
di …
al mo…
se sono …
se mi s…

159

Attilia: He was either working or training, and when he wasn't, he liked to be at home. He hardly ever went out socialising.

'Beppe: The longer and harder the races, the better he became.

He started having problems in 1991, when he turned amateur. They were eighteen-year-old kids, and Olivano Locatelli, the coach, was extremely strict with them. He'd be weighing them all the time, and Paolo couldn't stand that. He knew he couldn't eat, and he didn't need somebody telling him all the time.

Attilia: If he didn't agree with something, he said so. Locatelli didn't appreciate that, so Paolo left after a few months and Locatelli was livid. He had the other kids ride just to stop him winning, and once when Paolo won he was so mad that he made one of them ride home …

Little wonder they nicknamed him 'The Falcon'.

Base camp, 1996. Professional now, with Roslotto.

BEPPE SAVOLDELLI, ATTILIA BELINGHERI, MARIO MANZONI, SIMONETTA BETTINESCHI
PASSO SELVINO, MORGEX, COLERE, COLLE FAUNIERA, 1993–2000

Mario: I'm four years older than Savo', but people in the cycling community were talking about him.

I was a pro with Gatorade, and I remember we were out training one day. We were on the Selvino and by chance we came across his amateur team. You could tell straight away that he was different to the others.

How? Well, just by watching his pedal stroke. It's cycling: you know instantly.

'Beppe: I went to the Tour of Aosta the day after Diego Pellegrini died. He'd been trying to follow Paolo on the descent into Morgex, but he'd run straight into a car. Later, they looked at the data and Paolo had been doing 100 kph …

I think he bore the scar for a year or so, and he almost stopped altogether when they told him he had to wait another year to turn pro. That was a really delicate moment.

Mario: In 1996 he turned pro with my team, Roslotto. I was quite experienced, and one of my jobs was to help him find his way. He was new, but when we did a time trial or a hill climb he always did the fastest time. The point is that this wasn't in August or September, after a season of adjustment. It was in *January* and he was beating champions, guys like Maurizio Fondriest …

Then, over time, you realized he had the ability to recover. He'd train like an animal, and the next day he'd do it again. He was a kid, but you could see that he was a natural for stage races.

Simonetta: I'm from Colere, where the Savoldellis had their summer house. I knew Paolo's cousin, and he introduced us one evening at the village pub. I was twenty-seven and he was twenty-five, so it would have been late 1998. We played darts …

I was working in a clothing factory at the time. I said, "What do you do?" and he said, "I ride a bike." I said, "Yes, but what do you do for a *job?*"

I liked him, and thankfully he never talked about cycling.

'Beppe: He signed with Claudio Corti at Saeco for 1998, and he made a big step up. He won the Tour of Trentino, and I think he finished top ten at the Giro. He won Trentino again the following year, and he beat Pantani to do it. Then he won the famous stage over the Fauniera at the Giro and finished second overall.

Before the 2000 Giro he won the GC at the Tour of Romandy. He was one of the strongest now, and he was going really well.

Paolo and Simonetta having a grapple.

Paolo: At the 2000 Giro I was second in the prologue, but on the first road stage a *bidon* fell from someone's bottle cage and caused a big crash. I came down on my back. I should have abandoned, but you know what it's like. I finished the Giro but I was in a lot of pain. I went to the chiropractor's and they tried to straighten me up, but after a few days I was back to square one. All the connective tissues around the muscle were contorted, so the problem never got resolved.

'Beppe: They should have stopped him there and then, but the team was built around Cipollini for the sprints and Paolo for the GC. They didn't have anyone else, so he had to go and ride the Tour as well.

Paolo: Back ache all the time, and this terrible pain in my thigh. I couldn't push.

Simonetta: It was, "Lift him out of bed, give him a painkilling injection, put him on his bike." With the painkillers he wasn't *feeling* the pain so much, so he was just making the injury worse and worse …

Everything was bent out of shape, and that started to cause problems with his tendons. Bettini, the photographer guy, told him he was all wrong on the bike. He was riding with one leg, and it was terrible to see him suffer like that.

'Beppe: He was a thoroughbred, but they treated him like a donkey. The doctor said, "You'd have been far better off with a broken leg. That way you'd have had to stop and you could have sorted it out."

BEPPE SAVOLDELLI, ATTILIA BELINGHERI, SIMONETTA BETTINESCHI, PAOLO SAVOLDELLI, ROME, ROVETTA, MILAN, PARIS, 2000–2001

in Cuneo when we landed. Quaranta had become a father two months earlier, so there were two babies at the hotel that evening.

Giovanni: The most important thing is to keep everybody together. You need some skills as a diplomat, and to be able to resolve problems before they become issues. Mario had the ability to do all that.

Mario: I guess it helps if you can deal with the little day-to-day problems, but all a leader really needs is someone he likes. Savo' is easy to get along with, and so that's what we did. We just … got along.

Everyone's watching, everyone's racing hard and there's everything going on around the race. It should be stressful, but you wouldn't have thought that in our room. I'd become a dad, and Savo' was doing his house. They were the main topics of conversation, not the stress of the race. The Giro is supposed to be exhausting and tense, but to be honest what I most remember is that it was just a beautiful moment!

On the road, the best we could do was to try to get him to the bottom of climbs in decent shape. Once the real battle started, he was on his own.

Mario Manzoni in Index jersey with "Blue Merchandising" sub-sponsor.

Simonetta: We'd decided not to tell anyone that I was pregnant, because I was worried I might lose my job if they found out and work was hard to come by. We'd speak every day, but we never spoke about the race.

Attilia: It was too stressful as it was, never mind sitting in front of the TV watching it. The days when I knew he'd have to try something on the descent were the worst. They always used to say, "There's never anything to eat in this house when the Giro's on!" I'm not sure I was really functioning.

'Beppe: Sometimes I'd watch the stage while I was working, either at the site or at someone's house. Other times I didn't have the courage to watch, and I'd find out how it had gone on the way home, by the looks on people's faces.

Simonetta: I didn't finish work until 5.30, so I'd record the stages and watch them later. You can't be listening to the radio at work, so I didn't usually find out until I got home.

Giovanni: He got the time back on the stage to Varazze. It was raining, there was a long descent to the finish and he did his thing. Nobody paid much attention because the break had stayed away, and he wasn't considered a threat for the *maglia rosa*. It was a good sign, though …

Mario: I was pretty fast as a rider, and I'd won stages at the Giro, Romandy and Tirreno. So in actual fact my job at the beginning was to help Quaranta. He'd broken his wrist before the race, and we were trying to nurse him through it in the hope that he'd recover some condition.

Paolo: I was always alone. Lanfranchi and Bo Hamburger were riding for themselves, and the rest were trying to help Quaranta. As soon as we hit any sort of a climb, they were out the back. There was nobody to bring me a *bidon*, nothing …

Mario: Quaranta abandoned after about twelve days, and from there on in I just focused on helping Paolo as best I could.
     We weren't much of a team, everyone else had fancy busses and equipment, and at first we had a laugh and a joke about it. The first week was a bit like that, but then Paolo started to get stronger and, one by one, the others started falling by the wayside. Garzelli and Simoni were out, and there was still only about a minute between the top ten. At a certain point, Savo' said to me, "Mario, what's going on here?"

Giovanni: We thought he'd do a good time trial, but for some reason he didn't go particularly well that day. It wasn't a disaster, but he lost 90 seconds to Tyler Hamilton and we felt we'd missed a chance.
     Then Casagrande was disqualified, but Paolo was concerned about the Fedaia stage. It was a climb he'd always suffered on, so I just said, "Yes, but maybe in previous years you didn't have the condition you have now. Anyway, all we can do is our best, and what will be will be …"
     In the event, he finished second behind Pérez Cuapio, but he was the best of the GC group. I think he was sixth at this point, and he was really starting to motor. The last Dolomite stage

was the following day, 220 kilometres with two huge climbs to finish. I knew if he didn't lose time he was virtually guaranteed at least a podium, and possibly even a win. I was sure he'd do a good time trial.

At breakfast he said something I'll never forget. I wasn't one of those sports directors who's on his riders' case all the time, particularly when they're tired and they've just got up. I always tried to keep it brief, and he didn't need chapter and verse from me. He didn't have a team, and he knew exactly what he had to do. I just said, "How are you feeling, Paolo?" and he said, "Great! I feel like I didn't ride yesterday."

Simonetta: I must have had a premonition because I started work half an hour early that day. I wanted to watch the finish, so me and my friends arranged to meet at my place.

Giovanni: They started with the Gardena and the Sella, and then 100 kilometres of descent. Then they did the Santa Barbera and Bordala, which were effectively 20 kilometres of climbing with a brief descent between them.

The last climb was Passo Coe, and we knew that was where the race was going to be decided, because it's 20 kilometres, and it's really, really hard. Tonkov and Pérez Cuapio were up the road, but they were only concerned with the stage win.

Paolo: Cadel Evans was *maglia rosa* and he had Noè with him at the bottom of the climb. Then Caucchioli had Pellizotti and I think Gotti, and there was someone with Frigo. The others I can't remember, but I was on my own. There would have been about fifteen in the GC group at that point, and Noè was pulling hard so that nobody would be able to attack Evans. I felt good and I knew it would start to thin out.

Giovanni: I think Frigo was one of the first to be dropped, which was a big surprise.

Paolo: Hamilton attacked and Evans blew straight away – a hunger flat probably. I caught Hamilton riding tempo, then put myself on the front. Suddenly, when I looked round, he was 50 metres behind me, and I couldn't see the others.

Giovanni: It was something incredible. He finished second behind Tonkov, but he put 2 minutes into Hamilton and Caucchioli. We had the *maglia rosa*, and all that was left was a time trial and two sprints.

Mario: As an athlete he was just … a machine gun.

Simonetta: There we were, my friends and I all sitting round the TV, and suddenly he was winning the *maglia rosa*!

Afterwards, he was doing *Il Processo alla Tappa*, the TV show where they round up the stage and interview the riders. They were just finishing up and he said, "Can I say something? I want to dedicate this *maglia rosa* to my fiancée, Simo. We've just found out she's going to have our baby."

My friends all turned and looked at me …

'Beppe: They rang the church bells in the village.

Attilia: I suffered a lot, yes. All our lives had been conditioned by his career, and I think when you want something so much it becomes … We knew that with cycling you can lose it all in an instant.

Giovanni: He took the jersey at the perfect moment. We didn't even have to defend it, and the time trial was 40 kilometres of false flat. It was made-to-measure for him.

Mario: I remember riding into Milan vividly, because I'd made up my mind I was going to take it all in. It was the first time I'd been in a Giro-winning team, and I didn't want it to pass me by. So for me, it was *very* emotional, probably even more so than for Savo'.

'Beppe: We went to Milan, yes.

Afterwards, Felice Gimondi said to Paolo, "Are you going to share the prize money with the *gregari* or not, given that you won it on your own?"

Giovanni: So you see, if that sponsor had signed up, he'd have had one hell of a return on his investment … I don't know whether Paolo would have won the Giro had Garzelli and Simoni been there, but my understanding is that you have to finish the Giro to win it. And he was really, really strong. *Incredibly* strong.

Attilia: I remember seeing him in the jersey in Milan and laughing. Who would have thought it?

Giovanni: I'd worked and ridden for some of the biggest teams in the sport, and there we were with our little motorhome and our second-hand truck …

People say that Leicester City winning the Premiership was incredible, but I reckon what we did at that Giro was a real sporting miracle. I remember a meeting with my colleagues and saying, "Christ, in October he didn't even have a *team*!"

Mario: There had been times during that first week when I'd just wanted to be at home with my daughter. It's nature's call, but imagine if I'd left. It would have been the biggest regret of my life …

Paolo: Apparently, Ferretti, the boss of Fassa Bortolo, was going round saying, "What am I supposed to tell the sponsors now? I've spent €7 million and we've come away with nothing! That lot have spent half a million, they can't even pay their riders' wages, and they've won the Giro!"

Simonetta: Afterwards, I said to him, "Do you realize what you've done? You've won the Giro d'Italia!"

171

Simonetta finished work in the winter of 2002, and the couple's first daughter, Marika, was born in January 2003. By then, Paolo had signed for two years with T-Mobile, where he was joined by Giovanni Fidanza. His time there was plagued by ill-luck and injury, however. He never won any races, and never participated in a single Grand Tour.

In 2005 Paolo joined Discovery Channel, then in need of a Giro GC rider for the nascent Pro Tour. Once more fit and healthy, he won arguably the most dramatic Giro of the twenty-first century with a stupendous ride on the final mountain stage.

He later worked as the roving motorbike reporter for RAI, and then for the Bike Channel TV station.

Giovanni spent four years with T-Mobile, before being reunited with Paolo at Astana in 2007. The two of them worked together again in 2008, for the ill-fated LPR team. Giovanni stayed on until 2011, but these days manages a women's team. His daughter Arianna was junior world champion in the points, before signing a contract with Astana's women's team. Her younger sister, Martina, is a multiple Italian and European champion on the track.

Mario would ride the 2003 Giro as a gregario for Marco Pantani. He was reunited with Ivan Quaranta for the 2004 edition, his ninth and last as a professional cyclist. On retirement, Mario became a sports director, latterly for Nippo-Vini Fantini, an Italo-Japanese team attempting to locate and nurture Japanese riders. How the world turns …

'Beppe and Attilia still have the house in Colere, on the other side of the Presolana. They have five grandchildren, and 'Beppe still has the Marinoni bike he collected from the airport.

GIROTAPPA 16

UN GIORNO DA LEONE

(ONE DAY AS A LION)

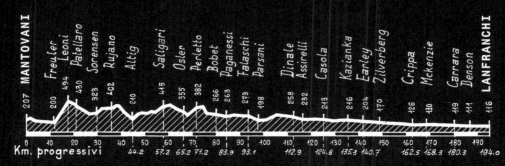

I turned pro in 1977, after the Montreal Olympics. Then, in January 1978, I was out sledging with my nephew. We attached the sledge to the horse, but he bolted and I had to try to protect my nephew. In simple terms, my femur broke in half and I finished up with my left leg behind my back, at right angles to my trunk. I literally had to reach round and throw it back into position. It still makes me shudder thinking about it …

They took me to hospital but they had no idea what to do with my leg and they left me there for two days. Eventually, I was taken to a sports injuries centre in Milan, to a surgeon named Lanzetta. He told me he'd do what he could, and that he ought to be able to get me back on my feet. Then he said I should start thinking about a new career, and you can imagine how that felt to a person like me. The bike was my entire world.

So he opened my leg up, cut all the muscle away and put a metal plate in. It was held in place by fifteen screws, and they hoped that the bone would knit back together. I was on crutches for six months, and by the time I got off them the leg was two centimetres longer than the other one. They told me that I could start doing some light physio, but that under no circumstances was I even to think about getting back on the bike. Of course, I wasn't having that, and I reckoned that, if I could walk, I could ride.

On 20 August I signed on for the Tre Valle Varesine and rode 120 kilometres alone at the front. Don't ask me how because I can't really figure it out even today, but I was out of contract and I needed to prove to people that I was still a rider. The surgeon rang me that night, because he'd seen the race on TV. He said, "What the hell do you think you're doing?" They took the plate out of my leg in November, and I started my rehab …

I was a sprinter, and I'd spent my amateur career tooth and nail with 'Beppe Saronni. He would win one week, I'd win the next, and so it went. That had been my level, but the accident left me with a leg and a half at best. Over time, I built the muscle mass up again, but my legs weren't really twinned anymore and the left one was way down on power. I couldn't stamp on the pedals the way I'd been able to previously, and I had to start my sprint with the right leg.

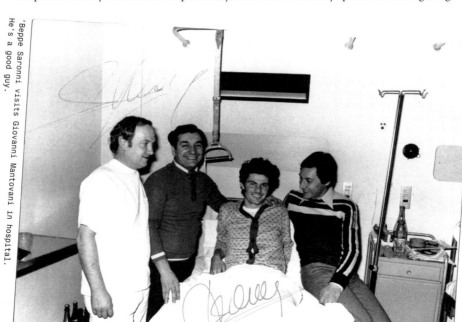

'Beppe Saronni visits Giovanni Mantovani in hospital.
He's a good guy.

I was still reasonably competitive, but I was riding in pain all the time and the right leg was carrying the left. In 1979 Saronni won the Giro, and I was *hors delay* on the fifteenth stage of the Tour. He'd become the champion I'd hoped to be, while I was just struggling to survive.

I signed for Dino Zandegù in 1980. I got a start at the Giro, and after everything I'd been through that was huge for me. I came close to winning at Imperia and Parma, but Saronni won them both. Then the eighth stage was an uphill finish at Fiuggi, and I finished second again because a Spanish guy managed to slip away. The following day was Sorrento, the longest stage of the Giro, and finally I managed to win one. It was pretty emotional for me, as you can imagine, and of course everyone in cycling knew my story.

I don't remember much about the sprint itself, but I do remember a moment later on in the evening. We were staying in quite a big hotel, and a few other teams were there as well. Then, of course, you had a lot of tourists, because Sorrento is a resort town. Obviously, as the stage winner I had to do the ceremonies, anti-doping, speak with the press, all that stuff. So one way or another, I was last to have a massage and, as a consequence, last into the dining room. As I walked in, everyone – my team, the other teams, the waiters, ordinary people there on holiday – just stood up as one and started applauding me. I was overcome …

Giovanni Mantovani's stage win was ecstatically received, and he repeated it the following day at Palinuro. He would ride professionally until 1988, and even represented his country at the 1985 World Championships. He won about twenty races all told, but never again landed a Giro stage because he never quite rediscovered the change of pace that had characterized his junior career.

Giovanni managed the Giro's publicity caravan for many years, and then became head of stage arrivals. He says he enjoyed working with race director Carmine Castellano a great deal, but couldn't get along with his successor, Angelo Zomegnan. When we met, he had just celebrated his sixtieth birthday, and was working as an agent for a cycling clothing company.

I'm from Monreale, near Palermo. To have a chance in cycling you needed to move, so I left home when I was seventeen. I rode for my country, and in 1980 Dino Zandegù came to see me. I was twenty years old, but he was offering me a professional contract. At that time, there was only one other professional from Sicily, so as you can imagine it was quite a thing …

I didn't get started until the Tour of Puglia in late April. I went to see my parents while we were down there, and it was obvious that my dad wasn't at all well. He actually worked at the hospital, but they couldn't figure out what was wrong with him.

175

After the Giro prologue there was a split stage. The second part was a team time trial up in Bibione, and we won it. We were basically a team of neo-pros, but we did it at 53 kph and beat all the stars. It was a major success for us, but something was wrong because my dad wasn't calling me. He and I had spoken every day on the phone for years, come what may. Now, though, he wasn't ringing, and I was worried. My mum said, "Well, he's not too good, but don't worry yourself. The reason he's not ringing is that he's gone to the house in the countryside and there's no phone there."

The tenth stage was in Rome. The owner of the junior team I'd ridden for there, Vittorio Cinque, came to see me. I'd lived with him while I was there, so obviously we were close. He told me they'd discovered that my dad had cancer, but they hadn't said anything because they didn't want to worry me while I was riding my first Giro. Then, a couple of days later, I had a call from the boss of my amateur team in Lombardy. He told me my dad had been transferred to a cancer hospital in Milan, and that he'd send someone to pick me up after the stage finish in Pavia.

So I went to see my dad and he was extremely ill. The cancer was in his lymph nodes, and he weighed 39 kilos. I was looking at my dad, but in some way it wasn't him.

I hadn't done much at the Giro because I'd developed a fever. Before I left, my dad said to me, "You could at least try to ride on the front of the group from time to time. That way, I'll get to see you a bit on the television."

I went back to the Giro, but obviously I was in pieces. I could barely eat – in fact, they brought my dinner up to my room the following day – and I couldn't sleep. My dad was forty-three years old, and he was dying …

Two days later there was Mantova–Borno, 215 kilometres with four big climbs. I wanted my dad to see me, so I took off after 15 kilometres. I hadn't realized Mario Noris had already gone up the road, but I caught him at the bottom of the San Fermo. I was going at twice his speed, because I had to make sure I was still away when RAI started the TV transmission. At the top I was still 100 kilometres from the finish, but they told me I had 20 minutes on the group.

So that was when I allowed myself to think about it. Next I did the Gallo, and the drag up to Clusone. I was floating, but then they told me that Faustino Rupérez had attacked out of the main group. He'd won the Vuelta, and he was a specialist climber. I actually knew the final climb really well, but it didn't alter the fact that it was ten hard kilometres, and I had to get to the top of it. Then, when I started it, I realized I was cooked. All I had left was my dad …

Like all Italian cyclists, I'd always dreamed of winning a stage of the Giro, but for the first time in my life I wasn't thinking of winning for myself. When I was on the stage afterwards, De Zan, the TV guy, asked me if I wanted to send a message to my dad. I don't know who had told him, but obviously I was quite emotional. I still have a tape of it here, but I struggle to watch it …

In August, the boss of the team called me up. He said, "You're done, Benedetto. Your season's over, so it's time for you to go home." I went home, and we were together as a family for the last few weeks of my dad's life. He died in September.

A couple of years ago I was in Sicily, just walking along the beach. A guy came up to me and said, "Are you Benedetto Patellaro?" I told him I was, and he said he had an old bike of mine, a Bottecchia.

I gave the guy my number, but he didn't contact me. I got to thinking about it, and remembered what had happened. At the end of the season you sent your bikes back, and they sold them off. A guy from Sicily had bought mine, a fan. So I called him up and asked him what had happened to the bike. He told me he'd sold it on at a certain point, and set about finding out what had happened to it …

The stage following Benedetto's epic 200-kilometre stage win began with the Passo Viverone. He was immediately dropped from the gruppetto, but they waited for him. They then pushed him up the Passo Tonale, and somehow he got home just inside the time limit.

Benedetto eventually located his bike, although it was in a
terrible state. He bought it back and, with the help of some artisans,
rebuilt it. It resides in his house above Lake Como, and is beautiful.
He's fifty-six now, but hopes to take early retirement and return home.
Home to Sicily …

MARCO SALIGARI
SEMPRE IN FUGA
SONDRIO, 1992
VALLE VARAITA, 1993
CASERTA, 1994

It was 166 kilometres to Sondrio. You'd Aprica to climb, then five tough kilometres up to Valico di Triangia, then the descent down to Sondrio. It was too hard for the sprinters and not hard enough for the GC guys. However, it's all well and good to say, "That's the one for me!" but you know for a fact that forty or fifty other guys are thinking precisely the same thing …

It was a miserable day, and that suited me down to the ground. Ten minutes before departure, Moreno Argentin was drinking coffee in his rain cape, winter hat, gloves … I was in my normal jersey and he said, "Are you not cold, Marco?" I said, "No, because in ten minutes it's going to get really hot!" He said, "Why?" and I said, "Because I'm off!"

Someone attacked straight away and it seemed like they were going to let him go. They brought him back, though, and I took off immediately with a Spanish guy. It was a long, steady drag, somewhere between a false flat and a climb. I remember I felt well as I saw the sign for 150 kilometres. I pulled off so he'd do a turn, but he didn't come through. He'd disappeared.

My legs were good, but I was on my own against 180 of them. The gap hovered at 20 seconds, 40, 50, 30 … Then, after a while, they sat up – though not for long …

Everyone knows when you're going well, so they never gave me more than five minutes all day. That's pretty hard, and it got harder when Chiappucci attacked. Don't ask me why, but when he went, the GC group had to follow. I hit the last climb with 4 minutes, but obviously the GC riders were better climbers than me. I knew that if I could get to the top I'd be OK, because I knew the descent really well. I had 36 seconds, and I won by 1'20". When I reached the finish, it was glorious sunlight … Indurain congratulated me in the hall afterwards. That evening at dinner, a magnum of champagne arrived at our table, courtesy of Miguel.

The following year, 1993, was Varazze to Val Varaita, another hard transition stage between the Dolomites and the Alps. Eventually, there were four of us left: me, my teammate Santaromita, Baffi and Bortolami.

Baffi was the key because he had the points jersey. He needed the break to stay away so he could get the intermediate sprint points, and he did a massive ride. By rights, someone like him shouldn't have been earning points on a hard stage like that, but he made a major contribution. So, in addition to the points, he got paid by me as well, just as Santaromita got paid. That was all perfectly normal because we were all helping one another. It was logical that, as stage winner, I'd pay, because otherwise I'd have got the glory *and* the money, and the others would have been left with nothing. That's cycling, isn't it?

Bortolami? No, he didn't get anything, because with him it was different …

Bortolami was the strongest, but he pulled the least. If the speed drops from 40 kph to 32 kph each time someone goes to the front, it's because he's recovering. To be honest, I'd probably have done the same in his shoes, but by the same token he understood that there would be no money if he didn't win. He wasn't pulling not because he was lazy, but because that was the tactic that he felt gave him the best chance of winning. However, it was implicit that, if he didn't, he wouldn't get paid.

So Bortolami was strong, but also too fast for me to risk dragging him to the finish. I decided I'd attack him on a climb 25 kilometres out, so I went to the car and spoke to Domenico Cavallo, our second DS. The main DS was Giancarlo Ferretti, but he'd stayed behind with the GC group. I said to Cavallo, "Give me something to drink because I'm going." I knew where the climb steepened, and I reasoned that Bortolami wouldn't expect me to attack there. I was close to a hunger knock by the time I got over the top, but I held him off and I was a better descender.

I found out later that Cavallo had spoken to Ferretti on the radio, and he'd gone berserk. He was convinced it was the wrong time to go, and apparently he'd told Cavallo to stop me. Cavallo didn't, though, because he agreed with me. Imagine the scene with Ferretti had I *not* won …

The last one? Martina, my daughter, had been born the week before …

By then it had become *very* difficult for me to get in the breaks. It's a bit like the GC group when Indurain moves: the shout goes up and they're all over it. The stage was Potenza–Caserta, down in the south, and it was incredibly hot. Extreme weather always favours the break, so that was good.

On one of the last climbs I gave it a go, and five of us got clear. Me, Gotti, Imboden, Ghirotto and Faresin. So all decent riders, and I knew straight away that we'd make it. Ghirotto and I were the strongest, but the others pulled as well and we were doing 50 kph. It would have needed three teams to bring that back, and we knew that wasn't going to happen.

We probably had six or seven minutes at 6 kilometres, and that was where the games started. Gotti was cooked, so he wasn't an issue. Faresin couldn't win a sprint, but he was a good friend of Ghirotto. I was faster than Ghirotto on paper, but Imboden was quick and hadn't done as much work.

So I knew that Faresin would go first, and that, if it didn't work, he'd be working for Ghirotto. Faresin

attacked twice and each time it was me who closed him down. I could see that Imboden was waiting for the sprint, but I'd been expecting that and I couldn't do anything about it. The third time Faresin went I didn't follow at first, and at 3 kilometres we were all sitting looking at one another. So now Faresin's got 100 metres, 200, 300 …

At that point Ghirotto made a big mistake. He offered me a lot of cash to close the gap, and that suggested that he didn't think he had the strength to beat me. So I reckoned I was the strongest and hopefully the fastest, and it was clear that the others couldn't or wouldn't go across. I didn't answer Ghirotto, but instead I set off after Faresin. I only needed to ride at eight-tenths to bring him back, and then when we turned into the home straight I realized it was a strong headwind. We caught Faresin at 600 metres, and then Ghirotto made another mistake. He found himself on the front, and that was perfect for me because I had all the time I needed to recover. With a headwind it becomes a test of strength more than speed, and that favoured me over Imboden. I won easily …

What a day that was. I've never seen so many people at a Giro stage finish.

Marco Saligari started nine giri, and finished them all. He was often referred to as a "breakaway specialist", but in reality he was simply a terrific passista with a very good cycling brain. He was able to ride prodigious distances on the front of a breakaway, or indeed on his own. He won the Tour de Suisse in 1993, and stages at Paris–Nice and the Tour of Catalonia.

For better or worse, cycling has become more "professional" and team-orientated in recent years. The sprinters' teams in particular are formidable, so the sort of 150-kilometre solo stage win Marco accomplished at Sondrio have all but disappeared. The Australian David McKenzie produced something similar at the 2000 Giro, but it seems that the epic, lung-busting solo rides of yore are no more.

ALESSANDRO PAGANESSI
SHOULD I STAY OR
SHOULD I GO?
ARABBA, 1983

My problem as a cyclist was that if there were three of us in a sprint, you could almost guarantee that I'd finish third. So there was only one way for me to win, and everyone knew it. I can assure you that it's not easy to ride away from everyone else in a bike race, and still less so when you've spent the last 150 to 200 kilometres fetching bottles for the leaders.

The day I won was the last Friday. The climbs were Campolongo, Pordoi, Sella, Gardena and Campolongo again, with the finish at Arabba. It was my second Giro, but that was the first time I was able to try for myself. The leaders were all out of the GC, so I had a free hand to go for it.

My memory isn't that good, but I reckon on the Sella there would have been about eight or ten of us. 'Beppe

Saronni had the jersey, but Visentini was only a few seconds behind. I think Saronni was on his own and wasn't feeling too good, so he asked me for a hand …

He wasn't offering me a "deal" as such, no. He and I knew each other, so obviously he doesn't need to come straight out and offer me money. It's more … well, you're a professional cyclist, aren't you? Everyone knows the game, so if needs be you can have that conversation just by using your eyes.

I didn't have long to decide, but I just felt really good so I sort of let him know that we'd wait and see. My instinct was to accept, but not because I was in it for the money. That's not the way I was, but I knew my limitations. He was a champion and someone I respected, and we were surrounded by Spanish climbers. You had Fernández, Rupérez and what have you, and they were really good. So I couldn't be sure I was going to win, and, given that I couldn't sprint, the only way was to drop them all.

Saronni was chipping away at me, and I had to decide because time was running out. In the end, I just went. The Spaniards caught me at the top, but they were never much use as descenders. I was only 63 kilos, but I was pretty good. I did more than thirty kilometres over the Gardena and Campolongo, and I won by over two minutes. That's it …

If you take a good look at my results, you'll see the pattern just repeats itself. Third at Lazio, third at Sabatini, third at Campania. Fourth here, fifth there, endless top-ten placings but very few wins. I'd beat myself up for having started the sprint too early or too late, but in reality it probably didn't make that much difference. I just didn't have the speed, and if you don't have it, you don't have it. You can analyse it all you like, you can discuss the team all you like and you can talk about tactics until you're blue in the face, but none of it makes any difference.

So people *said* that Bianchi wasted my talent, but maybe I wasn't quite as talented as they liked to think. Besides, it was my local team. Everyone lived within about thirty kilometres of Bergamo, the service course was here, and we all trained together. So it wasn't as if there was anything better. There were more Italian teams back then, but ten teams of thirteen riders is still only 130 pros. The competition for places was intense.

It's clear that I'd have had more liberty in a smaller team, but I'd have also been under more pressure. There are a lot of guys who went really well for the first couple of years and then vanished. Think of poor Pino Faraca, the Calabrese who was white jersey at the Giro. The flipside was that you did as you were told. You couldn't just go off in the breaks like they do today; there was none of that back then. There was work to do, and when it's time to work, what do you do? You work …

I never rode the Tour de France. I wouldn't say the Giro was its equal back then, but it almost was. Even a team like Bianchi had no appetite for it, and the sponsors weren't bothered. It would have been nice to try it, but the Italian calendar was so full that they didn't need to bother going over there.

In 1985 Sandro signed for Murella, a new team managed by a new face. Aldo Sassi had assisted Francesco Moser in preparing for the hour record, and sought to deploy a similar methodology with a road team. During the winter, they did interval training up and down the hill separating Bergamo's old town from its new one, as often as not on new-fangled "mountain bikes".

The snow was particularly heavy that year, but by the same token Rossin, the team's bike manufacturer, were the first Italian manufacturer to produce mountain bikes. The bikes were featured on the front page of Bicisport, *the monthly cycling bible, but on the road Sassi's methods were catastrophic. Sandro's stage win at Romandy was their only meaningful result, and by May they were so knackered that six of them abandoned a famously "light" Giro.*

Sandro packed it in two years later, and became double Italian mountain-bike champion in cross-country.

PAOLO LANFRANCHI
IN PANTA'S SHADOW
BRIANÇON, 2000

Of course I remember it! It was the most important moment of my career, a mountain stage of the Giro over the Agnello and the Izoard! I'd won Langkawi and the Tour of the Algarve but … Well, the Giro is the *Giro*, isn't it?

The following morning I couldn't wait to get the newspapers and see my name on the front pages. When I got the *Gazzetta*, the headline was, "THE RETURN OF PANTANI!"

He came up to me in the start village to congratulate me, and we were laughing about it. I said, "I get the Torriani Prize and win the biggest stage of my life, and all they're writing about is you, the bloody runner-up!" I was really happy anyway, and for me the fact that he was second made it even more valuable. He was Panta, after all …

I was still with Mapei, working for Pavel Tonkov. Francesco Casagrande had the jersey, and the Giro was between him and Garzelli. Pantani already had his problems, so he wasn't as good as he'd been before. Anyway, I was pedalling well that year, in the breaks a lot. I'd been third when Di Luca won at Peschici and fourth when Axel Merckx won at Prato …

I was a climber, so my job was to protect Pavel. That day, it involved getting in the break, and luckily it was a good one. There was a natural selection on the Agnello, but a lead group of five or six started the Izoard together. The GC group came up to us, but Pavel had drifted off the back of it. That meant I had to wait, and I still hadn't quite got him back by the time we reached the top.

When the descent started, it was touch and go whether we'd make it. The first four kilometres are technical, and after that you've a stretch of false flat. I knew I had to get Pavel back on before that, because, if not, they would start to pull and he'd be done for. I got him back on right at the start of the false flat.

As we rejoined, Pavel gave me a shove and I went to the front. He wasn't on a great day, and he wanted to avoid people attacking while he got his breath back. So I went and did a turn, but when I looked round they'd let a gap open. It was maybe ten metres, then twenty, and then I just went. That was it; I won by nearly two minutes *and* I'd also done my job for Pavel.

What can I say? Pantani was Pantani. He was a very reserved person who probably didn't have many friends, but he was fine. I'd known him for years, and I'd say I was quite friendly with him. I got on well with him but he wasn't someone who really confided in people. If he did, it was because he thought you were a person of value.

In 2000 he wasn't going like he had in 1994, 1995 or 1998, but then he'd stopped riding after Madonna di Campiglio. He was still decent, though, and he was getting stronger as the Giro went on. You knew there was a problem, but the really dramatic changes came later on …

I retired in 2004. I did six years training a junior team, but with globalization it's really hard for these kids to emerge. Only the absolute best of them are going to turn pro, and that means there will be progressively less Italians at the Giro.

When you think about how much it's changed and how *quickly* it's changed, it's incredible. I'm not one of those who are forever moaning that it was better back then, but it was certainly different. I suppose it's just a reflection of a totally different world. When I won the Giro with Paolo Savoldelli in 2002, the sponsor was from Bergamo, the staff were from Bergamo, and half of the riders were from Bergamo. I'm not talking about Italy, or even about Lombardy; I'm talking about thirty or so professionals in the province of Bergamo *alone*.

So I'd ridden for Mapei, the best team in the world, for six years. We were the Team Sky of the time, but I only won the Giro with bloody Index-Alexia! If I'm honest, I wasn't much help to Paolo at that Giro. Why? Ha! Good question!

Let's just say riding for Index was quite … *challenging*.

The 2000 Giro saw 179 starters, of whom 87 were Italian. Of the twenty teams, twelve featured an Italian company as title sponsor. By 2016, there were three Italian main sponsors, only one of which (Lampre) was operating in the World Tour. Of the 198 participants who rolled out of the Dutch city of Apeldoorn, only 53 were Italian. The figure has been stable at around 25 per cent of the peloton for some years now, but with Lampre's departure there are no Italian title sponsors in the top division. By the time the Chinese takeover of the team was announced, 'Beppe Saronni's outfit stood fifteenth in the UCI rankings. They had more Twitter followers in the UK than in Italy.

Perugia on the eve of the 1995 Giro. Paolo Lanfranchi is in the centre.

GIROTAPPA 17

ALTRE STORIE
DEI GREGARI

(MORE STORIES FROM THE *GREGARI*)

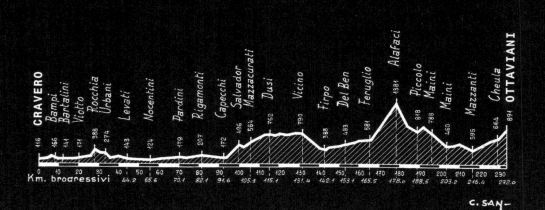

I didn't turned pro till I was twenty-six. By then I'd stopped cycling a few times, started again … I wasn't particularly talented, and I had quite a complicated relationship with cycling. At the end of the day it's a sickness, and I've never quite been able to shake it off.

CRAVERO MATTEO

Sanson

ha creato il gelato che soddisfa ogni palato

I signed for Sanson, and our captain was Gianni Motta. There were thirteen of us on the team, but only ten spots for the Giro. I was just starting out and I wasn't guaranteed a spot, but I finished tenth at the Tour of Tuscany and then fourth at the Tour of Romagna. I think it surprised them a bit, so when Motta cried off a few days before the start, I was in …

What I most remember about the race itself is the fact that Eddy Merckx just seemed to be everywhere. He won the time trials, he won the sprints, and he always seemed to be first over the top of the climbs. On the stage to Terracina, he did something I'd never seen before and never saw again. It was extremely windy, but Merckx just jumped out of the echelon and rode away. He won the stage on his own, and I couldn't really get my head around it. A normal human being wouldn't have attempted that, because objectively it was a sure-fire way to lose the stage. That was just Merckx I guess …

It was so windy that the temporary stand collapsed. A little boy was playing under it, and he died. It was a terrible moment for all of us, and I remember how upset Eddy was. I remember because it made me think that he was flesh and blood just like the rest of us.

How do I remember Savona? Like when a bomb goes off!

I went to the roll-out, but as we were starting to sign on someone said, "Merckx is positive!" After that it was just total confusion. You had Roberto Poggiali, who was a sort of shop steward, and then Rudi Altig was jumping up and down telling anyone who'd listen that we should all strike. I started to worry because it was my first Giro and I was determined to finish it at any price.

Merckx had stayed at a hotel in Albisola, just along the coast. A delegation went off there, although I don't know what was said. Anyway, Merckx was out and Felice Gimondi refused to wear the *maglia rosa*. Before we set off, the group decided they'd ride the stage as tourists, as some sort of statement of solidarity with Eddy. Of course, the tourist idea didn't materialize. After a while it was hell for leather as usual …

I finished the Giro twenty-second, which wasn't bad for my first attempt. At the end of the season, Sanson folded and I signed for Zonca. They didn't get a ride at the Giro, so I decided to retire.

In retrospect, my problem was that I never really had an objective. I fancied turning professional and riding the Giro, but beyond that I wasn't particularly ambitious. I wasn't one of those who was going to become some sort of *gregario di lusso*, and if I'm honest I probably wasn't good enough to do anything much on my own.

There are all sorts of theories about Merckx's expulsion, but most seem to discount the idea that he doped. The consensus seems to be that he wouldn't have needed stimulants for a meaningless transition stage, and that there were darker forces at play. We'll probably never know, but the notion that he alone was positive amid a 130-man peloton is ludicrous. The chances are that someone, somewhere, tampered with his sample.

Some have made reference to a mysterious Spanish soigneur working for Merckx's Faema team. Legend has it that this soigneur vanished, never to be seen again, immediately after the "Savona affair". Others suggest that Rudi Altig had offered Merckx a suitcase full of cash on behalf of Felice Gimondi's Salvarani team, but that Merckx had declined. Some say his bidon was spiked, and so on ad infinitum.

Matteo Cravero was much better than he'd have us believe. Like many small-town former professionals, he went on to open a bike shop. In 1996 his brother, Paolo, died of a heart attack while out on his bike.

Teofilo Sanson made ice cream. He was crazy for cycling.

REMO ROCCHIA
A WORLD OF HIS OWN
SAN GIACOMO
DI ROBURENT, 1977

I started my second season well. On the first stage of Tirreno–Adriatico, five of us escaped: Saronni, Moser, De Vlaeminck, Alfio Vandi and me. So I was fifth heading into the final time trial, but I was a pure climber. I lost two minutes in eighteen kilometres, and finished tenth overall. My captain was Franco Bitossi, and he said, "You've got the mentality of a true champion, Rocchia, but not quite the body of one ..."

I was supposed to ride for Bitossi, but my instinct was to attack and I never learned to curb it. I didn't have the head for tactics, teamwork, all that stuff. I'd have made a hopeless *gregario*, as I think I demonstrated on the Giro stage to San Giacomo di Roburent.

It was a summit finish just up the road from where I live, and suddenly there were hundreds of people cheering for me. My name was written all over the road, so as soon as we hit the bottom of the climb I attacked. The problem was that I managed to drag about twenty others along, and Bitossi wasn't one of them. I pulled all the way up the climb, then blew up two kilometres from the top. I finished fifteenth, and at the end of the stage the rest of the *gregari* were livid. They were saying, "You're supposed to be riding for Bitossi, you bloody imbecile!"

They were absolutely right, but, if I'm honest, Bitossi had been the last thing on my mind when I'd seen all those people cheering for me. It was supposed to be "all for one", and I'd

ridden it that way. The problem was that Bitossi was supposed to have been the one, not me …

It didn't matter that Bitossi was past his best, because it was a different kind of cycling. Nowadays, lots of guys are capable of winning, but in our day the system was almost feudal. The leaders were the symbols of their teams, and the thinking was that they generated the money that sustained the sport. The public was conditioned to the idea that one of them would win, and the whole business was structured around that. Bitossi was a nice guy, but he knew he didn't have the legs anymore. The problem was the rest of the guys in the team, because as far as they were concerned I'd got too big for my boots. I'd upset the natural order, and they weren't having that.

Anyway, I caught bronchitis just before we reached the Dolomites, and that did for me. I was twenty-third, but had I not got sick I'd have been in the top fifteen.

The following year, 1978, the captain was Roberto Visentini, and he wasn't terribly diplomatic. We were getting towards the top of a climb, and it was raining. Visentini said, "Rocchia, go and get me a cape!" so I put my arm up and waited for the team car. I took a cape for Visentini and one for me, and started trying to get back to the front. That's not easy at the Giro, believe me, but I reached Visentini about a kilometre from the summit. Then he just started hurling abuse at me. He said, "I wanted a red cape, for fuck's sake! Why didn't you get me the red one?" I said to him, "My dear Roberto, it looks like you'll be riding this particular descent without any cape at all." I put mine on, but he rode the descent without one. So much for trying to be a good *gregario* …

Ten days before the 1979 Giro I crashed at Trentino. I damaged my knee, and that meant I didn't get to race. That was a problem because the contracts were sorted out at the Giro and I hadn't had particularly good results beforehand. I'd also married by then, and my wife wasn't keen on my being away all the time. I stopped at the end of the season.

All told, I did four years and rode the Giro twice. I stopped aged twenty-eight, and I've regretted it ever since. I'm still convinced I had a lot more to give …

Remo Rocchia's attack on the climb to San Giacomo di Roburent was lost amid the fall-out from the first doping scandal of the race. Debutant Annunzio Colombo had been positive nine days earlier, at Isernia, and the results had just come back. Colombo was relegated to last place on the stage, penalized 10 minutes on GC and given a suspended one-month ban. That was all entirely academic, but not so the fine. In 1977, 1,000 Swiss francs equated to about 350,000 lire, two months' wages for an Italian factory worker. Ten days on, the results came back from the San Giacomo di Ruberent stage. It transpired that Spain's Miguel María Lasa, the stage winner on the road, had also been positive …

Having won seven of the opening ten stages, the Flemish race leader Freddy Maertens crashed out. His team (and, by extension, Belgian TV) was persuaded to stay in the race by race director Vincenzo Torriani, but the consequences for the Giro would be disastrous. One of Maertens's domestiques, Michel Pollentier, profited from the caustic rivalry between Francesco Moser and Gianbattista Baronchelli, and ran away with the pink jersey. Porca di una miseria …

VIRGILIO LEVATI
ONE DAY AT A TIME
SCANNO, 1969

I'd won a lot as an amateur. The longest stage of the Peace Race in Lublin, the amateur Tour of Lombardy, Milan–Asti, a stage of the Tour of Piedmont …

I had the chance to ride for Gianni Motta at Sanson, but I turned it down. Three of us had ridden together as amateurs, and we wanted to stay together. So we spoke to this new team, Sagit, and they told us that Pierino Baffi was going to be the DS. That was great, because he knew cycling inside out and he'd do anything for his riders. So we signed on, but then after the first *ritiro* he didn't appear anymore.

They hadn't kept their word, and instead of Baffi we finished up with a guy named Ludovico Lissoni. He worked as a rep for the sponsor, but he knew nothing about cycling.

I didn't find the transition from amateur to pro physically hard, but we needed help as a team and there wasn't any. We had the cheapest bikes, only one *soigneur* and one mechanic. I pretty much looked after my own bike, and we'd this idiot for a DS. No wonder that first Giro was such a shambles …

Ten of us set off from Lake Garda. We lost Carniel after a few days, but then Franco Cortinovis won the stage at Viterbo. That night at dinner, he asked the waiter for an extra piece of cheese, and Lissoni went mad. He said, "Is that the way you behave at your house? When you've finished eating, do you start demanding extra cheese?"

Cortinovis had been Italian amateur champion, and he was the best I'd ever ridden with. He had immense class on a bike, and he'd just won a stage at the Giro for Sagit, the smallest team in the race. He'd simply fancied an extra slice of cheese, but Lissoni felt like he needed to demonstrate that he was the boss by humiliating him. It was astonishing.

The following day, Gabriele Gazzetta crashed and had to be taken to hospital, and then the temporary stand collapsed at Terracina. Carminati finished at the bottom of it and he ended up in hospital as well. So we had a DS who was worse than useless, and one way or another we'd lost three by the end of the first week. That wasn't good, but it was about to get much worse …

The stage to Scanno – I think it was stage 11 or 12 – was terrible. It was only 165 kilometres, but it was up and down all day in ferocious heat. It was one of the hardest days I've ever had on the bike, and I think there were sixty riders over the time limit. They revised the limit, but Donghi and Belasso didn't make it.

The heat was terrible that year, but Baffi had always told me never to take water from a mountain spring. So I'd managed to resist, but then after the stage the rest of the team started coming down with dysentery. I went to see Lissoni but he just said, "What am I supposed to do about it?" I told him to find a pharmacy or at least go and see the Giro's doctor. He wouldn't go, however, and the following morning Cortinovis was too ill to start. Palazzi and Vanzin climbed off during the stage, so that just left me and Oliviero Morotti. With twelve stages still to go …

Ten feet tall ... Levati has won, Dad's pleased as punch.

CARMINATI   CORTINOVIS   BALASSO   DONGHI   PALAZZI   MOROTTI   LISSONI D. S.

INDUSTRIA CONFEZIONI

20050 **TREGASIO** DI **TRIUGGIO** (MILANO)

TELEFONO 30.172

Thankfully, we both made it round, and I got round again the following year. In 1971 I signed with Motta and Gimondi at Salvarani, and I won the Coppa Bernocchi. I rode the Tour that year, but then I made a mistake and went to Zonca. I did a season there, but I'd started to suffer with a stomach ulcer. I was struggling to digest my food, and I was in real agony. Eventually, the doctor told me I ought to stop. With my condition, it was just too stressful, and it was clear that I was half the rider I should have been …

Nine of the ten riders who started the 1969 Giro for Sagit were first-year professionals. All had obviously been outstanding amateurs, but collectively and individually their stories illustrate just how hard it was for a young Italian to make a career from cycling during the Eddy Merckx era.

At the end of the 1969 season, the gifted Franco Cortinovis moved to Ferretti, a much wealthier team. Antonio Carniel found a place at GBC, while Gabriele Gazzetta retired. The other six stayed put, but with Italian cycling contracting, teams were able to get much more rider for the same money. The original intake found rides increasingly difficult to come by, and at the conclusion of the 1970 season Sagit pulled the plug. The sport called time on Carniel and Cortinovis as well, and when the dust settled, only two of Sagit's ill-fated Giro team remained in professional cycling. Virgilio and Oliviero Morotti, the two who got round, would each ride a total of four years, but they too would be out of the sport before their twenty-ninth birthdays.

Virgilio still rides three times a week.

FLORIDO BARALE
A FAMILY AFFAIR
THE ABRUZZO, 1990

So I got a contract with Amore & Vita, but when I went for the tests they said I'd a problem with my heart. Apparently, I went tachycardic, and they wouldn't issue me the certificate I needed to get my racing licence. In fact, it was even worse because they issued a certificate stating that I *couldn't* race, as opposed to just not issuing one at all.

I was mortified. My dad and my uncle had both been professional cyclists, so emulating them was all I'd ever wanted to do. We come from a small town, Domodossola, and obviously they all followed me. As a cyclist in Italy, you become a bit of a local hero, don't you?

You know what it's like in Italy – you have to find ways to get around the bureaucracy. The third guy I went to, over in Imola … well, let's just say that he failed to notice any anomalies with my heart. So I had my licence a week before the Tour of Trentino, and finally I got to do my first professional race. I finished it somewhere in the middle, then set off down to Bari for my first Giro.

So now I'm there and they put me in a room with Pierino Gavazzi. He's thirty-nine and I'm twenty-one, and he'd been riding professionally when I was three years old. He's been Italian champion, he's won Milan–San Remo and goodness knows how many stages at the Giro. He's been one hell of a bike rider, and he doesn't give an inch. I'm expected to help him, but he's not helping *me* at all. It's my first time and I'm doing my best, but there's no encouragement, no advice, no conversation and no nothing. You know when you're young and insecure and you're just finding your way? Just an ounce of human kindness can make a world of difference, but there's none of that, not a crumb. I'm talkative anyway, as you know, but he's not having any of it. Grumpy old sod …

We're on a climb in the Apennines, and I'm really doing my best. I'm concentrating really hard and I think I'm doing all right, but then Gavazzi starts at me. He's going, "You youngsters, what are you doing at the front?" as if I've broken some sort of rule. I've had enough at this point, and I snap. I'm like, "Fuck! I've only been riding for a month and I'm turning myself inside out trying to do my best!" Now all of a sudden there's this terrible, deathly hush in the group – total silence.

Then, after a while, Gianni Bugno comes up to me in his *maglia rosa*. He says, "Don't worry about him. I had him when I started and he was exactly the same with me …"

So you know it's those little things. Gianni would probably never remember something like that, and I very much doubt whether Gavazzi would either. Those two were champions, but for me, just starting out aged twenty-one, what he said was a godsend.

I got round, and then afterwards I finished fourth in a stage at Midi Libre. That was the closest I ever got. I rode the Giro again the following year, and we did Mortirolo again, only this time from the harder side. The climb I'll always remember, though, is the Fedaia. I was really, really suffering. My dad was up there and he started giving me a push. I had to tell him to stop, however, because I was starting to worry about his health. He'd put a bit of weight on, and he was suffering more than I was!

Gregorio di lusso Germano Barale with his son, Florido.

I didn't get any offers for 1992, and in that sense I was probably lucky. Cycling was changing, and with my heart I'm pretty sure I'd have been at major risk. While I was sleeping, my heart rate was 34, and I knew that sooner or later I would have had to choose. Some might say that people like me were just making up the numbers, but I can assure you there were some seriously good riders making up the numbers.

I think I did OK given my possibilities, and I also made my dad proud. I tried it, and the good thing is I was young enough to start a real job when it finished …

Florido did two years as a professional, so he was out of the sport before Pierino Gavazzi. Although his career was brief and, on the face of it, not particularly notable, riders like him were the overwhelming majority. In one crucial respect he was lucky. Although he doesn't pretend to have been a paragon of virtue, he says he was already seeing incredible performances in 1991. He was at the bottom of the food chain economically, and he left cycling just as EPO use started to proliferate in Italy. Elsewhere, Joachim Halupczok, the immensely talented Pole who debuted with him at the 1990 Giro, died of a heart attack in 1994.

Florido runs a bike shop in Domodossola. His father, Germano, was a legendary gregario who won the 1962 Giro with Franco Balmamion; his daughter Francesca won the 2016 Italian National Championships for debutants aged thirteen.

I was twenty-one, a first-year professional full of ambition. The team I was riding for was new, and the best we could do was to get in the breakaways. We were hoping one would stick, but none of them did.

On the final Thursday there was a short, flat transition stage before the Alps. It finished south of Milan, and it was our last chance. It looked like a nailed-on bunch sprint, but I wanted to try because you never know. I was reasonably quick, and I figured I might be able to win a sprint out of a small group.

At a certain point the group was dawdling, so I shoved it into the 53 x 12 and took off on the right-hand side of the road. The problem was that the sprinters' teams reacted, so I only ever got about three hundred metres and they soon caught me. Oh well …

A bit later on, Bernard Hinault, who was *maglia rosa*, came up and grabbed hold of my jersey. He started gesticulating and hurling insults at me, threatening to hit me. Hinault was a champion, but I was young and full of testosterone and I wasn't having it so I told him to go to hell. He'd been my idol, but he was totally out of order treating me like that. I was a rookie, but everyone has to start somewhere, and I had as much right as anybody else to try to win a stage.

When I got back to the hotel, the team manager told me that if I didn't apologize to Hinault, I'd be sent home. I told him that Hinault ought to be apologizing to *me*, and went up to my room. Then, a little later, Pieroni, my DS, knocked on the door and explained what had happened …

Unbeknown to me, Hinault had stopped for a call of nature at precisely the moment I'd attacked. His lead at that point was only about a minute and a half, and Bianchi had Silvano Contini, Tommy Prim and Tista Baronchelli in second, third and fourth places on GC. When I'd gone, the sprinters' teams had gone to the front to drag me back, and the speed had gone through the roof. As a consequence, Hinault had been left behind, and Contini had become virtual *maglia rosa*. Through no fault of his own, Hinault had been in danger of losing the Giro, and Renault had been forced to ride a team time trial to get him back on.

Of course, I hadn't known Hinault was off his bike, and if I had I'd never have attacked. Equally, he didn't know that I hadn't known, and had assumed I'd attacked while he was having a pee because I was a wanker. As a consequence, when finally he'd got back on, he'd been livid. Guimard, his DS, had heard on the race radio that a certain Salvador had caused the mayhem, and Hinault had gone to Moser wanting to know who I was.

It was all clear to me now, and I felt terrible. I told Pieroni I'd apologize the following morning at the sign-on, but when I went down for dinner nobody spoke to me and the table

was like a morgue. Cycling was hierarchical, I'd pissed off the best rider in the world, and they were worried about the consequences for our team.

So the following morning we went to the *partenza*. The plan was that I'd sign on, then wait for Hinault and explain what had happened and beg his forgiveness. I signed on, and just as I was leaving the stage Hinault appeared and called me over. He took me to one side and I was thinking, "Here we go. He's going to humiliate me in front of all these people."

He looked me in the eye and said, "Listen, I was really nervous yesterday, but that's no excuse. The way I behaved was terrible, so I just wanted to say that I'm sorry."

Bernard Hinault. What a man …

Earlier in the stage, Bernard Becaas, one of Hinault's domestiques, had been rushed to hospital with a suspected skull fracture. A woman had tried to cross the road on a scooter, and Becaas had been unable to avoid her. In the event, he was fine, but it's little wonder that Hinault was stressed.

Two days later, the Giro repeated Fausto Coppi's 1949 odyssey from Cuneo to Pinerolo. Hinault was one against Bianchi's three, but they never looked remotely like unseating him. The following day, he flew round the time trial in Turin to clinch the second of his three giri.

In 1987, Ennio Salvador attacked on the road to Sappada. It had dramatic consequences, with Ireland's Stephen Roche ripping the jersey away from teammate Roberto Visentini. Ennio never won a Giro stage, but he finished each of the eight editions he started.

I didn't want to be a cyclist.

When I was a kid I was a good skier, but I broke my ankle. They put me in plaster, but when they took it off the ankle hadn't set properly. So they broke it again, straightened it up and left me in plaster for three months. When they took the plaster off, they said I should start riding a bike for twenty to thirty kilometres each day, but with toe-clips. The idea was that the toe-clips would keep the ankle straight, and the muscle would reform around it.

I wasn't interested, but my dad got me a "sports" bike from Pinarello, and I starting riding with some of the skiers who rode to keep fit during the summer. When we reached the climbs I tended to drop them, and they said I should race. I didn't like cycling, though; I liked motocross. In fact, I was working in a body shop, doing lots of overtime so that I could buy the bits I needed to build my own 'cross bike. I'd have been fifteen …

I got home from work one night and there were three blokes from the cycling club in the living room. They said they wanted me to join the club and that they'd sort the bike and the jersey out. They said all I needed were the shoes and a helmet, and I had to ride anyway because of the ankle.

They'd just asphalted the road I lived on, and installed some streetlights. I started going up and down the road as fast as I could, and I did that all through the winter. Five kilometres out, five kilometres back. Out and back, out and back, out and back …

The first race was in March, a criterium. There was a big pile-up in front of me, and it scared me. I didn't like it, so straight after the race I took the jersey and the bike and gave them back. I said, "Sorry, but this isn't for me," but they insisted I try again. They said, "Don't worry, because next week it's an uphill finish so it will be much safer." They persuaded me to give it one more go.

So at the next race I was always at the back, trying to stay out of trouble, but then we hit the finishing climb. It would have been two or three kilometres, no more, but I just started overtaking the others. There were lots of people there cheering, and I actually enjoyed it. By the time I reached the finish I was fourth, and people started giving me money! Five hundred lire here, a thousand lire there … I couldn't believe it! I was thinking, "Right, now I can buy a fork for the 'cross bike, now I can afford new tyres …"

The penultimate stage of the 1979 Giro was 250 kilometres. It started in Trento, then over the Tonale and Aprica, finishing with a climb up to Barzio. It was one of those that started at 7.30 in the morning, and Moser came up to me at the start. He said, "Hey, Bruno! There's a *prime* of 500,000 lire for the first to pass my bike shop."

I knew he'd just opened a new shop on the edge of town, and I reckoned it was only about a kilometre. I thought I may as well try, so I attacked straight away, and when I looked round nobody else had moved. Problem was that when I reached Moser's shop, there was nobody there. I thought he must have been playing a joke on me, but then I remembered that he'd another bike shop ten kilometres up the road at San Michele all'Adige.

So I decided to keep going, just in case he'd meant that one, but there were no judges there either. It had been a wind-up, but I thought I may as well keep going and try to get some publicity. I assumed they'd catch me on the Tonale, but my lead just kept getting bigger and bigger.

At a certain point I had 21 minutes, but then one of the motorbikes came up. The guy said, "I've been told by Panizza that you have to stop". Wladi' Panizza was riding for Moser's team, and they'd had enough because each minute I spent out front was a minute less publicity for them. They'd sent me on a wild goose chase for a non-existent *prime*, but now the joke was on them and they weren't happy about it. I said to the guy, "Go back and tell Panizza that if he wants me to stop, he'd better come and tell me himself."

I was starting to believe I might make it, but then a storm came. There was a terrible headwind and hailstones, and I started to suffer really badly. Meanwhile, they were forming echelons, and by the time they got to where the storm had been it had passed over. Gradually, the lead started coming down, and they caught me 12 kilometres from the finish.

I think it's one of the longest lone breaks in the history of the race, though …

Bruno Vicino was a better track rider than roadie. He was a stayer (he won the motor-paced world championships three times) and featured regularly on the six-day circuit. He rode his first Giro in 1975, as part of Fausto Bertoglio's race-winning Jolly Ceramica team. At the bottom of the Stelvio, he saw a friend with a transistor radio, swiped it, and rode up with it glued to his ear. He thus joined millions of other Italians in hearing on the radio Bertoglio's epic duel with Paco Galdós. Race director Vincenzo Torriani wasn't best pleased, but Bruno always was his own man.

Bruno retired from racing in 1987, and has worked as a sports director ever since. He was with Saeco for eight years, and when we met he'd just concluded his twelfth season with Lampre. He quite likes cycling now, but motor sport remains his great passion. He drives an Alpine A110, and competes regularly in historic events.

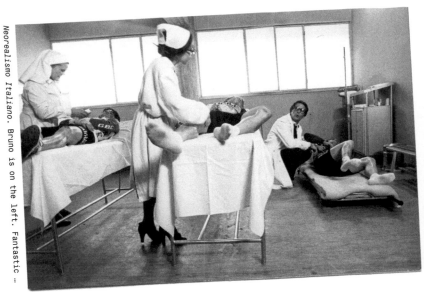

Neorealismo Italiano. Bruno is on the left. Fantastic …

I was only twenty. I was lucky because I didn't know anything and nothing was expected of me, and of course at that age you've no fear. I'd to fetch bottles and do whatever I could for the leaders, but for the most part I just had to ride my bike each day and go as far as I could. It was a bit of an adventure …

I probably had really bad moments along the way, but I didn't have any psychological baggage so I just assumed it was normal. I just got on with it, and one way or another I got round.

They had this idea to recreate the old "Gran Fondo" and use it as an epilogue to the Giro. It was 660 kilometres from Milan to Rome, and you had to sign in at various points along the way. It was an old concept from the heroic era, but riding through the night was a complete novelty for us. None of us had ever attempted it before.

The organizers' intention had been for all the stars of the Giro to take part, but they let the teams decide. In the end, none of the champions signed on, so what was left was the mass of riders, the ordinary ones. We were on our normal bikes, but the road was illuminated by the race vehicles and all the bikes were covered in these high-visibility strips. We set off at nine o'clock, and thankfully the weather was good. We weren't belting along, but nor was it just a dawdle. I think people wanted to get stuck in, and there were big prizes for anyone who got in a break.

You know that in cycling there's the tradition of letting the local rider go ahead to greet his nearest and dearest? I'm from Bologna, so as we entered the city limits I rode off the front to meet my mum and dad, my girlfriend and all my mates. It would have been two or three o'clock in the morning, something like that, and they sent a car to light my way.

So everyone was waiting by the side of the road, but as I slowed down to stop, the following car ran straight into me from behind. I was almost at a standstill when it hit me, but I landed right on my sacrum and it hurt like hell. Everyone had been ready to congratulate me on finishing my first Giro d'Italia, but instead they ended up lifting me off the floor. I tried to carry on but it was hopeless. I ended up in hospital having an X-ray on my backside …

I rode the Giro eight times, and I won a stage out of the break in 1985. I won a stage at the Vuelta as well, but I never rode the Tour de France. I've done lots of them as a DS, but the Giro is a much more interesting race. You have more interesting stages, the route is less formulaic, and you don't generally have one team controlling everything. Then the weather is far less predictable than at the Tour or the Vuelta, so all things considered there's just a lot more going on. It's not as big as the Tour, but as a bike race there's no question that it's superior.

Necessity is the mother of cycling invention, and the Gran Fondo d'Italia was a case in point. Following Eddy Merckx's dominion and wins for

The madness of the Gran Fondo d'Italia. For Orlando Maini, the end is nigh …

Michel Pollentier and Johan De Muynck, interest in the Giro was waning. As such, the Gran Fondo was conceived to recapture the imagination of the Italian public. Fiat was launching a new hatchback, the Ritmo, and forty of them were fitted with special headlamps to light the way for the riders. All told, the purse — 85 million lire — amounted to more than half that of the Giro itself. Sadly, though, it didn't work. The big stars wanted nothing to do with it, none of the top ten participated, and only fifty-nine set out from Milan. They were enthusiastically greeted until the pubs and clubs closed, but that was your lot.

Of the forty-one who made it to Rome's (deserted) Olympic stadium nineteen hours later, the fastest was a twenty-two-year-old named Sergio Santimaria. "Who's he?" you ask. Precisely.

ANGELO OTTAVIANI
BREAKING THE CHAIN
PASSO DEL SEMPIONE, 1965

On the big stage to Saas Fee in 1965, I was supposed to stay with our leader, Graziano Battistini. I felt really good, though, and I wanted to try. So I spoke with the DS, but he wasn't having it because he didn't know anything about cycling. I spoke to Battistini instead, and he said it was up to me. In the end, I just thought, "Bollocks to it!" and went …

I was getting stronger all the time, and I knew that a mountain-stage win at the Giro would have changed everything. If you pulled something like that off, the teams would come looking for you as opposed to the other way round. By the same token, if you go against team orders and fail, everyone knows about it, and they all remember it. Everybody is looking out for his own interests, and everything in the peloton is balanced in a certain way. That balance is very delicate, and if you set out to upset it you need to be pretty sure you're strong enough to pull it off.

Adorni and Zilioli caught me near the top. Then Balmamion, Marcello Mugnaini, Bitossi and Battistini got back on the descent. I finished seventh.

The other stage was Rocco di Cambio, the following year. I was away with Schiavon and Rudi Altig, guaranteed a podium, and they stopped me five kilometres from the finish because Vito Taccone, our leader, ordered it. I didn't know it then, but that was the beginning of the end …

I came out of that Giro well, and we went to the Tour of Switzerland. It was a wealthy race, which is why the Italian teams preferred it to the Tour de France. Each day there was an intermediate sprint and the winner got a car, a Renault. We earned a lot of money and our leader, Ambrogio Portalupi, won the GC. That was largely because of me – I was climbing like never before – and after the race Luciano Pezzi came up to me in Zurich. He was the sports director of Salvarani, the most powerful team in Italy. He offered me a contract for the following season, 400,000 lire. That was four times what I was earning at Vitadello, but I had some of my best friends in that team and I was very close to Battistini, who'd been runner-up at the Tour. My preference was to stay with him, so that evening I said, "Look, I have an offer from Salvarani, but if you can match it I'll stay here." The owner of Vitadello said, "Listen, Ottaviani, we want you with us, so we'll match it."

Then, after Lombardy, they put a contract in front of me for 100,000 lire. I said, "What's this? We agreed 400,000 in Zurich!" They just said take it or leave it, because they knew it was

too late to go elsewhere. I said, "Listen, I may be poor and ignorant, but at least I'm an honest man." I didn't sign it, and that was me done.

Jacques Anquetil was an absolute gentleman. He always said to me, "Angelo, you're a great climber. You've got the ability, just not the head." He was right because I'd forget to eat, go at the wrong moment, make all sorts of silly mistakes …

Anyway, this particular stage finished in Pesaro, and I punctured 40 kilometres from the finish. Nobody waits for a *gregario*, especially 40 kilometres from the stage finish. However, as chance would have it, Jacques punctured as well, and obviously his team stopped to get him back on. So I got back on as well, and then he and I were chatting together in the *gruppo*. At a certain point, one of his *gregari* appeared, Pierre Everaert I think it was. He had a fresh bottle and he gave it to Jacques. Instead of drinking it, though, he offered it to me first. He said, "Drink, Angelo! Drink!"

Sadly, Angelo passed away in July 2016, a few days after our interview.

He turned pro in 1963, and in riding his debut Giro unwittingly contributed to a pivotal moment in cycling history. The race heralded the beginning of live TV coverage, and also of the mythical Il Processo alla Tappa *post-stage show. It was expertly hosted by the great Sergio Zavoli, which was just as well, given cycling's manifest limitations as a live TV sport …*

There were no moving cameras, just fixed ones at the finish of each stage, and you couldn't know when the riders would appear, and thus when the two-minute thrill would occur. As such, advertisers were uncomfortable, and scheduling on Italy's one TV channel was a lottery. Then most of the sport's core constituents, Italian blue-collar workers, were still at work. Meanwhile, such stadium sports as football took place at the weekends and in the evenings, and had clearly defined start and finish times.

So while football (partisan, uncomplicated, absolute) benefited hugely from the new god television, the sport of cycling was always going to be the big loser.

GIROTAPPA 18
DIETRO LE QUINTE
(BEHIND THE SCENES)

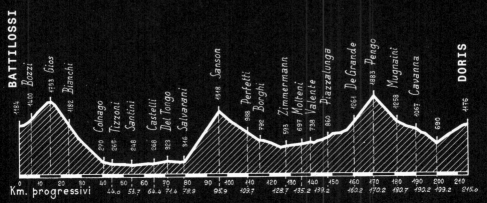

BATTILOSSI

Bozzi 1184
Gios 1153
Bianchi 1182
Colnago 290
Tizzoni 265
Santini 248
Castelli 268
Del Tongo 323
Salvarani 316
Sanson 1518
Perfetti 988
Borghi 792
Zimmermann 593
Molteni 697
Valente 738
Piazzalunga 860
De Grande 1261
Pengo 1883
Mugnaini 1258
Cavanna 1067
690
DORIS 1176

Km. progressivi

0 10 20 30 40 50 60 70 80 90 100 110 120 130 140 150 160 170 180 190 200 210

44.0 53.7 64.4 71.4 78.9 95.9 109.7 128.7 135.2 139.2 160.2 170.2 180.7 190.2 199.2 215.0

C. SAN-

My dad was a shoemaker, and when I was eleven or twelve he said, "What are we going to do? Your schoolwork's not up to much so you should probably go off and learn the trade."

This would have been just after the war, 1945 or 1946. I went off and started my apprenticeship, but I wasn't paid for the first two or three years. In fact, when you learn the job, you ruin a lot of shoes. So if I destroyed a sole because the knife slipped, or whatever, I'd take it to my dad and he'd have to replace it …

So I became a shoemaker, but also a cyclist. I used to follow the races, and I became friends with all the champions from Turin. They used to get their shoes from down in Tuscany, and one of them – I think it was Nino Defilippis – asked me why I didn't try making cycling shoes. So that's what I did.

I remember setting off down to Genoa with a pair for Gianni Motta to try. He was heading off to the Tour of Sardinia on the ferry, and he said he'd try them. I set off in my little Fiat 500 – it was on tick – and I remember thinking that if he didn't buy them I'd be struggling to get home because I'd no money and only half a tank of petrol. Anyway, pretty soon I was making them for all the big champions: Merckx, Maertens, Van Impe, Sercu, De Vlaeminck, Thurau, Contini, Baronchelli …

Most had contracts with Adidas, Colnago, Puma and suchlike, so I had to apply their branding to my shoes. I remember Colnago complaining about the price of the shoes I made for Maertens. They cost three or four times more than a normal pair, but they were handmade with the best materials. I remember thinking, "Yes, but how many of your mass-produced shoes are you going to sell off the back of my work?" To be honest, I was hopeless commercially. My brother was wealthy, but I never understood the value of what I did. I was good at making shoes and hopeless at making money. I don't mind, though, because cycling has been my life and I've had a great life.

The Giro? Well, the 1962 race finished on 9 June and I was married on 10 June. Does that answer your question?

I did it five times on a motorbike. I used to pilot a young journalist, Beppe Conti. This particular stage finished in a sprint, and I remember it well because the whole thing was a shambles. Van Linden won, but Sercu crashed into a camera operator fifty metres after the finishing line. He ended up in hospital, the riders threatened to go on strike, the usual Giro chaos …

At the time, I was making shoes for a lot of the riders, so I suppose I was quite well known. Given that the stage was local to where I lived, they asked me to go on to the stage for an interview with Adriano De Zan, the guy from RAI. I'd done it once or twice before, people seemed to like it, and I must admit I rather enjoyed it.

My workshop was a meeting point for cyclists. One morning shortly after the Giro, the phone rang and it was a woman from RAI. She seen my interview and they'd been impressed. She said they were interested in understanding the world of the artisan shoemaker, and they wanted to come to the shop and do a story about me. She said they'd get everything organized, and come back to me a few days beforehand to confirm everything.

You have to understand that being on TV was a really big thing back then, and even more so for someone like me. I'd grown up in Italy in the fifties, and the telly was quite a mystical thing for my generation. Today, there are hundreds of channels, but back then there were only two. Of course, everyone started pulling my leg about my new career as a TV personality, but eventually it was decided that it would be best to smarten the place up before the cameras came.

So I set about making everything look presentable. I scrubbed my workshop clean, tidied up and gave the place a lick of paint ready for my big day. I waited and waited, and everyone kept on asking me when RAI were coming. That woman never called back, though, and everyone seemed to find it hilarious …

Cycling's artisan traditions are in decline, but once upon a time they were central to the professional sport. The likes of Riccardo Battilossi and Luigi Colombini made beautiful shoes, while others produced wheels, bar tape, track mitts, saddles, brake levers …

A small army of framebuilders prepared the bikes on which the Giro was won and lost. During the 1970s and 1980s in particular, appearances could be deceiving. Still today, Giro-winning bikes feature heavily in the museums and marketing campaigns of the businesses whose brand names they carry. As often as not they were made by terzisti (third-party manufacturers) and branded up according to the sponsors' needs. One legendary framebuilder claims to have built more than half the bikes used during the 1975 Giro.

Riccardo is a legend, but it would be a year before he realized that "the woman from RAI" was in fact the wife of one of his friends.

PRODUZIONE
GIOS
TORINO
ITALIA

BROOKLYN
LA GOMMA DEL PONTE

ALDO GIOS
EASY RIDER
MILAN FAIR, 1971

I'd seen *Easy Rider*, the film with Peter Fonda and Dennis Hopper, so I built a bike just like their Harley-Davidsons. It was a Chopper with two front forks, shock absorbers and headlights, and we took it to the bike fair in Milan.

The owner of Brooklyn chewing gum, Perfetti, came to our stand. He said he wanted a hundred of them to promote his chewing gum, and that was the beginning of it.

Perfetti was talking to Franco Cribiori about sponsoring his team. They were using frames from a guy in Milan at the time, but the timing was perfect. An artisan named Giuseppe Pelà had always built our road frames, but he was ready to retire. He had the Giamè brothers working for him, and they were phenomenal. We took them on, and they taught me how to build road frames.

So we became the supplier to Brooklyn. Then, at a certain point, they said, "Why don't you come on board as mechanic?" From there on in I was with them all the time, and I loved the work. How could I not love working with Roger De Vlaeminck, Patrick Sercu, Johan De Muynck and the like?

I lived among the riders and I designed and built their bikes, so obviously I was the person best able to maintain them. They were the best in the world, and it's no coincidence that we won more races than anyone else. We had the best bikes and the least mechanicals. Why did De Vlaeminck win so often? How did De Wolf win Milan–San Remo? He won it on the descent of the Poggio, because his bike was the best in the race …

The 1976 Giro? You can have no idea how much anguish it caused us. We lost the Giro by 19 seconds, having been the best in the race for three weeks. All I will say is that, had that final time trial been in Flanders – or anywhere else but Bergamo – De Muynck would have won that Giro and not Gimondi. You can read what you like into that.

After Brooklyn we sponsored Zodiac, IJsboerke, then Vermeer, Jolly, Kelme, Relax … We had some great riders, but at a certain point you have to walk away. I guess it just had nothing to do with me anymore.

We had to come to terms with a new reality. We'd supplied the best teams and the best riders, and won hundreds of races. Then it became apparent that there was no place for a family business like ours in the World Tour, and that was difficult given our history. Eventually, though, you have to decide. Do you want to be part of the circus, or do you want to retain your identity and your business?

There are no Italian frames in the Giro anymore, and, to be honest, I find

The long and the short of it. Otherwise known as Didi Thurau and Vicente Belda.

that sad. "Made in Italy" doesn't actually mean what it says, because the frames are all built elsewhere. You might find Italian names and Italian *design*, but not Italian frames. I think that's wrong, and I think it's a trick. Some years ago my brother and I split the business. I took the smaller part because I wanted to retain the history and integrity of the Gios name. How can I put my name on a bike that's made in Asia?

We probably make about three hundred bikes a year, but they're made by hand here, in Italy. They're made-to-measure, they are made to fit, you can't buy them online, and they work. They're bikes for life, and me and my son are the guarantors of that. So we're at peace with it, and we have no wish to "capitalize" the business as some have. We're tiny and maybe old-fashioned, and it's that which sustains us. The bikes we make really matter to the people who buy them.

Gios remains an iconic brand. It's synonymous with Roger De Vlaeminck's Brooklyn, and was once widely regarded as the best frame in the world. These days, the company founded by Tolmino Gios in 1948 exists outside of the professional cycling industry, but retains its artisan roots. While the artisan tradition still exists, pro cycling is carbon-centric, and driven overwhelmingly by matter-of-fact commercial imperative.

The likes of Willier, Pinarello and Bianchi still sponsor World Tour teams, and inform us that the frames they supply are conceived in Italy. That's as maybe, but economic expedience dictates that their "Italian heritage" is largely engineered in the Far East. The vast majority of the frames used in the Giro are made there, and so too the componentry.

BRUNO RAGONA
THE NEW CYCLING
TRENTO, 1979

I was Roger De Vlaeminck's masseur at Brooklyn for three years, but then he went back to Belgium and I started working for Francesco Moser. When he lost the 1979 Giro to 'Beppe Saronni, he was extremely upset. He said he was going to give up trying, but then he changed his mind. He couldn't countenance the idea of not winning it at least once during his career.

Moser met a Polish trainer named Andrzej Żmuda, and this guy was extremely smart. He spoke several languages, and he had really evolved ideas about sport. He was a sports psychologist, he understood aerodynamics and he had radical new ideas about training.

At the time, Hinault was using really big gears to climb. Moser couldn't match that, so Żmuda started to work on his agility instead. He had him skiing and playing tennis in the winter, mountaineering … Then he'd have him standing up on the pedals on the flat for ten minutes, then ten minutes recovery, then another ten minutes. The things they were doing were incredible, and only someone like Moser would have been capable of coping with them. Żmuda would have him sprinting in his smallest gear for 200 metres, then recovery, then time trials in a tunnel up there in Trentino. He shortened the winter break, all sorts of new ideas …

So Żmuda moved to Trento to work with Moser and he was important because he was the precursor to *preparatori* like Ferrari and Conconi. He understood how blood values affected performance, and in that sense he changed the direction of cycling. It was through him that Moser started to understand the importance of haemoglobin levels in the blood. By measuring Moser's haemoglobin, they were able to programme the way he rode. If it was low, Żmuda would say, "Today you don't want to be doing too much – don't waste energy." Then, if the level was good, Moser was able to make the race, and so on.

The problem was that Żmuda started to exert a lot of influence over Moser, and the sports directors didn't like that. They felt undermined by Żmuda because they were former cyclists who were used to deciding training programmes. Now you had this foreign guy coming along and their athlete was being guided by what he said. Żmuda didn't last long, but it was the beginning of a big change. I guess it culminated in the hour and Moser's Giro win in 1984.

There was always a bit of a tug of war around the great champions, because there was so much invested in them. Broadly speaking, you had the rider and his *soigneur* concerned with winning, and the doctor concerned with health. Then the managers were concerned with the finances and the well-being of the team, and so it went. As often as not, the riders didn't want the sports director or the doctor to know what they'd taken.

Why is it that an athlete can't use things a normal person can? The important thing is that they are given the chance to understand the medicine, are educated about it. Beyond that, it's up to them, and the best wins. If you want sport to succeed, you have to give them all the same tools, and that doesn't happen anymore. You can say, "Yes, but they die!" but they probably wouldn't if they were informed and knew what they were doing ... People die because they abuse drugs and alcohol all the time.

So the growth hormone, human chorionic gonadotropin ... That's a case in point about educating the riders. It's a hormone found in women's urine that stimulates the production of testosterone, and I saw things with that you wouldn't believe ...

Then in Belgium they'd prepare with hormones extracted from a monkey's kidney, and allied to iron injections it gave you an increase in red blood cells. So when I was in Belgium I had to find a way to get hold of that, because you can't just sit back and watch your rider lose.

All of this was the precursor to synthetic EPO, so it was obvious that when it came on the market everyone would use it. Just look at Armstrong ... It was inevitable, and the only people who were surprised were people who didn't know anything about cycling.

You did what you were paid to do, which was to help the riders do what they were paid

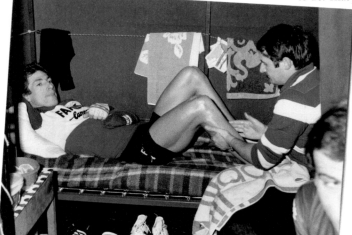

to do. That always was part of the sport, and part of the job of the *soigneur*. Another part was the ongoing quest to discover something more, something that gave them that little bit extra. That way, they could say, "This is my palmares, so now I deserve a pay rise ..."

Bruno did the Giro sixteen times between 1975 and 1992, and was employed by the biggest and best teams in Italy.

Following his time with De Vlaeminck and Moser, Bruno joined forces with Giancarlo Ferretti's Bianchi team, the one containing Tommy Prim, Silvano Contini and Tista Baronchelli. When that morphed into Sammontana (and later Gewiss-Bianchi and Ariostea), he worked extensively for the great classics champion Moreno Argentin.

Traditionally, the relationship between masseur and star rider tended to be quite intimate, simply because they spent so much time together. In addition to the races themselves, Bruno spent countless winter hours motor-pacing his charges, and also worked the six-day scene. In effect, wherever Argentin went, he went too.

SERGIO LEONE
THE COLD, HARD FACTS OF IT
BIELLA, 2016

The wider public sees a bike race, but for a town like ours it's much more than that …

This was always a textile town, and it was built around the wool industry. Everything was geared around it, and for decades it drove the local economy. For decades, nobody really considered the post-industrial reality, but then suddenly it was upon us. In 2005 the Multi Fibre Arrangement expired, meaning developing economies could export textiles to Europe without tariffs. From then on, products from India, China, Pakistan and Bangladesh started to invade the marketplace, and the industry was decimated. We still have a niche industry – high-quality names like Zegna and Cerruti – but it's a fraction of what it was. We've lost 20 per cent of our inhabitants in thirty years, and that's going to be terribly damaging for any town. We have 45,000 people now, and somehow we need to find a way to reverse the trend.

I'm part of the organizing committee for the stage finish we're hosting at Oropa in 2017. I'm the sports assessor for the council, and the assessors for tourism and mobility are also on the committee. Then there's somebody from the regional tourism office, the mayor himself and

a whole load of cycling people involved in the technical and operational aspects of the race. So it's a large group, and some of them have worked for many months to bring the Giro here.

It's the 100th edition of the race, and ours is one of the three stages dedicated to the memory of Pantani. We're going to use it to promote the natural beauty of our territory, because a Saturday stage finish is an amazing opportunity. Then, of course, the Sanctuary of Oropa is a major site historically, architecturally and culturally, and it's a perfect theatre for the race itself.

The cost is €120,000, but we should get €60,000 of that back from the regional council. That leaves us with €60,000 to find, and the aim is to recoup as much as possible from sponsors and benefactors. I don't know what a one-minute spot on RAI costs, but I have an idea it's about €50,000. We'll have an hour, and it will be broadcast in 197 countries. When

207

you think about it in those terms, and bear in mind that the hotels and restaurants will be full, it's extremely good value for money.

We see it as part of the development of the territory, a sort of relaunch. It's at the vanguard of a series of cycling-related activities and initiatives we want to roll out. People here are increasingly sedentary, and of course that has health implications. When I was a kid, my mum cycled to work, and people thought nothing of riding 15 or 20 kilometres to get to where they wanted to be. So our objective is to develop the cycling infrastructure, connect the various cycling paths we have, and promote bike use in general. We want people to see the value in leaving their car at home, and to create a new approach to getting around the city.

We also want to inform potential visitors that this is a great place to ride. Each May, we'll be running events and campaigns reminding people that we were chosen for the 100th Giro, in the hope of making our town synonymous with cycling excellence.

So it's a lot more than "just" a bike race. We're investing a lot of time, energy and money because, one way or another, we have a hell of a lot riding on it.

Smaller cities like Biella are increasingly the bulwarks of the Giro, and the race offers them unrivalled media exposure. However, in recent times, RCS Sport has reconfigured the Giro to enable it to visit new territories.

In winning the ferocious Giro of 1994, Evgeni Berzin covered 3,740 kilometres over twenty-two stages with no rest day. The 2016 edition, beginning in the Netherlands and won by Vincenzo Nibali, was comprised of twenty-one stages. Nibali rode 280 kilometres less, and had three rest days. Thus, for all that the Giro promotes itself as the hardest of the three Grand Tours, its percorso is increasingly designed around stolid commercial imperative.

A large part of the problem is the evolving character of the race. Under Vincenzo Torriani, it existed more or less as a financial sole entity, a festival of cycling and a brand driver for the Gazzetta. These days, it's answerable to shareholders, and part of an ailing media company. Furthermore, the crisis in public funding means that many of the host towns either can't pay or won't pay. As such, the race is compelled to make up the shortfall elsewhere, and foreign starts are (relatively) easy money. Some like them and some don't, but it's an incontrovertible fact that they've had a profound impact on the Giro. The question, therefore, is whether a three-week race with three rest days and virtually no time trials has a right to call itself a "grand tour" at all …

ENNIO DORIS
SPONSOR OF THE GIRO D'ITALIA
TOMBOLO, 1909

I come from Tombolo, a small village in the Veneto. About a hundred years ago it was an agricultural village, one of the poorest in the region. Back then, the villagers would have to walk 30 or 40 kilometres to the market in order to sell their produce. They'd set off at eleven o'clock at night, and the journey would take them five or six hours. They'd then try to sell what they had at the market, and then walk home again. Obviously, they didn't know any other way, and it was a pretty simple equation. Those who were able to do it ate, and those that weren't didn't. Most of the families of Tombolo didn't get to eat every day, and that was what was meant by being poor back then. Being poor meant going hungry …

One winter's night, the people of Tombolo, about three hundred of them, set off as normal about eleven o'clock. The market started at about four or five in the morning, so off they went. Just after Castelfranco Veneto it started to snow, and when it snowed the markets were called off because the animals couldn't get there. Anyway, somewhere along the route there was an *osteria* that used to stay open late. The guy there took pity on them, and gave them all a few pennies to get the train home. Only they didn't take the train. They walked home instead, because that way they saved a few extra pennies and had a little more to eat. So that gives you an idea of where I come from, and of the quotidian hardship people faced back in the day.

Occupational hazard.

Only the wealthiest possessed a horse at that time, and there was no public transport in places like that. However, the bike did exist, and slowly but surely it changed the face of this country. The Giro – and cycle racing in general – was a catalyst for that, and as demand went up, so the price was driven down. Progressively, more and more people were able to afford a bike, and they knew that if they could save enough money to buy one, the quality of their lives would be altered beyond recognition. Suddenly, they didn't have to walk, and they weren't limited to the 30 or 40 kilometres. They could travel 100, 150, even 200 kilometres, distances they'd never even dreamed of. So as a driver of social and economic progress, the bike was hugely important. It bestowed a genuine revolution on this country, and that explains the enormous passion Italians developed for cycling.

It's no accident that Mediolanum has been sponsoring the King of the Mountains jersey all these years. I suppose you could say that the idea for the sponsorship came from my marketing people, but the truth is it comes from my heart. Through the sponsorship, we play our part in the well-being of the Giro, but we also see it as a way of communicating some of the values of our business to customers and potential customers.

The sponsorship gives people the chance to touch us physically, and for a bank like ours that's important. We don't have branches because we're an Internet business, so we see the physical presence the Giro gives us as extremely important. The proximity is also one of the cornerstones of cycling, and that's why we invite people to ride with champions like Gianni Motta, Maurizio Fondriest and Francesco Moser. The real champions emerge when the race becomes more difficult, that fits perfectly with the mountains prize, and we like it as a metaphor.

What's interesting is that people here still have a profound respect for bike riders. All these years on, and after all that cycling has been through, they still revere them. We might take it for granted, but as Italians the bike is part of our DNA.

Ennio is the president of Mediolanum Bank, and one of Italy's wealthiest men. He grew up in the Veneto, one of the strongholds of Italian cycling, and his company has sponsored the King of the Mountains prize since 2003.

The first mountains competition, won by Alfredo Binda, took place in 1933. Gino Bartali won it no fewer than seven times, the great Spanish climber José Manuel Fuente four. The green jersey was introduced in 1974, but replaced (apparently at Mediolanum's behest) in 2012. Only Eddy Merckx has won the GC, the points and the mountains at the same Giro. He ran away with all three at the 1968 edition. The last maglia rosa *winner to win the King of the Mountains was Marco Pantani, back in 1998.*

GIROTAPPA 19
I DIRETTORI SPORTIVI
(THE SPORTS DIRECTORS)

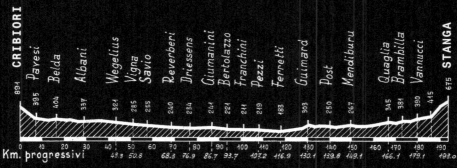

CRIBIORI · Pavesi · Belda · Albani · Wegelius · Vigna · Savio · Reverberi · Driessens · Giumanini · Bertolazzo · Franchini · Pezzi · Ferretti · Guimard · Post · Mendiburu · Quaglia · Brambilla · Vannucci · STANGA

891 · 395 · 404 · 337 · 324 · 285 · 255 · 240 · 234 · 244 · 221 · 241 · 249 · 183 · 303 · 250 · 267 · 345 · 381 · 390 · 445 · 675

Km. progressivi   43.3 50.8   68.3 76.9 86.7 93.7   107.2 116.9 130.1   139.8 149.1   166.1 179.1   193.0

0 10 20 30 40 50 60 70 80 90 100 110 120 130 140 150 160 170 180 190

C. SAN—

The biggest regret would be never having won the Giro with Brooklyn. Johan De Muynck should have won it in 1976, but he made two monumental mistakes. On stage 18, Gimondi had the jersey by a few seconds, but he crashed. The Giro was there for the taking, and all De Muynck had to do was keep riding. I told him this was his moment, but he wouldn't listen. He stopped to wait instead, and I couldn't believe what I was seeing …

De Muynck got the jersey back in the Dolomites the following day, and Gimondi was on his knees. On the penultimate day, there was a mountain stage to Bergamo, Gimondi's home town. He was cooked on the Zambla, and I told De Muynck to attack. All he needed was a minute or so at full gas, and Gimondi would have blown up completely. Instead, he decided to ride defensively, because there was a time trial the final day and he wanted to conserve energy. It made no sense because, if he'd ridden away, the time trial would have been academic anyway. Then, of course, he crashed on the descent and injured himself really badly. Gimondi hammered him in the time trial on the final day to reclaim the jersey, so that was that.

Everyone said they felt sorry for De Muynck, but they didn't really. What they actually felt was *grateful* to De Muynck. Grateful for his sportsmanship, but grateful most of all because he'd contrived to let Gimondi win. At the end of the day, the record books don't register the how and why of it, and the sponsors weren't much interested. De Muynck lost the Giro, but he didn't exist in a vacuum. His losing the Giro cost us all, and he didn't lose it because he was unlucky or because of some Corinthian sportsmanship. He lost it – and we *all* lost it – because he didn't have the killer instinct to go and win it …

I raced against Jacques Anquetil, I was a DS during the Eddy Merckx and Bernard Hinault eras, and a journalist during the Miguel Indurain years. So I saw them all, and I guess the one who left the biggest impression was Anquetil. I say that not because he was such a good bike rider, but because he wasn't. In fact, in many respects he was absolutely shocking …

In 1964 Anquetil smashed everyone else out of sight in the time trial, then more or less did as he pleased. He'd just hang around at the back of the *gruppo*, and as often as not he'd be stuck out in the wind. He was this great champion, and yet he turned up at the Giro with no sort of a team. They'd let really dangerous breaks go, and they wouldn't lift a finger. Anquetil would be at the back chatting away, and then Paul Wiegant, his DS, would roll up. He'd say, "They've got two minutes, Jacques!" Anquetil would say, "*Ça va*", and let them get on with it.

Eventually, he'd go to the front and bring it back *on his own!* There would be ten riders in the break, but he'd just pull for as long as it took. The whole peloton would be destroyed trying to cling on, but the break would come back. Then he'd drift off to the back again and carry on where he left off. It was literally unbelievable.

People say Merckx was the strongest, but I don't think he was. He was *better* for sure, but not *stronger*. Merckx rode to win every time he raced, and he had an incredible team. Then Indurain would let the rest win stages because he knew he'd be winning the GC. With Anquetil, it wasn't like that at all, because half the time he barely seemed to be taking part.

Brooklyn? When I finished as a rider I just got the telephone book out and started ringing around. I picked out companies I thought might be interested in sponsoring a team, and called them up. The first one was Dreher, and when that contract expired I rang Brooklyn Chewing Gum. The owner, Perfetti, was a big art collector, and I recognized some of his paintings in his office because I liked art myself. So there we were, talking about his paintings, and then, after about half an hour, he said, "Sorry, what was it you wanted to see me about again? I can't remember …"

So that was how the team began. They knew that cycling was a good brand-awareness tool, but they didn't understand it at all. I remember Perfetti rang me once and said, "I've had an idea. Given that De Vlaeminck wins all the time and that the others don't, why don't you just get rid of the rest and double his salary?"

In 1968 twenty-eight-year-old Franco Cribiori set up his own team. In 1972 the great Flemish rider Roger De Vlaeminck joined him, and the following year Brooklyn became title sponsor. Although De Vlaeminck is famed principally for his Paris—Roubaix exploits, he won nineteen Giro stages for Brooklyn, and three points competitions.

At the 1976 Giro, Brooklyn won ten stages with five different riders. De Muynck was easily the strongest in the race, but his dominance needled De Vlaeminck, his erstwhile captain. There was no way Cribiori could hope to retain them both, and De Muynck was lost to Bianchi in 1978. He won the Giro for them, while Cribiori, one of the greatest sports directors in Italian cycling history, never quite landed the corsa rosa …

I was twenty-nine when I became Eddy Merckx's sports director at Faema …

The general manager was Vincenzo Giacotto. He came from a marketing and public-relations background, and he'd revolutionized the sport with Carpano. He was the first to really think about how the team conducted itself *off* the bike, and the PR implications for the sponsor. So no more crappy hotels, no more lousy food and no more riders milling around the lobby wearing their slippers. They wore the team uniform, and they were expected to represent the sponsor well at all times.

Cycling teams were tiny by comparison to today, so you did everything. The role of the DS was different back then, more logistical than tactical. As often as not, I booked the

**MARINO VIGNA
ENTENTE CORDIALE
MONTE GRAPPA, 1968**

With Franco Balmamion at Learco Guerra's Mantua, having won the previous day.

hotels and restaurants, and took care of all the nuts and bolts involved in getting the team to the race.

Merckx was already world champion when he came to us, but he didn't actually know much. Like everyone else, he'd just followed what the others did, so we had to teach him about diet and recovery, and about using his head instead of just going to war every day. We also gave him a better bike and better geometry, and we helped him to become a much better descender.

The first problem was Vittorio Adorni, his teammate. Vittorio had won the Giro, and of course he was a big champion. He assumed that Merckx would realize that he was the captain, but it was obvious straight away that it was never going to be like that. We were preparing for the season at a training camp down in Reggio Calabria, and it was getting harder and faster. At a certain point, Adorni came to me and said, "OK, tell him to stop now, otherwise everyone is going to get dropped." For a star like Adorni it was difficult, but he was smart enough to mask his feelings about it.

We started the 1968 Giro with four Italians and six Belgians. Merckx wanted to win all the stages, and that wasn't ideal for all sorts of reasons. You have to work harder if you want to win, and over three weeks that has an effect. Then there's also a certain amount of politics involved, because it's no good upsetting people. At that point, Eddy didn't really understand those things, and, to be honest, we didn't really understand just how good he was. So we were trying to rein him in, when all he wanted was to be let off the leash.

On the stage to Monte Grappa, one of our Italian *gregari*, Casalini, attacked at the bottom of the climb. He was from Parma like Adorni, and Adorni told Eddy he had to wait because one of ours was up the road. So Eddy had to wait until the final kilometre, when Casalini had the stage wrapped up. As a consequence, he only put about twenty seconds into Felice Gimondi, and that caused some tension. As Eddy saw it, Casalini's winning had made him lose, and he was suspicious of Adorni's motives. He was young, he wanted to impose himself straight away, and of course he had a totally different mentality. The Italian rider gets up in the morning and opens the curtains. If it's raining, he either goes back to bed or waits until it stops. The Belgian comes down for breakfast ready to ride come what may. It's not that he's looked at the weather and decided he's going to ride anyway; not at all. He comes down because he hasn't even *opened* the curtains.

Two days later, at Tre Cime, Eddy was still needled by the incident with Casalini, and that was the best Merckx I ever saw. He got it all out that day, and we managed to keep him fairly calm after that. He wasn't happy when he lost the time trial to Gimondi, but I think that was a big moment because the penny started to drop about saving energy.

214

The following year Eddy wanted to ride the Tour de France, but Faema obliged him to ride the Giro. On the third stage there was the Abetone, and the mechanic fitted him a 20 sprocket. When we got to the start, he saw that the others all had 24, and he was panicking. He said, "Are you sure, Marino?" and I told him not to worry. He went up the Abetone on 44 x 18 and won the stage. The next day he won the time trial, and prior to Savona he won fairly well as he pleased.

I remember that Adorni, who was more of a manager than Eddy, said we ought to have a war chest, in case we needed cash during the races. I was the sports director for three years, and I never once used it. Why would I need it? I had guys like Swerts and Vandenbossche. Not even the flies could escape.

So there you go. If I made history in cycling, it's because I was the guy who manged to get Merckx to slow down …

Marino won Olympic gold in the 1960 team pursuit.

Vincenzo Giacotto, the Torinese responsible for bringing Eddy Merckx to Italy, died with Merckx in yellow at the 1970 Tour de France. His first foray into cycling had been in 1956. Mandated by the owners of the Carpano vermouth company to create a team, he'd engaged the great Fausto Coppi as its factotum. When the campionissimo left in 1958, Giacotto replaced the team's white jersey for the black-and-white stripes of his beloved Juventus. That was problematical with Turin's sports fans, and in 1961 he formed a second team to run in parallel. The riders of Baratti & Milano (a brand of chocolate) wore the claret jerseys of Torino, Juve's local rival.

Legnano. The DS, Pavesi, rode the very first Giro.

I was the youngest of nine kids, and life wasn't easy. I started work as a waiter aged eleven, then as a tailor, all sorts. I didn't have a bike but I desperately wanted to be a professional cyclist. I went to the local club, but they told me I was too skinny.

I was on my way home in tears, when the local priest came by on his bike. He was a real enthusiast, and he ran a club of his own nearby. He asked me what was wrong, I told him, and he said I could join his club, Olimpia Passinflex. So now I had a bike club, but still no actual bike. A friend of mine worked with his dad repairing bikes, and he helped me out. He'd lend me the repaired bikes to "test" before handing them back to their customers.

I turned professional in 1969, and I thought I was going to be a big star. On the second stage of the Giro I attacked, and somehow I managed to stay away and get the *maglia rosa*. That autumn I rode the Trofeo Baracchi with Eddy Merckx, and we won. Afterwards, though, I started to suffer badly with tendinitis and I was never the rider I should have been. I seemed to spend more time in hospital than on the road.

I started Inoxpran in 1979, and we won the Giro with Giovanni Battaglin in 1981. Then we signed Roberto Visentini, and then Carrera came on board as main sponsor.

Visentini was a massively talented guy, but also a very complex one. Something always seemed to go wrong, so I approached Stephen Roche after he won the Aubisque stage at the 1985 Tour de France. It was probably the best decision I ever made, and probably the worst. Roche contracted tendonitis, but Visentini finally won the Giro the following year.

I had them both at the 1987 Giro, and they were both in good form. The idea was that Stephen would work for Roberto there, and vice versa at the Tour. However, there was a downhill time trial on the second day, from the top of the Poggio into San Remo. Stephen was a good descender, so he won the stage. Then, when we won the team time trial a few days later, he took the *maglia rosa*.

There was another time trial on stage 13, and by now there was quite a bit of tension in the team. Stephen and Roberto were both champions, they both wanted to win, and the rest of them didn't really know what to do or say. We had to make a decision for the good of the team and the sponsor, so we agreed that whoever came out of the time trial with the jersey would be the undisputed leader in the final week.

With Giovanni Battaglin. The 1981 Giro is theirs :

Roberto won the time trial, so it was all clear. We were dominating the race, and Stephen was in second place, just in case. The problem was that Panasonic had Eric Breukink, and they weren't just going to lie down and let us win. It was logical that they would try something, and they were running out of time. They attacked on a descent, and Roberto was in the middle of the group. He was a good descender, but for some reason he was too far back. I can't say for sure whether it was premeditated, because the only person that truly knows is Stephen. What I would say is that we'd decided it was all for one, and he went with the break instead of staying to help his leader as we'd agreed …

Irrespective of Stephen's motives, it wasn't necessarily an issue for us as a team. Roberto had nearly three minutes on Stephen, so in theory there was no problem for him to be in that break. In point of fact, it made sense for us to have somebody in it, because there were some important GC riders there. Sappada is a long, steady climb, about thirty kilometres. At half distance the gap was only a minute, and it looked like it would come together again. As a matter of fact, Toni Rominger, who was third on GC at the time, was also left behind with the Visentini group. He actually bridged across to the break and overtook everybody except Johan Van der Velde.

However, Roberto was fragile psychologically, and as he saw it Stephen had betrayed him. We were trying to nurse him round, but he couldn't cope and he caved in. He lost three minutes in the final four kilometres.

Regardless of what people think of Stephen's behaviour that day, Roberto lost the Giro because he collapsed psychologically, not physically. If he'd had Stephen's head, Roberto could have done whatever he wanted as a cyclist. There's no question in my mind he could have won the Tour …

The story of the 1987 race is incredible even by the Giro's standards. In essence, Visentini, the reigning champion and maglia rosa, was ambushed on the road to Sappada, by a group including his teammate Stephen Roche. The Irishman thus claimed the jersey, went on to win the Giro, and would add both the Tour de France and the World Championships in a single calendar year. After the stage, Roche told Italian reporters that he was "taking care of my own interests". Subsequently, however, he disseminated a different version of events. He had simply followed the breakaway in the interests of the team, while Visentini had paid for his inattention.

The Italian version, broadly speaking, is that Roche, at that point in the race a gregario, committed one of the most grievous crimes in the history of the Giro. He had agreed to work for the maglia rosa, but instead was instrumental (or, at the very least, complicit) in the ambush. And that constituted no less than a heresy …

GIANLUIGI STANGA
THE BEGINNING OF THE END
MILAN, 1990 AND 1999

We won the Giro, but we were in a vicious circle. I knew it was going to have terrible consequences for all of us …

I was running Polti, and it had been clear to everyone that Marco Pantani couldn't be beaten. I'd thought that Ivan Gotti might be able to stay with him on the stage to Madonna di Campiglio, but he just couldn't. Afterwards, I said to Ivan, "Look, we can't win the Giro, but second behind Pantani is a good result."

I was in the corridor the following morning, because I had to go and get Gotti's tests. I was outside Pantani's room, and I could tell that something was wrong. There were too many people, too much commotion and too much anxiety. When it became apparent that it was a doping infraction, my first reaction was, "Fuck! Pantani!"

The real loser was cycling, and above all *Italian* cycling. You only have to look at what's happened since. It's been seventeen years since Madonna di Campiglio, and the prosecutors have only just archived it. It's one of the saddest, most miserable episodes in cycling history, and yet for some reason they've made it into an industry.

Think about all the nonsense that's been written and spoken about it. The Mafia, illicit gambling rings, the underworld, the UCI … Most of these people know nothing about the rules of cycling, the protocols, not even the basic facts. They write things like, "They switched the samples." Why would they switch the samples? At that point, they don't even know who the sample belongs to – it's just a number! Then you have the president of the jury, the doctors, the person from anti-doping, the chemists themselves … So five or six people and all of them are complicit?

There's no ambiguity, just tittle-tattle. It's a very sad case, but what else could they do? It's ridiculous to blame Carmine Castellano or Hein Verbruggen, because everyone was operating within the rules. You can't say, "Yes, but it was Pantani! It would have been better for cycling if we'd let it go." There was only one course of action, and sadly that was it.

When I won the Giro with Gianni Bugno, he held the pink jersey from the first stage to the last. It may sound like a lot to defend the jersey for three weeks, but I don't remember a single moment when I felt like it was unravelling. It was much harder to finish second with Honchar, or third with Guerini.

Bugno's *performance* was incredible, but there was much more to it than that. We'd had the Francesco Moser and 'Beppe Saronni era, but then foreign winners for three years. So Italian cycling was in a hole, and Bugno dug it out. People really warmed to him because he was shy and extremely modest, but also very charismatic. At the end of the day, though, you can talk all you want, but it's what a cyclist *does* that counts. When Chiappucci came along, the rivalry between them was good for the sport, but Claudio never had Bugno's class, either on the bike or off it. It was Bugno who relaunched Italian cycling …

Winning with Francesco Moser.

The following year Bugno finished fourth at the Giro and second behind Miguel Indurain at the Tour de France. The time trial was 60 kilometres, and Indurain only put about thirty seconds into him. Bugno also won the Italian championships and the World Championships in Stuttgart, so he said, "Next year I want to focus on the Tour." I agreed with him, and it made sense to have the Tour as his objective. Of course, when the *Gazzetta dello Sport* found out he wouldn't be at the Giro, they set about us; in their eyes, Bugno couldn't do right for doing wrong. They *massacred* us …

Anyway, there are Giro winners and Giro winners. I suppose they're defined by the impact they have, but also by things they have no control over …

Over a thirty-year career, Gianluigi "Gigi" Stanga directed (among others) Francesco Moser, Gianni Bugno, Laurent Fignon, Richard Virenque, Djamolidine Abdoujaparov, Tony Rominger and Erik Zabel. His idol and inspiration was the legendary Dutch sports director Peter Post, the boss of Ti-Raleigh and later Panasonic.

The great Gianni Bugno remains one of only four riders to lead the Giro from the first day to the last. The others are Costante Girardengo (1919; ten stages), Alfredo Binda (1927; fifteen stages) and Eddy Merckx (1973; prologue and twenty stages). Bugno never repeated his Giro win, but his two rainbow jerseys and the splenetic nature of his rivalry with the climber Claudio Chiappucci defined an era.

Ivan Gotti won the 1997 Giro when he and second-placed Pavel Tonkov effectively called a truce on the Mortirolo. Many argue that the 1999 maglia rosa, won following Marco Pantani's expulsion, was something of a curse. Gotti was an outstanding climber, but the best he could hope to do was cling on to Pantani's wheel. In inheriting the Giro after Madonna di Campiglio, he became a scapegoat for the Pantani legions. He declined to be interviewed for this book.

The year is 1985, and the second sponsor is Allegro Wurstel. Italians like wurstel a great deal.

supermercati **BRIANZOLI** *allegro* wurstel

Da sinistra:
ZOLA - MANTOVANI - CHINETTI - FERRETTI - BEVILACQUA - CORTI - BARONCHELLI G. - COLOMBO - BARONCHELLI G.B. - BOTTOIA - D.S. STANGA

GIROTAPPA 20
I GIGANTI DEL GIRO D'ITALIA
(THE GIANTS OF THE GIRO D'ITALIA)

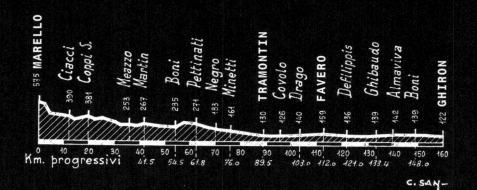

I lived through two great sporting tragedies.

The first was the day the plane carrying the great Torino football team came down at Superga. It was 1949 and I'd only just turned fifteen. I'd been working full-time for five years by then, though, because I'd started as a barber when I was ten. I can only really describe Superga as desolation on a huge scale. It was as if part of us had been ripped away.

The second was the death of Fausto Coppi. That was much more personal, because Fausto was such an intrinsic part of who I was and of who we *all* were ... I was a grown man when it happened, but I'll never forget it and I'm not ashamed to say that I cried.

Everyone I knew followed cycling, and I mean *everyone*. People always draw parallels with football today, but that's illusory. Football is much more diffuse, there are dozens of teams, and money is central to it. With cycling it was different because it was man against man, and it was the sport of the ages. It had been handed down to me by my father, just as it had in all Italian families. For his generation, it was Belloni, Brunero and Girardengo, and for us it was Coppi and Bartali. You knew all the riders, and you appreciated some more than others. However, everyone was either *Coppiano* or *Bartaliano* because it was impossible not to be. Guys like Astrua, Soldani and the Rossello brothers were good riders, but Coppi and Bartali were cycling.

I was on the roadside at Cuneo–Pinerolo in 1949. I remember Fausto passing and then one minute, two minutes, three minutes ... The Stelvio stage in 1953 – I wept that day – and listening to the radio during the famous 1946 Milan–San Remo. Fausto came in fifteen minutes ahead of the rest, and they didn't know what to do or say. Eventually, the presenter said, "We've decided to play some dance music while we wait for them to arrive." Now I ask you, who else could have done something like that? Eddy Merckx was the cannibal, yes, and Bartali was Bartali. If you want to talk about greatness, though, there's no comparison ...

It's true that TV changed cycling, and some would argue that it changed it for the better. You see it better because you see everything, but you don't feel it and you don't *live* it. When TV came along, the material effect was that people stopped going, and that made a big difference. You can watch sport on TV, but really it's just a facsimile. There's no sport without physicality.

One day when the Giro came, my dad and his mate got two bikes, caked their legs in mud – at the time the roads were all dust and mud – and dressed themselves up as riders. They put dossards on their backs with the numbers 16 and 69. In Italy, the number 16 is synonymous with the backside, and 69 is, well ...

Angelo Marello (left, crying) with mum and brother Stefano.

Yashin? Banks? Bacigalupo?

Anyway, they waited for the peloton to pass, and then the voice went up that there were two lost riders and they were about to pass through the village. Suddenly, everyone ran to the roadside, and when they came through the whole village started laughing at them. My mum was quite a sensitive soul, and at first she had no idea that it was my dad and his mate playing a joke. She thought they were ordinary riders who were off the back, and that people were making fun of them because they were last. She said, "Don't be cruel to them just because they're last!" but then my dad came closer and she finally realized it was him.

The thing is that the Giro used to create these stories. That all happened ninety years ago or whatever, but it's become part of the folklore of the village …

Those who rode with, for and against Fausto Coppi are becoming fewer and fewer, and Angelo's is the last generation to have witnessed his exploits first-hand.

It's impossible to overstate Coppi's historical importance. He remains arguably Italy's greatest sportsman, and certainly her most influential. The likes of Costante Girardengo, Alfredo Binda and Gino Bartali were great cyclists, and of course others have emerged across the sporting spectrum. However, none ever resonated with the Italian public in the way that Coppi did, and nor for as long. Not for nothing do Italians say that "Merckx was the best, but Coppi was the greatest". Put simply, his legend continues to inform Italian sport seventy-five years on from his first Giro win.

For ten years, Angelo knocked on doors and canvassed business leaders, and by 2002 he'd generated sufficient political and financial capital to build a beautiful Coppi monument on the doorstep of Turin's old velodrome. He's eighty-two now, but he and his like were formed by cycling, and in cycling. As such, the love they have for the sport burns as brightly as ever.

FILIPPO GHIRON
MALATO DI CICLISMO
PECETTO, 2016

It's my birthday today; I'm sixteen …

It was 2005 and it started with the village *pizzaiolo*. He said he wanted to start a cycling team, so me and my two brothers signed up. Aldo would have been fifteen, Giorgio nine, and I was five.

I think there were about fifteen of us at the beginning, but one by one they packed it in. I think they understood that cycling is a hard sport, and that to do it properly you have to make sacrifices. At the end, there were only three of us left: me and my two brothers. Aldo didn't manage to turn professional, but he still rides Gran Fondos and he wins quite a lot. Giorgio has stopped now, because he's at university.

At school, most of the others either play football or follow football. The others either play on their computers or they don't do anything. Everyone else goes out at night, and they eat what they want and drink what they want. They think I'm strange because I don't do any of those things, but I don't care. From the beginning, I dreamed of becoming a professional cyclist, and I still dream of becoming a professional cyclist. It's taken hold of me, and there's nothing I can do about it.

I don't know if I *like* it in a normal sense, but I know that I love it. My mum and dad tell me that I have to try to combine my studies with riding the bike, because school is important. I know it's important and I'm trying, but it's not easy because I have to train every day. I try to concentrate, but I think about cycling a lot.

I didn't win a race for five years, but then this year I had the best form I've ever had. I won the regional championship, but then I crashed on a descent while I was out training. That was June, and my season finished there. I had two operations, and I have one leg shorter than the other now. I'm still doing physio, and they're working on rebuilding it because it was just bone. It's 1.5 centimetres shorter than the other, and it's a delicate moment because I'm growing quite a lot. This year I pass to the junior category, and I know it's going to be hard. I'm not giving up, though. No way …

If I have to choose between the Tour de France and the Giro, I'll take the Giro. People say the Tour is bigger, more prestigious and wealthier, but I'm not so bothered about that. I'm Italian, so riding here, in my country … The Giro is my dream.

Filippo Ghiron is an Italian racing cyclist.

Filippo Ghiron (left), winner of the 2027 Tour of Lombardy.

On the rivet. Ghiron leads …

Ai postumi i'ardua sentenza …

At least one of the testimonies contained in this book is pure
invention. The interviewee recounted it to me in explicit detail,
but the fact is that it simply never happened. I have no problem with
that per se, and I include it here because the story — for all that
it's a figment of his imagination — is absolutely intrinsic to who he's
become. He's told it so many times over the years that he's probably
unable to distinguish between fact and fiction, and in that sense he's
the perfect bike-racing metaphor. He's a cycling Walter Mitty, but it's
not for me, a mere hack, to denude him of his identity. And besides,
who's to say that the other ninety-nine were telling the truth?

So I make no apology for including it, and I'll leave you, dear
reader, to try to deduce which one it is.

Thanks to everyone who contributed in the writing and production
of this book.
— Herbie Sykes

Editor's acknowledgements.
Many thanks to all those whose talent helped to create this book.
To Melanie Mues for injecting her unique energy into the design.
To Mark Ralph, Linda Duong and Edwin Ingram for their exceptional
attention to detail. To Simon Mottram, Jack Saunders, Eve Issak
and Daniel Blumire at Rapha who shared our enthusiasm and vision
for realising it and finally, to the Giro 100 and to Herbie Sykes
for taking us all on this fascinating journey.
— Taz Darling